Beware of Dog

"Dogs in Our World" Series

*Beware of Dog: How Media Portrays
the Aggressive Canine* (Melissa Crawley, 2021)

*Dog of the Decade: Breed Trends and What They Mean
in America* (Deborah Thompson, 2021)

*I'm Not Single, I Have a Dog: Dating Tales from
the Bark Side* (Susan Hartzler, 2021)

*Laboratory Dogs Rescued: From Test Subjects
to Beloved Companions* (Ellie Hansen, 2021)

*Dogs in Health Care: Pioneering Animal-Human
Partnerships* (Jill Lenk Schilp, 2019)

*General Custer, Libbie Custer and Their Dogs:
A Passion for Hounds, from the Civil War to Little Bighorn*
(Brian Patrick Duggan, 2019)

*Dog's Best Friend: Will Judy, Founder of National Dog Week and
Dog World Publisher* (Lisa Begin-Kruysman, 2014)

*Man Writes Dog: Canine Themes in Literature,
Law and Folklore* (William Farina, 2014)

*Saluki: The Desert Hound and the English Travelers
Who Brought It to the West* (Brian Patrick Duggan, 2009)

Beware of Dog

How Media Portrays the Aggressive Canine

MELISSA CRAWLEY

DOGS IN OUR WORLD

Series Editor Brian Patrick Duggan

McFarland & Company, Inc., Publishers

Jefferson, North Carolina

ALSO BY MELISSA CRAWLEY AND FROM MCFARLAND

The American Television Critic: A History (2017)

*Mr. Sorkin Goes to Washington: Shaping
the President on Television's* The West Wing (2006)

LIBRARY OF CONGRESS CATALOGUING-IN-PUBLICATION DATA

Names: Crawley, Melissa, 1971– author. | Duggan, Brian Patrick, 1953– editor.
Title: Beware of dog : how media portrays the aggressive canine /
Melissa Crawley, Brian Patrick Duggan.
Description: Jefferson, North Carolina : McFarland & Company, Inc.,
Publishers, 2021. | Series: Dogs in our world | Includes
bibliographical references and index.
Identifiers: LCCN 2021016154 | ISBN 9781476685243 (paperback : acid free paper) ∞
ISBN 9781476643243 (ebook)
Subjects: LCSH: Dangerous dogs. | Fighting dogs. |
Dogs in motion pictures. | Dogs on television.
Classification: LCC SF428.85 .C73 2021 | DDC 636.7—dc23
LC record available at https://lccn.loc.gov/2021016154

BRITISH LIBRARY CATALOGUING DATA ARE AVAILABLE

ISBN (print) 978-1-4766-8524-3
ISBN (ebook) 978-1-4766-4324-3

Front cover image July 31, 2018, © 2021 Nick Bolton / Unsplash

Printed in the United States of America

*McFarland & Company, Inc., Publishers
Box 611, Jefferson, North Carolina 28640
www.mcfarlandpub.com*

For Max

Table of Contents

Preface   1

Beginnings   7

Chapter One. Dangerous Dogs   11

Chapter Two. Urban   29

Chapter Three. Working   58

Chapter Four. Screen   116

Endings   165

Chapter Notes   173

Bibliography   195

Index   199

Preface

Walking Max

I have an adopted Greyhound named Charlie. In another life, this ex-racer chased a mechanical lure for 100 starts, a statistic that earned him some fame in his native Queensland, Australia. Charlie's retirement is mostly about sleeping. He barks so infrequently that it's startling to hear and rarely does he spend more than 30 seconds paying attention to other dogs. To give you a sense of who Charlie is, the joke around my house is that he skipped the puppy stage and was born fully grown. He is a low-energy gentleman.

Greyhound adopters, like other dog people, are fond of the saying that dogs are like potato chips. You can't have just one. In my case, that's true. Charlie is my third Greyhound. First was Helen, who taught me how wonderful it is to be a dog owner. Then came Elle, who out of all the dogs who have graced my life so far, had the sweetest personality. After Elle and Helen died in the same year, I contacted Greyhound rescue organizations in both Australia and the U.S. mainland to adopt another, but no rescue was interested in sending one to Hawaii, where I live. Most of them had a policy of home checks, which meant only selecting adopters in their area. Others found it too challenging to deal with the wait period that is required for Hawaii, a rabies-free state. Disappointed, I scrolled through the local humane society website and saw a picture of a too-thin German Shepherd Dog. His name was Clooney.

A German Shepherd Dog showing up at a shelter in Hawaii is rare. Clooney ended up there because he has diabetes and when I met him, he was a tail-wagging mess. His scrawny body gave him the appearance of a too big head. He anxiously paced and frequently urinated, a sign that his diabetes was not under control yet. He barely made eye contact and spent most of our time together barking at all the other dogs. I found out that he had been adopted a few months after being dumped on the shelter's doorstep but was surrendered several weeks later in worse shape than when he left.

1

The adopter had stopped giving him insulin and he was about 40 pounds underweight. Then the shelter attendant said that the cloudy look in his eyes was the result of cataracts. Without an operation, he would eventually go blind.

I left the humane society mentally listing all the various deal breakers that would stop me from going through with an adoption and silently wished Clooney good luck. My husband was more enthusiastic and suggested that we talk to a vet and learn more. The vet said that Clooney's diabetes was completely manageable once his insulin was regulated, and at age three, he had every chance to live a full life. He assured us that after a week of giving insulin shots, we would be old pros. That part turned out not to be true.

Administering twice-daily insulin shots to a German Shepherd Dog you barely know is a task that could break you, and it almost did. It took months, and the long road to success was paved with patience, practice and one or two emotional breakdowns. Once Clooney, who we renamed Max, learned to trust us and relax a little, the routine became manageable, but I would not describe it as easy. In my fantasy, Max is like a German Shepherd Dog I recently saw in a video who stood completely still until his shot was over. In my reality, Max's routine consists of one or all of the following: squirming, jostling forward and backward, turning in one direction and then the other. When he relents, and he always does, it's only for a split second so the shot has to be lightning fast. As for him ever standing still, we live in hope.

Once we cleared the insulin shot hurdle, we scheduled cataract surgery and after many, many eye drops, Max was chasing Frisbees that he could actually see. It was incredibly rewarding. Then one day, he wouldn't put pressure on his back-left foot, and we found out that he had a partial tear in the cranial cruciate ligament of his knee.[1] So, another surgery was scheduled. Max was an excellent patient and a surprisingly calm airline passenger (both of his surgeries required a short flight). He is now well on his way to chasing more Frisbees. As for my husband and me, we're practically veterinary technicians at this point.

While Charlie is independent, Max gets involved in everyone's business. We joke that he has a severe case of fear-of-missing-out. He goes crazy over the garden hose and will drop a toy by your feet, take a few steps back and stare at it, silently willing you to throw it. He is smart and good-natured, follows commands and likes people. Dogs are different. They typically get his full and vocal attention during walks, and we swiftly guide him away. A pit bull[2] type named Bonnie, for reasons only known to the two of them, was his mortal enemy.[3] Their interactions always began with a solid stare, like two gunslingers facing off, daring the other to draw. One of them would bark to break the tension. The other would respond and the

Max on the way to TPLO surgery. His second time in an airplane. January 2020 (photo by Alan Crawley).

noise level would rise. When Max and Bonnie crossed paths, people turned their heads and looked.

A quick internet search of the German Shepherd Dog will tell you two things: They are number two in the American Kennel Club's breed popularity ranking, and they are considered an "aggressive" breed, right along with

Dobermans, Rottweilers and of course, the variety of bull terrier breeds and mixes commonly referred to as pit bulls. Max is reactive more than aggressive. His interactions with dogs other than Charlie typically involve a lot of barking, but with Bonnie, his fear-based reactivity reached a different level.

Walking Max in the morning, I was always on high alert for Bonnie, scanning the horizon and expecting to run into her around every corner. The strategies to prevent Max from running at his nemesis full speed were both physical and emotional. A firm grip on the leash coupled with what dog trainer Cesar Millan would call "calm, assertive energy" would typically control and correct his behavior. On the day that Max finally reached Bonnie, I didn't do either of these things successfully.

It started as it always did. Separated by a wide street, they launched into stares. Max barked. Bonnie responded. The sounds grew louder. Max pulled harder. I like to think I had his reaction under control, at least for a few seconds, but I never did. His reactivity and my anxious response to it took over. He ran full speed, straight at Bonnie and I held on tight, determined that if I could just keep a grip, I could stop him from reaching her. I lost my balance and the fall broke my hold on the leash. My hands, knees and shoulder scraped across the road as Max hurled himself at Bonnie.

The American Kennel Club describes the German Shepherd Dog as a "bold and punishing fighter, if need be." On the day Max reached Bonnie, he was bold but not so punishing. He pounced on her a few times. They tussled. My husband, who was still on the other side of the street with Charlie, called Max's name and he stopped. Bonnie was pulled from the scene. Neither dog was hurt. If Max didn't feel a "need" to release the punishing force of his breed's fighting capabilities, it was little consolation. It suddenly felt like he was a potentially dangerous dog, and in some states, his encounter with Bonnie would have met the criteria for the official designation.

At the time of writing, there are over 35 states and several municipalities in America that have dangerous dog codes. The codes define when a dog is dangerous, the legal procedure that determines whether a dog is dangerous, the condition for owning a dangerous dog, provisions for euthanasia and penalties for the dog owner. In Delaware, Maryland, Minnesota, Nebraska, New Mexico and the District of Columbia, where state codes, with slight variations, define potentially dangerous dogs as "any specific dog with a known propensity, tendency, or disposition to attack when unprovoked, to cause injury, or to threaten the safety of humans or domestic animals,"[4] Max could be an offender. His attack may not be considered unprovoked and he may not have caused injury, but he had a disposition to threaten the safety of a fellow domestic animal. In Massachusetts, he might be called a "nuisance dog" because he has "threatened or attacked" a domestic animal but "such threat or attack was not a grossly disproportionate reaction under all the circumstances." I imagine Max would agree that under the circumstances, his reaction to Bonnie was not disproportionate, considering that she gave as good as she got.

When the Max and Bonnie morning show was canceled thanks to Bonnie's relocation to Northern California, Max lost his main adversary, but he continues to bark at other neighborhood dogs—his latest enemy is a Golden Retriever called Matilda. Still, he's all bark and no bite. And much less bark than he used to be. As surprising and troubling as it was, the Bonnie incident challenged me to consider the complexities of the canine-human bond in my relationship with Max and in the broader relationship we all have with dogs, specifically when things go wrong with man's best friend. Whether we own them or not, dogs are part of the fabric of American life and one of the primary ways we encounter "dangerous" dogs is through media narratives. The following pages explore these stories and the impact they have on how we understand both "bad" dogs, and the persons on the other end of the leash.

Beginnings

A dangerous dog is an aggressive dog or a dog that attacks, and this has legal consequences, but beyond state codes and breed-specific laws are tragic outcomes tied to social and cultural attitudes. In 2015, a police officer knocked on the front door of a home in Florida City, Florida, and was greeted by the family's two-year-old Bulldog mix, Dutchess [sic]. Believing the dog had charged him, the officer fired three shots into her head before the family even knew why he had come to their door. Surveillance cameras outside the home showed Dutchess running out but according to her owner, who is seen directly behind her in the footage, she was not barking or growling.[1]

In the case of Rosie, a Newfoundland living in Des Moines, Washington, who got loose from her backyard while her owners were out of town, it was three police officers rather than one who sealed her fate. Responding to a call, they used a Taser on her twice, chased her for blocks and then shot her four times with an assault rifle. The neighbor who had called 911 reported that a "big black dog" was running loose and said she feared the dog might "get killed" but did not say that the dog showed aggression, even to the kids who she witnessed trying to catch her. Rosie's owners were awarded $51,000 in the largest settlement reached in Washington State for a case of animal-related litigation.[2] The complaint allegations against the officers stated that "Rosie had completed extensive dog training; had never been found by any jurisdiction to be vicious, potentially dangerous, or dangerous; had never been the subject of any complaint by any person for exhibiting vicious propensities...."[3] Yet, the officers who shot her only saw a monstrous dog. They responded out of fear.

Irrational and persistent fear of dogs, or cynophobia, is a product of environmental conditioning and a predisposition to anxiety. It may start with a fear of Rottweilers, but it doesn't discriminate and can quickly include Chihuahuas. I witnessed it once when my friend had to frantically leave a party after the resident Chow Chow took advantage of an open door and joined the fun. When she spied him across a sea of people, she

7

instantly panicked. Her fear was real and diagnosable. Assuming that the
people responsible for the deaths of Dutchess and Rosie did not have a similar, clinical response to all dogs (they may even have dogs), it's reasonable
to assume that their fearfulness is culturally mediated, a result of images
and narratives that disrupt the position of the domesticated dog. Minus the
actual victims of dog attacks, the primary way in which humans most often
encounter dangerous dogs is through representations.

The stories and pictures that document the actions of aggressive dogs
often detail gruesome injuries to children, to the elderly, to police officers,
or to postal workers, and these accounts are awful to read. We feel empathy
for the victims. We may even develop an irrational fear of an entire breed
or type. But the truly horrifying idea is that dog attacks challenge how we
understand our dominance over nature by casting doubt on our ability
to tame a dog into man's best friend. Toys, treats, licks and belly rubs are
no guarantee that an uncontrollable monster isn't lying somewhere deep
inside our faithful companion.

Almost 90 percent of dog owners say their canine is a member of
their family.[4] It's a mindset that means dogs, as Donna Haraway writes,
"are not here just to think with" but to live with.[5] As with any relationship, the dog-human dynamic, whether they live with us or pass us on
the street, comes with expectations. Most of us relate to dogs by imagining that their feelings are like our feelings. For dog owners, this allows a
comfortable give and take of love and affection along with a level of disci-
plinary authority that aims to prevent unwanted behaviors. For non-dog
owners, the imagining may be somewhat the same, even if it includes
indifference or hostility. Either way, a dog's part of the bargain is that he
or she won't show us a wild side or at least the side that is capable of causing us physical harm. The narrative of the dangerous dog, which suggests
that the civilized cultivation of the dog from wild to tame has experienced
a profound breakdown, threatens to dismantle the deal. While it doesn't
bring everything crashing to the ground, it's an uncomfortable reminder
that dogs are both animal and pet, living in a created world of good and
bad and right and wrong.

Particularly in the western world, the popularity of beautiful dogs,
goofy dogs, hero dogs, and countless puppies, in news, films, television
pet programs, social media accounts and viral videos suggests that our
cultural attention span for dogs is endless. Media gives us access to these
dogs and offers information about them, but it also shapes what these
dogs mean. As an audience for all the media sources that catalogue the
vast world of dogs, we actively make our own meanings, rather than pas-
sively absorb them, but these sources nevertheless help form our attitudes
and beliefs about dogs. Representations of animals are not neutral. They

impact how we understand our relationship to dogs as well as their lived reality.

For those dogs the media labels dangerous, the stakes are high for both canines and humans because animal representations are often a reference for saying something about ourselves. When the media talks about dangerous dogs, it is with a mix of the symbolic and the real, but it is always deeply connected to the human presence accompanying the dog. A dog's most transgressive act is to attack or to disobey a human, and that rarely happens without human involvement, whether it is in the form of neglect, abuse or poorly executed training.

This book explores the story of dangerous dogs as told in the press and on the screen. Because these dogs are also considered "bad" dogs, you will find both terms used throughout. Fear is a central theme of their story and while it is something to consider in its own right, as a deeply primal, perhaps even evolutionary, response to a predator, it also underlies a broader set of social concerns. How we talk about dangerous dogs in the media articulates issues of class and race, reveals shifting power dynamics, and provides a commentary on the anxiety we feel when the human-dog relationship profoundly breaks down. Within this breakdown lies a deeper fear of the human becoming animalized.

Chapter Outline

Chapter One explores the dog-human world as one that began with our capacity to identify with other species. It traces the development of anthropomorphism and discusses various studies that investigate the social and emotional roles that dogs play in peoples' lives. From health benefits to social support in times of crisis and transition, research in the fields of social anthropology and contemporary psychology reports that many dogs are valued for a companionship that echoes the most intimate of human relationships. The problem is: Dogs are like us, until they're not. When dangerous dogs reveal their animal nature or their "creatureliness," it is often an unsettling reminder of the fluidity of their identity, the fragility of our uneasy alliance and the role we play in both.

Chapter Two considers the bad dog within the context of urban landscapes, from rabies-carrying strays wreaking havoc on nineteenth century city streets to twentieth century canines causing chaos in dog parks. As the cultural attitude toward dogs as pets began to change in the nineteenth century, city residents took to their newspapers to discuss their duty to an ethic of kindness versus their desire to eradicate nuisance dogs. The ensuing debate made a clear connection between undesirable human behavior and bad dogs. When dogs got their own parks, the bad behavior of pet owners who allowed their four-legged friends to be unruly was quickly policed by other owners, who made their feelings known in the press.

No discussion of dogs and the urban environment would be complete without investigating the complex image of pit bulls. The chapter explores pit bulls' history and their starring role as the scariest of all dogs, which in the press is never far from an association with human criminality and cruel ownership practices.

Heroic war dogs and brave police dogs make for good press, but there is a darker side to dogs with jobs. Chapter Three examines the problematic relationship between working dogs and racism, dehumanization and death. It looks at press coverage of dogs who navigate the battlefield and walk the beat, as well as those who were trained to hunt slaves. When a dog's publicly sanctioned role requires and rewards aggressiveness, the person on the other end of the leash is not exempt from the consequences.

Chapter Four explores dangerous dogs on screen with a focus on western animal horror cinema and reality television shows featuring dog rehabilitation experts. In these visual narratives, the depiction of dogs as either fictional deadly killers or real domestic nightmares is deeply rooted in how humans treat them. Whether they are characters fighting off bloody attacks, or real people trying to reclaim their domestic space from out-of-control pets, the human-dog relationships that collapse on screen are all about people failing to recognize their role in the breakdown.

Chapter One

Dangerous Dogs

Man's Best Friend

It's hard to avoid dogs in America. In 2017, there were 89 million dogs living in 60 million U.S. households.[1] For these 60 million American households, pet keeping is the act of choosing a specific animal above others and it comes with several characteristics, which historian Keith Thomas identifies as: Allowing the animal in the house, giving it a name and never eating it.[2] For academic Katherine Grier, these characteristics offer a solid foundation for understanding pet keeping but need some revision. Not all pets live inside or have names, and a few may in fact, get eaten. What pets do have in common, she argues, is that they have been differentiated by people who intend to care for them, whatever they may understand that care to mean. In her history of pet-keeping in America, she notes that the practice is a significant part of the history of everyday life and "connected to changing ideas about human nature, emotional life, individual responsibility, and our society's obligations to all kinds of dependent others, including people."[3]

How Americans came to think about emotional life through pet-keeping is about feeling something toward a pet but it's also about how they believe that pet might feel. This is anthropomorphism, or the application of human mental states, including thoughts, feelings, motivations and beliefs, to non-human animals.[4] In our relationships with the dogs we have deemed special, their "feelings," which are suspiciously like our feelings, often take center stage. How this developed is unclear, but one archeologist has an idea.

Scholars have argued that the basis for anthropomorphism lies in the human aptitude for "reflexive consciousness" or the power to use the information about what it is to be a person to then understand and predict others' behavior.[5] In his research on how reflexive consciousness grew to include animals, archeologist Steven Mithen argues that site evidence from the Upper Paleolithic points to a shift in human attitudes toward animals that may have taken place 40,000 years ago due to an increase in "cognitive fluidity," or better connections between the different areas of the brain.

A bulldog dressed in a flowered bonnet and paisley dress with a bow, circa 1905. Pets were taken to photographic studios beginning in the 1840s. Dressed up in ladies' clothes, this bulldog's fancy attire reflects people's changing attitudes toward pet-keeping (Library of Congress).

Mithen theorizes that when the "social intelligence" section of the brain, which deals with the ability to use self-knowledge to understand and anticipate others' actions, started interacting with other brain areas, early humans were able to make inferences about the thoughts and feelings of other animals and the natural world. He points to evidence that early humans carried out more complex hunting practices than their Neanderthal ancestors, theorizing that their superior skills came from using plans and strategies based on predicting their prey's behavior.[6] James Serpell, using Mithen's theories, suggests that our ancestors' shift to anthropomorphic thinking may have "opened the door to the incorporation of some animals into the human social milieu, first as pets, and ultimately as domestic dependents."[7]

How the practice of pet-keeping may have evolved from the early development of anthropomorphism is easier to theorize than why it has lasted for thousands of years. Chickens and pigs, with their eggs and meat, offer a return on investment, but it's harder to find the evolutionary value in cats and dogs. Certainly, it's not cheap to care for them. In 2017, Americans spent $69.51 billion on their pets, an increase of almost $3 billion from 2016.[8] Bob Vetere, President and CEO of the American Pet Products Association attributed the increased spending to an environment where pets' owners have "a top priority in pursuing longer, healthier lives for their pets."[9] Some researchers suggest that this priority stems from parental instinct and our seeming inability to resist a cute face.

A Darwinian view of pet keeping proposes that pets, without conscious intent, manipulate human responses in a way that uses and releases our innate parental instincts.[10] We are naturally drawn to young animals because they share perceptual features, including big eyes, chubby cheeks and short and thick limbs with human infants.[11] This is referred to as the "cute response" and along with it is a theory that proposes why humans are interested in animals in the first place.

Biophilia is defined as the inclination of humans to focus on life and lifelike processes, with an emphasis on the emotional connection that we have toward other forms of life, including animals.[12] Work on biophilia suggests that our inclination to seek an emotional connection with animals is formed from a set of learning rules and the rules spark different emotional reactions to animals, ranging from attraction to aversion.[13] People across

A hard to resist brown-haired puppy is ready for his close-up. The "cute response" theorizes that we are naturally drawn to young animals because they share features like big eyes with infants. April 24, 2020 (photo by Taylor Kopel. unsplash.com https://unsplash.com/photos/XdI7msXc6ps).

**Dog meat, along with a dog head, is on display in a backstreet market in Shen-
zhen, China. The fluid status of dogs means that some are companions while others are food. Photo by Paul Keller. December 9, 2006. Creative Commons. https://
ccsearch.creativecommons.org/photos/96af9049-1d84-4ee1-a986-ef9a2f9a5385**

cultures and social classes interact with and own animals but attitudes vary
as to their care and social identity.

In the Western world, our set of learning rules were shaped by the
domestic ethic of kindness, which expanded how the nineteenth-century
middle class understood the place of animals in the household.[14] In America for example, dogs may be considered companions, commodities,
objects of art, children, friends, workers and family members but in South
Korea, dogs may be all these things plus food. The co-evolution of animals
and humans across cultures suggests that our emotional reaction to animals, including how we apply anthropomorphism to our pets, follows different sets of learning rules but is a deep-seated and extensive drive. It also
might be good for our health.

Pet RX

In 1977, British psychiatrist Kenneth M.G. Keddie published a paper
that was one of the first studies about mourning a pet. "Those who do insist

on a special relationship with their dog or cat," he wrote, "put themselves at risk from a mental health point of view."[15] He illustrated his point with three medical cases. A 16-year-old girl developed a rash on her hands, could not swallow and constantly played with her fingers after the death of her King Charles Spaniel. A 55-year-old suffered from severe depression for 18 months following the death of her poodle and a 56-year-old breeder had nightmares and attacks of breathlessness when one of her champion Yorkshire terriers passed away. Keddie suggested that the patients' grief stemmed from each woman's creation of a family relationship with her dog. The young woman's spaniel was the sibling she never had while the breeder's dog stood in for the sympathetic husband she lacked. The poodle was a second child for a woman who had always wanted one.

While later studies reported that the percentage of people undergoing major pathological responses after the death of a pet was relatively low, at less than five percent,[16] Keddie's work pointed to the significant connection between pets and health. Like the women in his study, many contemporary pet owners consider their companion animals members of the family[17] and research shows that these members are often good for your health. Studies suggest that pet owners have fewer risk factors for heart disease than non-owners, higher survival rates following heart attacks[18] and appear to be more resistant to stress.[19] Researchers in New Zealand found that owners who reported a high level of behavioral compatibility between their pets and themselves showed better overall mental health, less stress and anxiety and fewer symptoms of illness.[20] In the elderly population, the literature reports that pet ownership can improve quality of life through increased physical and mental health.[21] One study found that having a dog was associated with fewer chronic illnesses, higher functional ability, and higher levels of subjective success when the aged lack human support.[22]

It's not all good news, however. Collectively, the body of work on the link between pets and positive health outcomes is inconsistent in its findings. While some studies show benefits, others demonstrate no advantage to pet owners' health. A few show poorer health outcomes for pet owners as compared to non-owners.[23] In a review of the literature, Judith Siegel suggests that what may be more useful is to think of the circumstances under which pet ownership may facilitate good health rather than whether or not it does so.[24]

For James Serpell, the link between pets and good health might lie in their role as a form of social support. Social support is defined as information that leads a person to believe that he or she is cared for and loved and part of a network of mutual obligation.[25] Theoretically, the positive health effect of social support may be applied to any relationship with the same characteristics. "By behaving in ways that make their owners believe that the animal cares for and loves them, holds them in high esteem, and depends on them for care and protection," pets could be considered a form of social support.[26]

Pets have been shown to help children develop respect, empathy, kindness and responsibility[27] and to aid people in coping with crisis and transition.[28] Pet owners report that bonds with pets are particularly important in times of illness and loss, helping to stem off loneliness and grief.[29] A study of social interaction between couples found that those with dogs had greater well-being and those who talked to their dogs (in addition to their spouse) about difficult situations reported greater life and marital satisfaction, as well as better physical and emotional health.[30] In a 2002 study, which measured cardiovascular changes of 120 married couples while performing two stressful tasks, the participants had lower heart rates and blood pressure when doing the tasks in front of their pet than when completing them in front of their spouse. The researchers noted that while the idea of a pet as social support "may appear to some as a peculiar notion," the study's results combined with the participants' descriptions of what their pets meant to their lives suggested that social support "can indeed cross species."[31]

An earlier study offered a similar conclusion after participants expressed a deep connection with their pets that was grounded in the animals' understanding of their moods and feelings. The study, which focused on the role of pets in family systems, surveyed 60 families with a variety of companion animals. The author found that most respondents believed that their pets understood when they talked to them, were sensitive to their moods and knew when they were feeling happy, excited, tense, sad or angry.[32] In one Australian study, the social support benefits of pets were expected even before the animals were adopted. A survey on the benefits and challenges people expected from dog ownership found that 89 percent of 3,465 prospective adopters expected happiness, 74 percent reported an expectation of decreased stress and 61 percent expected dog ownership to result in less loneliness.[33]

It's not hard to imagine that the same expectations for happiness and stress reduction that people have for their animal relationships is what they also hope for in their personal relationships. In a study conducted at Warwick University in England, researchers asked 90 people from 40 pet-owning households to use the Network of Relationships Inventory to describe the social support they received from human and non-human relationships. The respondents characterized their animal companion relationships using the same terms as they did for their relationships with other people. While human relationships scored better overall in terms of social support, pet dogs scored higher than people in the areas of "reliable alliance," "nurturance," and "companionship."[34]

The fact that the respondents were interpreting the behavioral signals of social support they got from their pets as if they were coming from people is directly connected to anthropomorphism. The ability to attribute human mental states to nonhumans is what allows people to socially, emotionally and physically benefit from their pets.[35] Talking to pet owners, it is not uncommon to hear them say that their dog misses them when they leave and is "happy" when they return or that their dog loves and needs them. Whether or not these beliefs are unrealistic is less important than the idea that without them, pets lose a significant aspect of their meaning. An interpretation of a pet's behavior that is not anthropomorphic, that might be guided by something besides human feelings, would cause the pet-human relationship to lose value.[36]

If attributing mental states to pets allows us to find value in our relationships with them, it also may be the case that we are influenced by a pet resembling us in intelligence and behaviors. In a pioneering study, social scientist Stephen Kellert surveyed 3,945 Americans on their attitudes toward different species. He found that a variety of influences impacted species preference, including aesthetic value, assumed

Print of a tobacco label showing a dog as a well-dressed man who prefers the finer things in life. Social psychology argues that dogs are typically perceived as having human-like traits, making canines preferable over other animals. Hatch & Co. September 14, 1869 (Library of Congress).

intelligence and threat.[37] While Kellert notes in this study and others[38] that similarity to humans is a factor that influences our attitude towards a species, other studies consider this idea in greater detail. In one, subjects were asked to indicate the likelihood that each of 30 animals could engage in three complex cognitive tasks and to rate the extent to which they felt each animal was similar to themselves and experienced the world in a similar manner to which they did. For pets (cats and dogs) and primates, the research found that there was a marked increase in perceived similarity.[39]

Social psychology offers a theory on why people show preference for similar animals, and it is linked to the idea that we are more empathetic and more attracted to those whom we perceive to be similar to us. So, if certain animals are perceived to share traits including sociability and intelligence with humans, they are preferred over others. The implications for an issue such as conservation are clear, as one study suggested when it found that respondents preferred to save species that they considered to be most similar to people.[40] To put it another way, if two conservation campaigns, one for jellyfish and one for elephants, were competing for the public's attention, it is highly likely that the elephant campaign would come out on top.

Animals Like Us

Anthropomorphizing an invertebrate, like a jellyfish, which is understood as physically, socially and behaviorally dissimilar to humans, is difficult for most people, at least when compared with an elephant, chimpanzee or dog. In fact, research suggests that humans actively dislike invertebrates because they are perceived as so dissimilar.[41] Yet, liking certain animals can also turn to dislike when the similar becomes too familiar. That is, when animals remind us of our own animal nature or "creatureliness," they potentially turn into a source of anxiety. Social anthropology and contemporary psychology offer some theoretical insight.

Social anthropologist Ernest Becker believes that creatureliness is an emotionally unsettling reminder of humans' biological nature, vulnerability and mortality. He suggests that the key to people elevating themselves above their animal nature is through the capacity for culture. Through culture, the behaviors humans share with other animals are given a special meaning beyond biological necessity and for Becker, culture is a "heroic denial of creatureliness."[42]

Using Becker's theories, psychologists developed Terror Management Theory (TMT), which proposes that culture partly developed in order to reduce the anxiety that comes from understanding that death is inevitable. When we are reminded that we share a creaturely nature with animals, that we too are mortal, it challenges the idea that we are different or special and therefore may be a source of worry.[43] Showing negative attitudes towards animals may be a way that some people relieve the tension. One Australian study set out to investigate this proposition by testing the hypothesis that people show more negative attitudes towards animals as a response to reminders of their creaturely nature.

In the study, participants were asked to evaluate animals under conditions that experimentally manipulated thoughts of human creatureliness. In order to prime these thoughts, subjects were shown a short video of chimpanzee mating behavior. The instructions were to think about how similar or different the behavior was to human reproduction.[44] As the researchers predicted, the participants who were reminded of their creatureliness gave more negative evaluations of the animals.[45] It turns out that when it comes to sex, giving a mental prompt that essentially says: Chimpanzees, they're just like us! did not create a positive association between people and primates. The chimpanzees became an outgroup.

It's easy to think of all animals as part of an outgroup. In fact, "us" and "them" may be a natural state of mind. Scholar David Berreby argues that humans have a natural inclination to divide their social world into these two categories.[46] Animals have, for most of history, been identified as "them" but a shift from farm life to city life changed this. Historian Richard Bulliet suggests that the shift from domesticity, where a farming existence meant daily contact with domestic animals, to what he calls "postdomesticity," where people live far from animals, both physically and psychologically, had an interesting effect. The farther away we got from "them," the animals that produce the "food, fiber, and hides" we depend on, the closer our relationships with pets became, which we often relate to "as if they were human."[47]

Of course, for some people, dogs are "them" no matter what. Whether it is indifference, hostility due to a bad experience or simply a preference for cats or parrots or a tank of tropical fish, dogs are not part of everyone's in-group. But the basic approach to understanding dogs for most people, whether those dogs are pets that are considered family members with similar feelings, household workers that are valued for their guarding, retrieving or other skills, or roaming strays that are considered a nuisance, is that dogs and humans have a complex level of co-existence. The common thread connecting all these categories of dogs is that being part of the daily rhythms of human life has a few conditions.

When dogs meet our behavioral expectations, they confirm the power dynamic of the human-animal bond. Dogs who engage in dangerous behavior by biting or attacking trouble this dynamic in two ways, but in both cases the wild side wins. When our pet dogs bite or attack, they have exposed our vulnerability and replaced us at the top of the hierarchy. Nature has beaten culture, however temporarily. When our working dogs bite or attack at our direction, as do police dogs or war dogs, the boundary between human and animal temporarily collapses, reminding us that we are perhaps not so civilized. Media accounts of dangerous dogs are an unsettling reminder that the deep bond we have with dogs has a dark side. Despite some sensationalized reports of bites and attacks that paint a picture of monster canines acting on their own, aggression in dogs rarely exists in a vacuum.

Biting the Hand That Feeds: Some Notes on Aggression

The National Safety Council wants you to worry—about the right things. The nation's leading safety nonprofit organization, it produces statistics on the lifetime odds of death for selected causes. The idea is that if you're going to worry about dying from miscellaneous risks, you should have some facts. According to its 2016 assessment of the biggest risks we face in the United States, you are right to worry about dying from heart disease, as it kills one in six of us, but you are causing yourself unnecessary anxiety if death by sharp objects is on your list (the odds are 1 in 27,407). Dog attacks number 23 out of 25 risks, with the odds of dying by dog at 1 in 132,614. Lightning, hot surfaces and substances, sunstroke and stings by hornets, wasps and bees are more likely to kill you than a dog.[48] Instructor and author Janis Bradley, who has prepared hundreds of students to become professional dog trainers at the San Francisco SPCA, puts it this way:

> Dogs are dangerous. And they are more dangerous to children than to
> adults. Not as dangerous of course, as front-porch steps or kitchen utensils or
> five-gallon water buckets or bathtubs or strollers or stoves or lamp cords or
> coffee-table corners or Christmas trees or balloons or bedroom slippers.[49]

Bradley's argument may not be very comforting to those who are bitten by dogs, which according to two widely quoted studies, is estimated to happen to 4.5 million Americans a year. The data are the result of a telephone survey of all types of injuries sustained by members of 5,238 households in 1994 and 9,684 households during 2001–2003.[50] The results include all bites that the respondents could remember during the previous year, including those that did not cause injury, a point that Bradley argues makes the numbers unreliable.

Another limitation of the study is that its estimates for persons aged 15 to 17 years old were extrapolated on the basis of rates for 10 to 14 year-olds.[51]

The numbers also come under scrutiny when compared to the CDC's Web-based Injury Statistics Query and Reporting System (WISQARS), which is a consistently maintained record of injurious dog bites. It records injuries presented for treatment at emergency departments across America. Since 2001, the WISQARS rate for dog bite cases averages 339,000 per year.[52]

In a 2001 presentation at the annual convention of the American Veterinary Medical Association, pediatrician and CDC epidemiologist, Dr. Julie Gilchrist, explained the difficulties in collecting data on dog bites. Dr. Gilchrist noted that if the injury was not serious from a pet dog bite, an owner or family member may not report it. In addition, there is no centralized reporting system for dog bites. "Incidents are typically relayed to a number of entities, such as the police, veterinarians, animal control, and emergency rooms, making meaningful analysis nearly impossible," she said.[53] While Gilchrist suggests that statistics on dog bites often lead to more confusion than clarity, Janis Bradley argues that the reason for collecting them in the first place is based on fear. In an interview with author Bronwen Dickey, Bradley argues, "We measure bites—or try to—because we're hardwired to react with fear to predators with sharp teeth." It's a response she believes we can learn to question, if not to disconnect from: "We can't teach ourselves not to flinch when the cobra at the zoo strikes from behind the glass, but we can learn that we don't have to run screaming outside because of the terrifying cobra."[54]

Dog bite data grow murkier when attempts are made to link the numbers to dog breeds. In 2013, researchers published a study that examined 256 dog bite–related fatalities in the United States between 2000 and 2009. They reported that most of these were characterized by coincident, preventable factors, including the absence of an able-bodied person to intervene, no familiar relationship of the victims with the dogs, and the failure of owners to neuter the dogs. Breed, the authors noted, was not one of the factors and the study's results supported previous recommendations for multifactorial approaches to dog bite prevention.[55] The researchers' findings should be taken into account when considering the results of an earlier CDC study, which made clear connections between breeds and attacks in an examination of over 300 dog-related deaths between 1979 and 1996. It reported that 60 deaths were caused by pit bull types, 29 by Rottweilers and 19 by German Shepherds Dogs.[56] Additionally, the American Veterinary Society of Animal Behavior says that identifying a dog's breed accurately is difficult, even for professionals, and visual recognition is not always reliable,[57] while multiple other studies have discredited visual breed identification.[58]

Pit bull types are particularly vulnerable to mistakes in dog breed identification practices. Research has found that the breed identification of these dogs by shelter staff and veterinarians is an inconsistent and unreliable means of identification.[59] In one study, half of the dogs labeled as pit bulls lacked DNA breed signatures of breeds typically classified as pit bulls.[60] While it's not just pit bulls that get mistaken—in one survey of over 2,000 bite reports, researchers found that any medium-sized black and tan animal was likely to be recorded as a German Shepherd Dog[61]—pit bulls are the most impacted by visual mislabeling and labeling in general. In a study on how the perceptions of a breed impact how potential adopters view it, the pit bull spent more time at a California shelter than its lookalike counterparts when it was labeled as a "pit bull." The removal of breed labels lead to more adoptions and a shorter number of days awaiting adoption for nearly all the dogs in the shelter, but it was most successful for the group of pit bulls.[62] As for the CDC, it stopped collecting breed data in dog-attack deaths after 1998, citing difficulty in identifying a dog's breed as one reason for the change.

Despite these challenges, dog bites and dog-attack fatalities have led to breed-specific legislation (BSL) that bans or restricts ownership of dog breeds and while these laws can apply to Rottweilers, Doberman Pinschers and other large breeds, pit bull–type dogs are often the prime targets. They are certainly in the crosshairs of dogsbite.org, a website dedicated to banning pit bulls, which reports that 433 people died from dog bite injuries over the 13-year period of 2005–2017. The site claims that pit bulls accounted for 65.6 percent or 284 of these deaths.[63]

Colleen Lynn, the creator and administrator of dogsbite.org, started the website after a pit bull bit her on the arm. She is not a professional in the field of statistics or animal behavior and some of the information on the website is sourced from the work of Merritt Clifton, who, like Lynn, is not professionally credentialed. Clifton has admitted to shaky research methods that are based on reading media reports rather than relying on primary source materials and speaking to investigators.[64] Various groups argue that the statistics provided on dogsbite.org are inaccurate and misleading, while author Bronwen Dickey suggests that what appears on the website "should not be confused with credible scientific information."[65] Yet, dogsbite.org is often used a source in journalistic reports, and its data compared to that of other organizations, including the American Veterinary Medical Association,[66] which problematically suggests that an anti-pit bull website with questionable critical analysis is on equal footing with organizations that have rigorous standards for statistical research.

The controversy over BSL is rooted in the relationship between dog bite–related fatalities and the circumstances that contribute to them, and one of the first of these variables to be investigated by law enforcement and journalists is a dog's breed. The intention is good. Identifying causal factors, like breed, is done to prevent future harm to people. But, as research has reported, visual breed identification is fraught with problems and studies that link bite-related fatalities to this type of breed verification often rely on weak and unreliable data. Another factor to consider in this debate is that research suggests serious injury due to dog bites is uncommon. Using data for treat and release injuries that are tracked by the CDC, the National Canine Research Council reports that 96 percent of dog bite injuries that end up in the country's emergency rooms are minor, and less than 1.5 percent require hospitalization. Children aged 1 to 12 are three times more likely to be hospitalized after going to the ER for an object stuck in an ear, eye, or nose than they are after receiving a dog bite.[67]

Deaths related to dog bites, while rare, are undeniably terrible. A strong emotional response to them is understandable because they are largely preventable and because they are widely viewed as disproportionately impacting children and the elderly. Yet, the idea that dogs bite more children than adults is not without controversy. While several studies note that children are the most common victims of dog bites and require more medical attention from those bites than adults do,[68] the largest survey conducted on dog bites, known as the second Injury Control and Risk Survey (ICARIS-2) and performed by the CDC, revealed something different. When the rates of dog bites to adults and children were compared using percentage of the population in the U.S. (counted as persons affected per 1,000), adults were more likely to suffer a dog bite. While it's natural to try and determine why a dog attacks, the answers are complex and particularly limited when an attempt is made to connect bite to breed.

Making Monsters: The Media and Dog Bite Stories

Most of us know about dog bites because we read about them in the press and the language used in these accounts matters. Popular press reports about dog bites have been shown to exaggerate the risk and to ignore the complex factors that may have contributed to the incident.[69] This impacts public perception and often finds its way into studies that investigate dog breed related attacks on humans, where media reports are sometimes used as the primary source for data. The loaded language of a newspaper or magazine article about a dog attack, particularly one that is described as "unprovoked," is an affective rhetorical device that generates fear by creating the idea that dogs suddenly turn vicious without human involvement.

In a March 2020 story about a pit bull that bit a Rochester, New York, toddler named Jayden, the reporter writes that the dog, "seemingly

unprovoked, clamped its jaw on her face at a family gathering" before listing the girl's many injuries.[70] A month earlier, a report on an Idaho police
officer who shot a dog after being attacked quotes a witness who says, "I
don't understand what's going on…. He doesn't usually attack people like
that."[71] In the same month, an account describing a pit bull that attacked
multiple members of the family who own him, resulting in one death, says
that the family told officials that the dog "had not been provoked before it
attacked."[72] In a 2002 article in *Good Housekeeping* magazine titled "Bred
for Trouble," the language used was similar and then the reporter went a
step further by constructing dog bites as a profound social problem.[73] The
writer named Mastiffs, Rottweilers and pit bulls as having "violent track
records" before quoting the president of the San Francisco Society for the
Prevention of Cruelty to Animals: "Ownership of dogs trained for aggression seems to be growing," he said. "These dogs are raised to be vicious.
Some people even say it's like building a bomb in your basement."

The *Good Housekeeping* piece also claimed that pit bulls "can clamp
their jaws down with up to 1,500 pounds of pressure—enough to snap a
human limb in half." It's a frightening sentence that may have led readers
to believe that pit bull types have more lethal bites than other dogs, which
is not true. (Scientific evidence suggests that the biggest determinant of a
dog's bite strength is its body mass, not its breed.[74]) The article also cited
several examples of dog attacks, including one fatal attack, made more
alarming by the choice of language. Two dogs "leaped free from confine-
ment and bore down" on "terrified" children. One of the children, whose
"little legs were no match for the mixed-breed pit bulls," suffered injuries
that he did not survive. The article did not discuss contributing factors in
any of its attack stories.[75]

It's not just journalists who are guilty of discussing dog attacks using
loaded language. A qualitative content analysis of 156 published papers
on dog bites written by health care professionals between 1966 and 2015
found "misinformation including factual errors, misinterpretations, omis-
sions, emotionally loaded language and exaggerations based on misunderstood or inaccurate statistics."[76] It may be the case, as the authors of the
study point out, that health care professionals are influenced by images in
popular culture and may rely on sources that reinforce their perceptions
or feelings about clinical situations when writing about dog bites. Regard-
less of whether or not health care professionals are allowing personal biases
to seep into their writing, their work has an important social impact. As
experts in the field, they are in positions to influence public policy decisions. Generalizing about certain bad breeds, as many of the authors in the
content analysis did by using, among other things, statistical percentages
of their sample size that were too low to allow for generalizations about the

entire sample, leads to stereotyping. It also stigmatizes particular breeds as dangerous.[77] When a health care professional writing a study or a reporter writing for a popular magazine or a newspaper about a dog attack uses misinformation or exaggeration, emphasizes a victim's terror, or creates a picture of a dog's viciousness with no reference to the complicated factors that may have caused the animal's reaction, it's a choice that has broader consequences for dogs, their owners and society.

There is something else at play when the media, in particular, reports on dangerous dogs. Priming is a cognitive process that relates to how one thought may generate other, associated thoughts. Exposure to related external stimuli, or the "primes," unconsciously triggers mental constructs of a target stimulus.[78] Priming is about offering a prior context that will be used to interpret subsequent information. It influences how ideas are evaluated and demonstrates how easily specific stimuli can shift how we think. In the fields of social psychology and political science, studies find that even short exposure to biasing information alters people's judgment. When participants in one study were shown violent video images, they listed more aggressive words in a free association than those exposed to nonviolent video images. Other research reports that slight racial cues in televised political advertisements primed racial attitudes.[79] In terms of animals, priming was a significant factor in the Australian study of creatureliness. The results were a negative view of chimpanzees but if the participants had been primed to see chimpanzee behaviors, like cooperation, as similar to their own, it's likely that they would have identified with the animals in a positive way.[80]

When it comes to dogs, the results are similar, in that priming plays a significant role in shaping how we think about them. One study examined whether negative and positive priming cues in written words and pictures influenced how people assess the traits of the German Shepherd Dog.[81] The hypothesis was that negative priming cues would trigger negative perceptions of them and closely related breeds. When the participants, who were exposed to words and pictures designed to portray the German Shepherd Dog negatively, rated the breed on various dog-related trait scales, they were more likely to perceive the dog as more aggressive, dangerous and less approachable than those exposed to the positive media cues. The results found no significant effect on perceptions of breed-related traits when breeds other than the German Shepherd Dog were considered, suggesting that priming may be breed-specific.

Repeated exposure to the same primes may determine public perception of an issue like dog attacks. By making certain aspects of dog attacks easy to recall, media influences the standards we use when forming attitudes about those attacks. Language that emphasizes the viciousness of a dog attack in a newspaper or magazine article makes recall of the topic easier in general because a story about a violent encounter between a dog and a person that results in gruesome injuries to that person is impactful. Processing the information from a dog attack article may then influence the standards readers use when forming future attitudes about the issue of dog attacks.

The priming effect is easily reduced by the flow of time as issues come and go and dog breeds that have been deemed dangerous change, but one dog has endured a bad reputation for decades thanks to consistent primes about its traits and behavior. In her history of pit bulls, author Bronwen Dickey argues that when dogfighting increased in the 1970s, activists used media campaigns to emphasize to its cruelty, but the crusade had the opposite effect. Instead of saving the dogs from a form of torture, reporters who cast them as natural born fighters "biologically hardwired to kill" condemned them to the margins of society, where conditions had already created a market for aggressive dogs.[82]

The negative image of pit bulls endures, and the media continues to prime audiences. A 2003 Nike television ad featured images of chained pit bulls lunging for each other cut with face-offs between basketball's biggest celebrities of the time.[83] In early 2018, social media users shared a video clip that showed scenes of cheering crowds and football imagery overlaid with the text statements: "Do not adopt a pit bull," "They killed the most kids," and "They killed the most family members." Kenneth M. Phillips, an attorney who specializes in dog bite law, created the video,[84] but the primes about pit bulls aren't limited to a lawyer's attempt at publicity. Dickey writes:

> Take a walk through any American shopping center, and you are likely to find pit bull sunglasses, pit bull soccer cleats, pit bull tires, pit bull colognes, even pit bull energy drinks, wines and hot sauces, all of which trade on the idea of a Nietzschean Uberhound who "won't back down" or "won't let go."[85]

Encountering primes about pit bulls or any dog deemed dangerous is impactful because these cues play upon a complicated relationship with an animal that has been an intricate part of humanity for over 30,000 years.

*   *   *

There is little doubt that certain breeds of dog exhibit certain types of behavior, but this becomes less convincing when that behavior is labeled as aggression and applied to an entire breed. Early canine domestication most likely included a selection for tameness, and when this was followed by the formation of dog breeds, various aspects of behavior were selected. The large amount of behavioral diversity among the hundreds of recognized breeds of dog worldwide suggests that a dog's behavior may be specific to his or her breed and will continue even without training or motivation. Pointing, hunting, tracking, herding, chasing— are all specialized tasks, selected for over generations and likely to be controlled, in some part, at the genetic level.

But no research has identified a specific aggression gene and use of the word may be problematic. One researcher described it as "a poor scientific term [that] chiefly functions as a convenient handle to relate phenomena described in more objective terms to practical human problems."[86] Aggression is also a normal behavior. Dogs, like their ancestor the wolf, exhibit aggression to protect themselves or their resources and to compete for food, territory or status and fear is a common cause. In her work with dogs that have acted aggressively, applied animal behaviorist and professional dog trainer, Karen London, notes that roughly 80 percent of the aggression she has seen is fear-based, and while it may not be the only factor, it is "typically the main issue."[87]

Trying to link aggression to the genes of specific breeds is also complicated by the interaction between genes and the environment and between genes themselves. Both interactions play a complex role in regulating canine behavior. If a dog that has potentially aggressive tendencies is then mistreated, the result may be antisocial behavior. Without the environmental factor, the antisocial behavior may be absent or different. How we respond to the reputations of certain breeds may also play a role. The biologist Ray Coppinger writes, "the fearful responses of people to a perceived aggressive breed 'teaches' the shepherds or the pit bulls to be aggressive with people.... It is a feedback system, where each time a person steps back ... the dog becomes more responsive to the move, and the people react more demonstratively to its movement."[88]

The National Canine Research Council takes the position that it's nearly impossible to reliably predict why a dog bites. It argues that a response resulting in a bite cannot be linked to an individual characteristic or a combination of them. Rather, a bite that injures is a rare occurrence that takes place due to multiple circumstances and variables in both the past and the present. Pointing to specific factors as causes of bites, such as being intact (unneutered) or simply looking like a pit bull, pulls attention away from other considerations that should be discussed when dealing with safety and the idea of a dog that is dangerous. Characterizing dogs without also thinking about the humans in their life or the situations that those humans have placed them in does them a disservice. For example, an adult's presence and supervision may prevent a dog harming a child. Sexually unaltered male dogs, which may show aggression, have owners who can choose to spay and neuter. Correctable factors like improper care, abuse, neglect, or lack of positive human interaction have all been connected to dog bites and related fatalities. Responsible animal stewardship has a direct impact on other factors that influence canine behavior.

In a 2014 review of primary literature, empirical data, public safety records and published veterinary accounts, researchers concluded that behavioral differences among breeds and within breeds exist and they were influenced by genetics, the environment and experience.[89] When it comes to unwanted behavior like aggression, dogs can be affected by numerous conditions that lead to it. My purpose here is not to deny that aggression in dogs exists. Rather, it is to offer evidence that media plays a central role in shaping how we understand dog aggression and that aggression is not an innate characteristic or gene found in certain breeds. It is the result of a complex set of factors, and every dog has the potential to bite. As author Bronwen Dickey writes, "If we want to own dogs, their teeth come along. It is up to us to learn how and when dogs use them and to keep our dogs out of situations where they feel they need to.... As much as we may want them, there are no simple answers."[90]

CHAPTER TWO

Urban

Mad Dogs and the City

> *We believe however, that City dogs for the most part, are an unmitigated nuisance, and from the entire race we conscientiously withhold our sympathy.*[1]

The practice of regarding specific dogs as favorites, or treating them as pets, stretches back to the late Paleolithic of Europe and North America, where some of the earliest known archaeological remains of domestic wolf-dogs were found buried with humans in a way that indicated mutual attachment.[2] Ancient pet-keeping however, was not without its rules. Canine animal control was on the minds of the Sumerians who laid down a few laws in the Mesopotamian Eskunna Law Code, circa 2300 BC: "If a dog is vicious and the authorities have brought the fact to the knowledge of its owner, (if nevertheless) he does not keep it in, it bites a man and causes his death, then the owner of the dog shall pay two thirds of a mina of silver."[3]

It wasn't just dogs that made the code. Oxen guilty of goring were also mentioned, along with instructions on how owners should be compensated. For the Sumerians, the costs of your ox's and your dog's antisocial behavior were steep, particularly if you failed to heed the warnings of your neighbor, who may have mentioned that your dog had a tendency to bite.

If you were a resident of Ipswich, Massachusetts, in 1644, things got more serious for your dog. A town meeting on May 11 ordered that "all doggs for the space of three weeks after the publishing hereof shall have one legg tyed up, and if such a dogg shall break loose and be found doing any harm, the owner of the dogg shall pay damages."[4] Refusal was an option, but if your dog was found "scrapeing up fish in a corne fielde" you had to pay twelve pence plus damages. The town of Exeter, New Hampshire, decided to take things to the next level: "It is agreed that all dogs shall be clog'd and side lined in ye day and tied up in the night and if any dogs shall be found trespassing in the lots they that shall find them shall shoot them."[5]

Despite these attempts, early animal control efforts did little to decrease the population of wandering dogs, which existed in most of America's cities well into the twentieth century. Some of the wandering dogs were owned while others were abandoned or feral, but most were considered a nuisance by a city's residents because the dogs spent much of their day harassing people for food, eating from the gutters and fighting and fraternizing with their fellow wanderers. The large canine populations quickly became one more problem for growing urban areas already struggling to regulate city life and maintain public health.[6] But it was fear of rabies (also called hydrophobia) that turned wandering dogs from a nuisance into a serious problem, as no animal-borne illness caused a greater sense of terror in people, particularly during the summer months, when it was falsely believed that rabies was most prevalent.

Rabies was a serious issue in nineteenth century American cities because the close contact of urban life made it more likely that a dog suffering from the disease would encounter a person or animal to potentially infect. But it was not a common one. The *Virginia Clinical Record* noted in 1872 that rabies was "an extremely rare disease" and gave the number of cases for New York during the six-year period 1866 to 1871 as 22, which worked out to be three cases of rabies a year to every million people.[7] Yet, the low number of rabies infections due to urban dogs did little to quell the growing anxiety over their presence, as newspaper reports routinely emphasized the chaotic nature of an outbreak and the number of dogs wildly out of control. In New York City, one dog in particular was to blame.

The "spitz" dog breed, which was loosely defined and included today's Pomeranian, was singled out by doctors as a main carrier of rabies, and the *New York Times* heightened the panic. In September 1881, a report on hydrophobia noted that the paper was the "first to point out that the Spitz dog is far more liable to rabies than is any other animal."[8] Readers did not have to look too hard for evidence that the dog and the disease were connected. "There can be no doubt that the comparative infrequency of cases of hydrophobia in this country during the last three years has been due to the progress which has been made in the extermination of the Spitz."[9]

Not that residents of New York City needed proof that the spitz was dangerous, since the paper had been sounding the alarm as early as 1875. One editorial made the paper's position clear. "There are but four venomous beasts among the fauna of the United States. These are the rattlesnake, the copperhead, the moccasin and the Spitz dog, and of the four, the latter is by far the most aggresive [sic] and deadly in its hostility to man."[10] It went on to say that the "ill-tempered and treacherous" dog was responsible for "every case of hydrophobia" in the city. According to the editorial, spitz dogs were monsters with one purpose. They "have devoted themselves with

An article praising the effectiveness of New York's dog-muzzling law, enacted to reduce hydrophobia or rabies infections. A plea was made for "toy dogs" weighing less than 15 pounds to be exempt (*Richmond Times-Dispatch*. November 14, 1915. Pg. 8. Library of Virginia. Richmond, Virginia. Chronicling America: Historic American Newspapers. Library of Congress).

startling energy to the work of thinning out the human race by inoculating it with hydrophobia."[11]

As reports of bite incidents and canine madness due to hydrophobia spread throughout nineteenth-century newspapers, panicked citizens demanded a solution. Some cities, including Philadelphia, implemented dog taxes and required expensive licenses meant to curb the dog population.[12] A more gruesome plan was implemented in some cities, where sanctioned dog killings took place, either in the streets or in pounds, and men were paid to either club dogs to death or drown them.

For the most part, the public responded positively to the dog killing ordinances. A May 29, 1840, commentary in the *Baltimore Sun* quoted remarks from the *Philadelphia North American*, which argued that while a country dog was in a "proper sphere" displaying "his wonderful powers of scent and sagacity, and guarding his master's property with untiring vigilance," city dogs had no useful purpose and were occupying a space where they didn't belong:

> We have no respect however for your town curs, yelping baying disturbers of sleep; howling occupants of back yards ... sneaking, mangy interlopers into small yards ... pests and calamities to a whole community, for the bite of one of these, so small that you see it not till you kick it over in passing, *may* [italics in original] entail death. On all such we cry aloud and spare not. May the "ketchers" thrive and multiply; and we hold him no good citizen who thwarts them in their duties.[13]

The Baltimore writer added that the sentiments were "not inappropriate to our own city" and expressed a desire that Baltimore's new ordinance "will be rigidly enforced."

The public's fear of rabies was so pronounced and widespread that the number of dogs didn't seem to matter. In 1886, an article in *Hall's Journal of Health* alarmingly noted that "there has been a spasm of hydrophobia scare at Newark, that has awakened the whole world within the last few weeks, owing to the running about of a furious, large, black dog."[14] One infected dog was powerful enough to create the perception of uncontrolled chaos.

Reports of a hydrophobia outbreak in one part of the country would reach newspaper readers in another, adding to the idea of a national epidemic. In 1889, a report in a San Francisco paper told readers about a situation in a West Virginia county. Despite killing two to three hundred dogs suspected of having the disease, the county was nevertheless "overrun with canines in a dangerous condition."[15] While some would come to recognize the panic for what it was—a commentator in an 1868 piece in the *New York Times* wrote that the "fear of the disease has worked far more harm than the malady"[16]—many people had powerful emotional responses to the topic that ranged from polite requests to angry rants. In an 1845 letter to the editor of the *New York Tribune*, the writer respectfully urged the paper's editor to call upon the Mayor "to put the 'Dog Law' in force" after a "worthy citizen" died from rabies and a child was bitten. The editor's attention to the matter would be met "with the warm response of the community at large."[17]

A less warm plea was made a few years later in 1856 when the *New York Daily Times* responded to reports of dog bites and a death from rabies in the nearby city of Paterson, New Jersey:

> It is villainous that our pounds should be so little patronized, and such swarms of dogs allowed to run unmuzzled.... In a brief walk of not more than a third of a mile yesterday, we counted no fewer than twenty-seven ugly yelping rascals, every one of whose snouts ought to, but did not enjoy the protection of a wire network.[18]

The commentary warned that the people may soon gather publicly to demand a new dog law and "hang those who have failed to execute the old one." While some citizens were angry over the failure of the pounds to curb the dog menace, others sounded an early warning by expressing doubt over their usefulness.

As early as 1845 when the Common Council in New York City proposed a change to the system, a commentary from the *Evening Post* argued that the process of catching and impounding dogs for a three-day period, after which they would either be sold or killed (rather than the current system that all unmuzzled dogs found at large could be killed by anyone)[19] was costly and unnecessary:

> Perhaps the city rulers have forgotten that the plan of catching dogs was tried many years since, and found to be utterly unpracticable, and it was not until several of our citizens were bitten by these rabid animals ... that the ordinance to destroy all dogs found running at large at a certain season of the year was enacted.... The dogs that are really dangerous, no man would dare to take hold of, while the city would be subject to the expense of keeping a dog pound, and paying the keeper, for the purpose of allowing a few worthless curs to live a few days longer.[20]

By 1850, the dog problem earned even more bureaucratic attention and a Dog Bureau was created in New York City. Made up of three squads of ten men with a captain and receiving full municipal encouragement, the office holders patrolled the streets with clubs and demonstrated their "prowess upon poodles, mastiffs, greyhounds—anything that went unmuzzled or without a collar."[21]

A year after the men of the Dog Bureau were clubbing dogs, the city's first pound was opened but, as a reporter for the *New York Times* noted in 1857, "it is not a very easy matter to get a good location for a dog pound,"[22] and residents resisted. The controversy over dog pounds in New York City

continued for years as newspaper commentaries called for their abolish-
ment or defended their use. In 1868, one concerned citizen, who warned
that without some means to reduce the dog population they would become
a plague of Egyptian proportion, had a solution. If dog pounds were
abolished, all dog owners should pay a heavy tax and the remainder of
unclaimed dogs should be shipped to China "where the usual Celestial fate
of the canine race in that country would end them."[23]

The debates surrounding control of urban dogs in the nineteenth century, framed around the widespread fear of rabies and how to contain it,
raised larger questions about political power but also about the complex-
ity of human-animal interactions during a time when attitudes toward
pets were changing. When the domestic ethic of kindness became part
of middle-class culture in the United States in the 1800s, the ways people thought about dogs and their place in the household expanded and
was reinforced through popular images. Historian Katherine Grier suggests that several metaphors emerged, including dogs as trusted servants, beloved children and friends. Together, these changes lead to more
emotional engagement in the act of pet-keeping.[24] For those who began
to relate to dogs as an emotional experience, "civilizing" their companions, or elevating an undeveloped mind, became an important part of the
arrangement.

Beginning in the 1840s, instructional books and essays on pet-keeping
began to appear, promoting the notion that a happy pet was one that a person thoughtfully cultivated in both its physical and mental characteristics.[25]
While the literature on training or "dog breaking" often stressed punishment, some writers started to approach the process differently. T.S. Hammond, in his 1894 book *Practical Dog Training*, described the traditional
mindset this way:

> Nearly all writers upon the subject of the dog agree that there is but one course
> to pursue; that all knowledge that is not beaten into a dog is worthless for all
> practical purposes and that the whip, check-cord and spike-collar, with perhaps
> an occasional charge of shot or a vigorous dose of shoe leather, are absolutely
> necessary to perfect his education.[26]

Hammond wanted to change the training narrative, and his ideas had some
impact. In an 1896 article from *Christian Statesman* called "How to Train
the Dog," the writer advised that the first step in training was to make sure
your dog was very fond of you, "so that the slightest cross word you may
speak will be punishment enough, without resorting to a stick."[27]

The notion of not inflicting physical harm on your dog reflected the
influence of the domestic ethic of kindness, particularly among middle-
class families who applied Victorian culture's principles of sophistication

and decorum to their lives. The ideal society reflected the ideal home, and in this home, animals were treated in a humane way, which distinguished their caretakers as good neighbors and good citizens. The sanctioned, inhumane killing of scores of wandering dogs involved issues of urban governance, public health and the duties of municipalities versus those of citizens and voluntary associations[28] but also at stake was the moral life of some of the city's residents. Dog killers did not make for good neighbors or good citizens.

As public anxiety grew over the corrupting influence of dog ordinances, reformers argued that the bounties encouraged the development of a criminal underworld full of unruly dogcatchers and street kids engaged in a cruel trade. Stories of dogs brutally clubbed to death in the streets by gangs of "urchins" and pets brazenly stolen from unsuspecting owners began appearing in newspapers. In 1848, a commentator wrote a lengthy piece for the *New York Daily Herald* describing several incidents where large numbers of street kids were seen chasing and killings loose dogs. Expressing alarm over the gruesome scenes, the writer told a story about a child who was employed by a "German sausage dealer" who left his beloved dog, Wella, in the boy's care. The boy and his friend killed the pet and shared the fee.

If the loss of poor Wella wasn't bad enough, the sausage merchant had a small riot on his hands after the boy, seeking revenge for being fired, caused a scene in front of customers by making it appear as if the dealer had sold him cat flesh disguised as sausage. Despite the merchant's assurances that his sausages were not made of cat, the women who were present "threw down their purchases, demanded their money, and left the place perfectly horrified at the idea of eating cats."[29]

For another editorialist, the corrupting influence of the city's payment for dead dogs was a shameful act that not only debased street kids' personal principles but also reflected deep disparities in social class:

> How would his honor the Mayor, or any one of our city fathers, admire it, if on his return from church, or at any other time, he met a young son or grandson of his, with bloodstained hands, bearing, instead of his school-books, a bloody bludgeon in his hand, and savage, bloodthirsty joy and avarice, beaming from his eyes. And yet, these same city fathers pay a premium from the people's pockets, to get the children of the poor to do these things.[30]

The commentator's pleas for empathy aside, the response highlights a clear distinction between those responsible for instituting the policy on dog collection as wealthy and respectable and those doing the dog catching as poor and engaged in a disreputable business. When organized animal welfare advocates joined concerned citizens in publicly expressing their alarm over

the impact of dog-catching on the morality of urban youth, reform was on
the horizon.

The formation of New York City's American Society for the Prevention of Cruelty to Animals (ASPCA) in 1866, the first animal welfare organization in the United States, gave the domestic ethic of kindness organized
expression.[31] Founded by Henry Bergh, the society was based on Britain's Royal Society for the Prevention of Cruelty to Animals. Bergh joined
the growing chorus of people who criticized the bounty system's corrupting influence on street kids. In 1874, he wrote: "With a bribe of fifty cents,
the idle youths of this city have been, in many instances, for the first time
seduced into the temptation of stealing and betraying their friendly companions, the dogs."

The dog pound's location close to a public primary school was also
on Bergh's mind and he worried that "along with the A, B C's the screams
of their condemned four-footed playmates might facilitate the scholars'
acquisition of immorality and prepare them for the State Prison and the

**Dog catchers pose with their quarry. 1924. While this group of men look quite
respectable, the general feeling among the public during this time, particularly
in New York City, was that those responsible for canine control were from the
wrong side of town (National Photo Company Collection. Library of Congress).**

gallows!"[32] Bergh's dire warning over the moral crisis facing the city's "idle" youth reflected a class based social vision of order but Bergh and other activists in the ASPCA also consistently aimed their efforts at all segments of society, not just the poor and working class.[33] Bergh had some modest success in limiting, and, in some years, halting the summer dog round-up, and in 1868 the ASPCA persuaded the mayor to cut the bounty reward in half and forbid persons under the age of eighteen to participate. Unfortunately, the change only benefited a growing group of middlemen dog brokers who would skirt the rules by giving street kids a small percentage to catch dogs, which they would then turn in.

By 1894, the ASPCA's push to remove children from the corrupt trade in dogs advanced as a result of a new law that gave the society control over the care and disposal of homeless animals. The municipal pound was closed, and licensing fees were introduced, along with a collar and tag requirement. Unlicensed dogs seized by the society's agents were taken to a new shelter facility. The aim was to find homes for dogs, with humane euthanasia by gas the last resort. In a press report announcing the change, a distinction was also made between the city's "brutal dog catchers ... recruited from the roughest classes" who tore dogs "away from their helpless mistresses in the streets" and the society's agents who would be "salaried and uniformed men ... held responsible for their actions ... and civil in the performance of their duties."[34] It was a point emphasized by John P. Haines, the ASPCA's president at the time, "You will not read any more complaints in the newspapers that Mrs. or Miss So and So has been knocked in the breast and has had her pet dog taken away from her by force."[35] The disciplined and authoritative agents of the ASPCA would no longer pose a safety concern for the respectable women of the city or their dogs.

Bergh's organized animal welfare movement spread to other states, and some advocates persuasively argued that society owed animals more kind and gentle treatment. Based in Philadelphia, the Women's Branch of the Pennsylvania SPCA (WPSPCA) successfully convinced the city's mayor to allow them control of the dog pound. By 1870, they had constructed a new facility, which they called a "shelter," instituted changes in how dogs were captured, and took care of them with a proper amount of food and water.[36] The Women's Branch also attempted to reform how dogs were killed and used "carbonic-oxide gas, generated by means of two charcoal furnaces."[37] Between 1874 and 1882, the society used this method to euthanize "nearly 30,000 dogs."[38] An influential organization with resources, the Women's Branch would go on to construct a shelter facility that vastly improved upon the municipal pound on land that the organization owned.

Despite the advancements of the WPSPCA, reform moved slowly. In

1885, the humane officer for the District of Columbia pound shot 3,000 dogs, while the pound in Pittsburgh was still drowning 25 dogs simultaneously in a large tank of water in 1891, fifteen years after the WPSPCA started using gas for euthanasia.[39] Fourteen years after the ASPCA took over animal control in New York City, it had presided over the killing of an estimated 200,000 dogs.[40] The numbers are remarkable, but animal advocates believed that the society's willingness to take on the task was a necessary community service, and it was framed as a preferable alternative to starving, diseased or troublesome dogs causing havoc on city streets.

The efforts of animal welfare advocates had an element of social control aimed at the poor and working class but their work also reset the image of the urban dog. Physical risk from rabies took a back seat to the ethical peril of a corrupt bounty system. The dangerousness of city dogs, which were now associated with disreputable dog catchers, moved from actual harm to spiritual harm. Animal control processes led by "bad" men were recast as a corrupting influence on poor children that transgressed a moral boundary.

Animal Welfare and the Underdog

Despite the fear of rabies declining among a public concerned with dog catchers' impact on the moral character of their youth, the disease continued to be a topic of conversation. Scientific, political and institutional developments, including French scientist Louis Pasteur's rabies vaccine, strengthened the conviction that the disease must be eradicated, and some of America's state health departments added its management to their agenda. The problem was that while public health officials became more actively involved in rabies prevention in the period leading up to World War I, the ASPCA, along with a second wave of animal welfare organizations, turned their attention to providing shelter, veterinary services and humane euthanasia. The two movements found little to agree on.

In New York City, confrontations between the Board of Health and the ASPCA reflected differing attitudes over rabies and animal control. Both organizations supported culling strays, but the ASPCA's central focus was protecting dogs from a harsh life on the street, with the health of the public a less important advantage of animal control.[41] While the state and volunteerism struggled to work together in the area of animal control, rabies outbreaks continued, and the press singled out stray dogs as a problem. A 1936 article in the *Chicago Tribune* quoted a "recognized authority on canine health and diseases" who said, "the stray is the carrier in almost all cases."[42]

But when it came to rabies, categories could be unstable. Writing from Hawaii in 1916, a state that was and remains rabies-free, a commentator addressing hydrophobia outbreaks in Washington and California argued that being designated a pet did not override animal instinct: "The lap dog and pet terrier are dogs first before they are pets" with "cantankerous dispositions toward all other canines." It was this animal nature that made them victims: "Fido, out for exercise ... snaps at the less pampered and wholly unpedigreed and unrestrained cur dog of the alleys" and gets a "dose of rabies" in return.[43] In a complex negotiation of animal identity, the writer categorized certain breeds as privileged yet still capable of uncontrolled behavior, which made them victims of both their animality and the less civilized "cur dog" of the streets.

Articles soon began to stress prevention rather than panic. In 1944, the *Pittsburgh Press* published an article titled: "What NOT to Do If You're Bitten by Dog with Rabies Is Explained." Approaching the topic scientifically, a "West Penn Hospital expert" took readers step by step through the process of dealing with and treating a suspected rabies bite, emphasizing the things they should not do. Shooting the dog was discouraged, as were extreme emotional reactions:

> It is safe to say that the greatest damage being done by the long continuance of the current rabies epidemic is not damage to the tissues of the body ... but damage to the nervous and mental equilibrium of ... mothers, whose often unnecessarily extreme apprehension over dangers to their children may attain the grade of an actual hysteria.[44]

Newspapers across the country took a scientific approach to the subject with long explanatory articles, including one in a Missouri paper from 1939 that outlined cause, symptoms, prevention and treatment. The article dispelled myths and rumors, "Hot, thirsty dogs, anxious for a drink have been accused of being 'mad' by misguided people," and stressed that there were "many false ideas prevalent among people" regarding the disease.[45] Along with the changing public discourse on rabies came a push toward adoption, which would reframe the dangerous urban dog.

Beginning in the late 1800s, groups including the Animal Rescue League of Boston and Chicago's Anticruelty Society devoted much of their time to protection and medical care and advice. They also made it easier on the public to turn in unwanted dogs and cats rather than abandon them. They established depots and receiving stations and sent agents to pick up relinquished animals. Their efforts to systemize adoption programs laid the groundwork for rethinking the place and value of stray dogs in communities.[46]

In the early 1900s, with the Women's League for Animals advocating for services to the dogs of the poor, and the Massachusetts SPCA launching the country's most advanced animal care facility in response to the demands of the residents of Boston and surrounding communities, owners of all economic classes had more professional care available to their dogs. As humane societies' involvement in companion animal care increased, the SPCA's association with pet keeping also intensified. Adoption was promoted as a commonsense solution to overpopulation, while the various societies' services including affordable care, and in some cases, subsidizing the high cost of redemption fees at pounds, made pet ownership a more economically appealing practice. Another strategy was to promote shelter dogs as deserving underdogs.

Establishing the animal shelter as a source for adoptable pets, advocates often stressed a dog's stray status. One welfare group described their shelter's canine residents as "drawn from the miserable multitudes of the lost and stray, the stolen and tortured—literally the 'under-dogs' of their world."[47] Press reports profiled humane society workers' brave rescues of dogs in peril with photospreads of them happily feeding stray dogs in their organizations' "adoption pen."[48] The celebration of strays would soon expand to celebrity dogs that had a tough start. Famous film dog Rin Tin Tin's origin story was often repeated in the popular press. One headline read: "Lee Duncan Found the First Rinty in a Bombed-Out Kennel in 1918 and Thus Discovered the Greatest Dog Family in History."[49] Igloo, a favorite dog that belonged to Admiral Byrd, was profiled in 1931 with an emphasis on his role in "sharing all the hardships as well as the triumphs of the recent polar expedition."[50] Igloo, the piece noted, "was found by Mr. Byrd on the streets of Washington and at once found his way into the admiral's heart."[51]

Using the discourse of stray dogs as faithful servants and companions, second-wave animal welfare advocates sought to reclaim a pet status lost or never conferred on street dogs. With no home or family, the loose dog belonged to no one but became everyone's problem as a potential carrier of disease. Adoption redeemed the street dog by reestablishing domestic ties and the hierarchies that went with them. As belonging was restored, so was human control over a dangerous problem.

From the Street to the Dog Park

Roaming dogs in the eighteenth and nineteenth centuries occupied a range of categories, from companion to wild and feral, to somewhere in between. Moving between these categories, they challenged social, cultural and conceptual boundaries that divided animals from humans or nature from society. If they had rabies, they transgressed a public health boundary that had political implications for municipal structures and in time, the decisions made to reduce their numbers in the name of public health would align the idea of dangerous dogs with dangerous men. The conflicting views of public and private institutions over the best way to solve the problem of the urban dog framed them as a health threat, a moral danger to wayward youth and eventually, worthy of being restored to pet status. In each of these roles, humans took an active part. As a health threat, dogs represented a human loss of control over nature that was reclaimed when dogs were once again promoted as valued pets. As a threat to morality, dog catchers engaging in inhumane practices were cast as monstrous as the canines they were tasked with controlling.

One of the effects of animal welfare organizations' focus on caring for loose and abandoned dogs was the promotion and subsequent growth of pet ownership in urban areas. Where to take all these pet dogs quickly became an issue, and owners increasingly lobbied municipal governments to provide more spaces for their canine companions. By the 1950s and 1960s, a few state and regional parks allowed dogs to run free or off-leash on certain trails, but in most urban areas, dogs were required to be on-leash when in public. The idea of an urban, enclosed public space exclusively for dogs off-leash was developed in California, and the first dog park was established in Berkeley in 1979. In 2018, 774 dog parks were in operation in the 100 largest American cities, an increase of 40 percent since 2009.[52] While these parks have become an acceptable mode of urban canine management and a positive experience for many dogs and their owners, they are also contested spaces full of disputes and debates over the relationship between humans and dogs in cities.

For dog owners, off-leash sites offer a legal area where they can exercise and socialize their dogs. Research suggests that the benefits extend to the owners as well. Dog parks are spaces where dogs facilitate relationships among strangers. The common identity of "owner" allows for safe and comfortable social engagement with easy topics of conversation that revolve around the care and activity of a pet.[53] One study reported that 77 percent of dog park users believed that dog parks helped people meet neighbors and develop a sense of community.[54] A dog owner and frequent user of her local dog park in Tennessee told a reporter, "You meet a lot of people and even your neighbors through the dogs. It's good for the dogs and the neighborhood, as far as keeping the neighborhood strong."[55] A dog may facilitate interactions between humans that create inclusiveness, but in the dynamic world of the dog park, the possibilities for conflict are always present.

Dog Park Danger

As a politician, I have learned that there are two things you never do: You never change parking restrictions and you never get yourself involved in a dog park.[56]

The scarcity of green space in densely populated urban centers and concerns over the noise and smell produced from dog parks has often led groups to complain and demand tough municipal policies against their development. United States community leaders preside over board meetings that can draw hundreds of people with strong opinions on both sides of the dog park issue. In California, a pro–dog park group worried that anti-park people suffered from "constricted intellects" and wondered if maybe getting them dogs would "help brighten their worried lives."[57] In Indianapolis, one opponent of a dog park had a problem with pet owners: "It's the owners at 5:30 a.m. slamming the doors of their SUVs and shouting, 'C'mon Bosco! Here boy! Here boy!' Who wants to live next to a kennel?"[58] For those against the development of dog parks, canine companions (and sometimes their owners) are just as problematic as were their free roaming ancestors. For the users of these sanctioned spaces, the world of the dog park presents opportunities, but they are not trouble-free.

When urban dogs went from running loose in the streets to running loose in permittable public spaces, the problem they represented shifted from disease, which required control and detention, to troubling behavior (particularly around the issues of feces and aggression), which needed regulation and management. The solution was to erect signs that establish the boundaries of acceptable behavior, for both humans and their dogs. Telling park users to remove dog feces and how to prevent dog aggression, signs position the dog as a problem and establish the meaning of responsible pet ownership, marking the park as a site of urban civility.[59] Opponents to dog parks fear the absence of this civility because it would create foul-smelling and noisy areas near their homes. Supporters of off-leash sites claim that self-policing among users ensures this civility because most people supervise and clean up after their dogs, signs or not. But the dog park environment is a dynamic one and the idea that pet owners, rather than rangers or police, manage dogs outside the familiar environment of the home means that appropriate dog behaviors may not be a shared understanding. What one owner sees as bad behavior in need of regulation, another may view as a dog being allowed to be a dog.

Conflicts naturally arise when people with different expectations for responsible pet ownership encounter each other, and as one study reported, how they resolve these conflicts varies. Observing the participants of his local dog park, researcher Patrick Jackson found that pet owners became "control managers" who used various strategies to both negotiate problems related to dog behaviors and to manage their and other's understanding of what constituted appropriate behavior for dogs in public spaces.[60] While some owners avoided potential trouble areas like crowded gate entries, others walked away from situations they found problematic but could not avoid (like unwanted mounting of their dog by another), so as not to heighten the tension between themselves and another owner. Some used humor to diffuse a situation. Others publicly disciplined their dog to demonstrate their attempts at responsible control. In the world of the dog park, owners often define what it means to be a good or bad dog. Whereas a dog is constructed as a problem in need of managing, so too are the owners who fail to do the managing.

The Pit Bull Problem

In a dog park, a negative perception of a dog's breed or behavior may extend toward owners, which may limit their opportunity to form positive relationships. For the owners of pit bull types, the chance to bond with fellow canine caretakers in off-leash spaces is often stopped at the gate. In the Tennessee dog park mentioned earlier, the posted rules of 2007 stated that the following were not permitted: Dogs in heat. Dogs under four months of age. Dogs without supervision. Aggressive dogs, pit bulls or dogs having the characteristics of the pit bull breed.[61] More than a decade later, pit bulls are not welcome in some dog parks in Georgia, Indiana and New York.

For some pit bull owners dog park entry is the least of their worries, because their pit bull is prohibited from being housed at kennels, boarding facilities, rented residences and homes that are part of HOAs.[62] A few large insurance carriers will not underwrite the properties of pit bull owners, while others may offer a policy but stipulate that claims involving a pit bull won't be covered. Private housing is off-limits to pit bulls on all major U.S. military bases. According to pit bull advocacy nonprofit organization, Animal Farm Foundation, as of this writing, 350 cities ban pit bull–type dogs and 44 have declared them "dangerous." In 24 locations across the United States there is a mandatory spay/neuter law for these dogs in place, while in 85 towns and cities, pit bulls are declared "vicious." Across 80 places in America, pit bull–type dogs have more restrictions placed on them than do other breeds. (More than 180 towns and cities add Rottweilers, Doberman Pinschers and other breeds to their bans, restrictions and regulations.) The road that led to pit bulls being banished from dog parks, rental properties, insurance policies, cities, counties and military bases is a long one. It began in the fighting pits, where the dogs were considered as dangerous as the spectators who cheered them on.

Fighting Dogs for Fighting Men

If a pit bull was fighting in 1868 New York City, it was likely in the pits of Christopher Keyburn, or as he was more well-known, Kit Burns. Kit was an Irish immigrant whose love of dogfighting grew from working in the saloons of the impoverished and criminally overrun Five Points neighborhood of lower Manhattan.[63] His tavern, Sportsman's Hall, was the center of New York City dogfighting, and the press remarked on the crowds as much as the dogs. According to one reporter, the events attracted an audience of "ruffians who howled with delight" during fights.[64] Another journalist, who Kit invited as his guest in 1866, described the audience as having "faces lowering and strongly set about the jaws, so that they bore no weak or fanciful resemblance to the brutes who were yelping and rattling their chains in impatience below ... all of them talked slang and drank incessantly."[65] It was the dogs' association with objectionable members of society that marked them more than anything else. In the fighting pits of Sportsman's Hall, pit bulls were dangerous dogs for dangerous men.

All forms of animal fighting were outlawed in New York in 1867 and Burns would eventually be arrested during a dog fight in 1870, with SPCA president Henry Bergh leading the charge. (Burns would die before being formally sentenced.) The end of Burns's dogfighting empire in New York City didn't stop the enthusiasm Richard K. Fox had for the practice. Fox was publisher of the *National Police Gazette*, a paper that focused on sports, theatre gossip, crime and scandal. Despite the animal fighting ban, Fox published a piece in 1889 that outlined the stages of a dog fight, including the selection of the contenders, "the first grapple," rules for washing a dog before the fight, "the death struggle," and finally, the winner. Lushly illustrated, "Some Points on the Management of Canines in the Pit" was an instructive guide for practitioners and spectators.[66]

Fox's admiration for the "sport" of dogfighting and its canine athletes came up again in 1905, when he published an article extolling the virtues of Dewey, a white pit bull terrier owned by a saloon owner in Detroit named Archie McFeeter.[67] Dewey, whose scars were described as "marks of honor," was a good earner. Not only did his winnings pay off the mortgage on McFeeter's saloon, which was said to be several thousand dollars, but they also paid for the annual $500 saloon license. Dewey gave McFeeter financial security and had an interesting life outside the pit. He played a starring role in a romance, helping to establish "one happy home in Cleveland," and even captured a burglar. But it was Dewey's heart for fighting that set him apart. Matched with a champion pit bull named Spider that hailed from Cleveland, Dewey's first big match had high stakes. McFeeter placed a $700 bet and Dewey "seemed to know that his master's all was at stake." During the fight, Dewey was "cool, decisive and fearless." He fought for an hour and a half and then "seemed to be weakening." McFeeter was nervous but then something remarkable happened. Dewey somehow summoned the strength to win and McFeeter proudly said he "knew that there was the heart of a hero in him."[68]

Despite the good press that Dewey received as a loyal gladiator, pit bulls' association with unsavory characters like Kit Burns and his crowds made them generally unappealing as family pets until a man named John Colby came along. A native of Massachusetts who loved animal fighting, he saw an opportunity to capitalize on the public's declining interest in dog-fighting by promoting and selling fighting bulldogs as pets. Famous clients bought his dogs and Colby's success in transforming the pit bull from fighter to companion inspired breeders beyond Massachusetts to do the same.[69]

Soon, bull and terrier dogs were publicly celebrated in newspaper ads as gutsy, loyal and steadfast. In a 1916 advertisement, a Wichita, Kansas, breeder named A.O. Smith declared, "I am breeding the Pit Bull Terrier [*sic*] and the well known English Bulls. If you desire a faithful watch dog for your home and family, for your auto, your chickens, guard and companion for your children, these dogs are unequaled."[70] He continued with an appeal to dogfighting enthusiasts, "Boys, if you desire to raise a fighting dog that has a perfect unbroken record of the best Pit Bull Terrier [*sic*] blood lines in the country, these pups will meet your approval."[71] A breeder in Knox-ville, Tennessee, advertising his services to newspaper readers in Missis-sippi enticed potential customers with a similar appeal, "The Pit dog … is now probably without exception, the most courageous animal in the world … he is a perfect companion for a walk or drive and a lady accompanied by such a bundle of energy and loyalty has a protector which will defend her with his life."[72] In terms of fighting prowess, the ad claimed that pit bulls' stamina was only matched by their agreeableness in the face of death, "In fact it often occurs that two well bred dogs of this species will both die in the pit without either making a sound of complaint or an effort to quit."[73] The public, once skeptical of pit-type bulldogs, began to embrace them.

Homeward Bound

While the public was starting to fancy the pit bull, the American Ken-nel Club was less enthusiastic. The dogs' association with the disagreeable men of the fighting pits excluded them from the club's breed standards but the rejection didn't stop smaller canine clubs all over the U.S. from proudly displaying their dogs. Pet pit bulls formed a new class at the 1911 Madison Square Kennel Show, where they were represented by Cid and Zab, who were declared "two fine specimens of the breed,"[74] and said to be particularly suited for the pet realm. In the show, Cid and Zab were harnessed and pulled a wagon driven by a young girl, a spectacle that prompted Brooklynites to wonder at "the obedient, gentle conduct of the team."[75] A few years later, readers in Texas opened the *Houston Daily Post* to a photo spread of eight dogs who would be part of a stock and pet exhibit. Seven were pit bull terriers, one was a "Boston bull."[76] By 1925, the pit bulls of Houston wouldn't have to share the stage with livestock or other dogs. The American Bull Terrier Club of Houston and South Texas advertised its "first exclusive pit bull terrier show," which would be held at a Houston park. The contest had fifteen categories. Two cups and a variety of prizes were awarded.[77]

It wasn't long before stories about pit bulls that were wonderful children's playmates and brave protagonists filled the pages of magazines and novels.[78] The dogs became university mascots, military morale boosters and symbols of the country's prevailing attitude that anything was possible with grit and hard work. They were considered so appealing that advertisers used them to promote products. They made the cover of *Life* magazine three times, the only dogs to do so.[79] Teddy Roosevelt had a bull terrier at the White House called Pete. Helen Keller wrote about her beloved bull terrier dog Phiz. Pal the Wonder Dog would appear in over 200 films. One pit bull named Luke would become as well-known as his famous owner.

The real-life pet of comic actor Roscoe "Fatty" Arbuckle, Luke moved from background player in Arbuckle's films to playing crucial comedic roles. His tricks included climbing ladders, which he performed in several films, and his parts were often designed for sentimental and narrative purposes.[80] Luke's exploits, from eating an actress' slipper to getting lost for three days, much to Arbuckle's distress, were detailed in fan magazines and newspapers.[81] During Arbuckle's infamous trial in 1921, the *Los Angeles Times* wrote that the actor had at least one "sincere mourner." Luke "sits, disconsolate, at the door, waiting for the familiar step and the well-known voice. He doesn't eat. He waits. Whatever befalls Fatty, Luke will not forget."[82] Part of popular culture, Luke's stardom rose and fell with Arbuckle's, but his impact on the Keystone film studio was significant, as he contributed to expanding the appeal of its movies to family audiences.[83]

Whether they were promoted as perfect family companions, brave heroes, or lovable movie stars, pit bulls had risen from the fighting pits and achieved a deep well of goodwill among the American public. It would take decades before this well would turn rancid, and when it did, the pit bull would never be able to fully climb out of it.

Return of the Gladiator

Sheriff W.R. Taff was curious. His brother's entire motel in Shell Point, Florida, the town's only motel, was leased for Saturday night, August 28, 1971. In rural Wakulla County, population 6,000, that many travelers seeking accommodation was unusual. Early Sunday morning, Taff and his four deputies followed the motel traffic to a small dirt road. They radioed Sheriff Raymond Mamlin, who oversaw neighboring Leon County. He sent five deputies and two investigated the scene. What they found were families, some with small children, pressed against a 15-by-15 canvas and wood pit, watching two pit bulls fight. When the second fight started at 7:30 a.m., the two deputies signaled for the others to raid the area. Of the 260 men, women and children in attendance, some ran away through the high weeds of nearby woods but 87 were arrested and charged with cruelty to animals. Found at the scene, described by the chief deputy as a pit of "solid blood," were eight pit bulls, along with plastic and wooden wedges, which were used to pry open a dog's "death grip" on the throat of another dog, and drugs used to "revive exhausted winners."[84] Taff said that he believed it wasn't the first dog fight in the area and it wouldn't be the last. "The next time this happens," he warned, "I'm going to go as far as the law allows me to."[85]

It's not clear whether Taff busted up more dog fights after that sunny Sunday in August but he wouldn't have been alone in trying to stamp out the illegal activity as it rose in popularity. All over the country, crowds gathered to watch two dogs tear each other apart, and while the numbers weren't as alarming as animal welfare advocates suggested, organized dog fights were routinely taking place and the press was there to report all the gruesome details.

By 1974, Washington lawmakers started paying attention and in the fall, a congressional subcommittee held hearings on dogfighting, gambling and illegal activity associated with the fights after inquires "corroborated newspaper accounts of widespread, organized pit-fighting of trained and untrained animals at locations from coast to coast."[86] Many of these newspaper accounts referred to Duncan Wright, the executive director of the American Dog Owner's Association, who told *New York Times* journalist Wayne King that dogfighting had "quadrupled."[87] King later named Texas as "a capital of dogfighting"[88] and Texas journalists were quick to pick up on the story.

In Austin, reporter Mike Kelley, writing for the *Austin-American Statesman*, told readers about a man named Dewey and his pit bull who was bred only to fight. Dewey believed that he was simply facilitating a natural inclination. Kelley wrote:

> Dewey concedes that putting those dogs together in the pit is cruel and brutal and generally bad. But, he says, that is what they are born to do. It is instinctive in them to fight, he says. Dewey doesn't teach them to fight, he just makes it possible for them to do what comes naturally.[89]

The idea that pit bulls are innate fighters was stressed several times in the piece. Dewey told Kelley that "the fighting instinct" began to show at the age of four or five months and Kelley's description of a sparring match suggested that the theory was true. "The dogs do not seem to understand it is only practice," he wrote. "They fight in earnest: twisting, maneuvering for position, for a vise grip in a vital area." The dogs only stopped fighting when men "jam 'break-sticks' between their straining jaws." Painting a picture of dogs that only know one thing from the age of four months, Kelley resurrected the gladiators of the fighting pits, but this time they were cast as natural-born killers. The men in charge of these killers made it into Kelley's article as well. He noted that the spectators at dog fights carried guns, "so sometimes while the dogs are ripping each other apart in the pit, the men who bet on them are laying into each other too."[90] The connection made between violent men and their aggressive dogs, first reported in the stories of Kit Burns' fighting pits, was back in the press.

More sensational than bad men and bad dogs was the theme of pit bulls as monsters with the blood instincts to rip each other apart, and it was repeated in articles across America. Pit bulls were identified as specially bred for fighting and classified as "throat fighters," or nose, front or back leg specialists, depending on which part of their opponent's body they preferred to attack.[91] When Duncan Wright showed footage from a dog fight during the 1974 congressional hearing, papers reported that the film was "so gruesome that many persons in the crowded hearing room either averted their eyes or stepped outside until it was over."[92] While there's little doubt that the film was gory, some of Wright's facts, as author Bronwen Dickey notes, were doubtful. His claim that the number of dog fighters, which he told *New York Times'* journalist Wayne King was five thousand and had "quadrupled," was countered by some of the practice's most well-known organizers. They put the number of dog fighters across the country at fifty to a few hundred at any given time, while match reports from the early 1970s suggested that the number of people attending fights was also low.[93]

Details about dog fights grew more scandalous, and dubious, when Wayne King was invited to watch a match in Chicago. King was a guest of

Pat Podzianowski, who bred and fought Staffordshire terriers. King wrote a detailed description of Podzianowski's multiple tattoos, which included "a pair of dogs, their jaws open, fighting with fangs and straining muscles"[94] and noted that the trainer's advice to a novice on how to develop a puppy's "blood instincts" included the following instructions:

> What you want to do is get yourself one of those cats and put it in an onion bag and string it up on a rope from the top of the garage.... You want to get yourself some clippers and clip the claws off. Then you let the puppy at it.[95]

Podzianowski's callous comments were fiction according to Jack Kelly, editor of *The Sporting Dog Journal*. Kelly said that King had asked Podzianowski so many silly questions about dogs that he had decided to have some fun and tell him ridiculous stories he didn't expect King to believe.[96] Podzianowski may have been having fun with a reporter but his words fed into a narrative about pit bulls that would only continue to grow.

Five years after King's interview with Podzianowski, a law enforcement officer quoted in an Ohio newspaper article said he had received information that people were taking pit bulls and "turning them loose on other animals."[97] A regional director for the Humane Society supported the claim, saying that she was familiar with pit bull owners who used "10 to 12 cats and several small dogs" to condition their dogs for a fight. Pit bull owners, she said, will "stop at nothing to work up an animal to a good fighting state," and small animals gave the dogs "a good taste of blood."[98] The article quoted a man named Flapjack who said he fed stray cats and dogs to his five pit bulls because "they need that blood."

It's worth noting that the police officer mentioned in this article said he had received information. He did not witness it firsthand. The humane society executive claimed to be knowledgeable about pit bull owners engaging in bad practices but said nothing about seeing those practices personally, and a man named Flapjack offered a cruel detail about his training practices that may have been nothing more than a misguided attempt at shocking the reporter.

Like other frenzied reports of pit bulls spreading across the pages of 1970s newspapers, the Ohio newspaper article left readers with what had become a running theme in the cultural conversation about the nature of the dogs and their owners.[99] The *Today* show would eventually repeat the baiting stories, telling viewers that live animals were used to train pit bulls to fight,[100] while a fundraising appeal letter from the Humane Society of Greater Miami would call fight promoters "sadistic inhumane individuals."[101]

After years of exposure to stories about killer dogs and cruel trainers, newspaper readers and some television viewers were primed to equate pit bulls and their owners with violence. Over and over, the message was that the dogs were bloodthirsty monsters and so were the unscrupulous men (and a few women) who bred them to fight. It wasn't long before pit bulls, marked by these associations, were reframed as the dogs of an urban criminal class.

Living in a Gangster's Paradise

> There's something a little scary about wondering, "Is there a time bomb ticking in my dog?"
> —Dr. Franklin Loew, dean of Tufts Veterinary School[102]

When journalists characterized pit bulls as savage fighters who barely needed prompting to kill another dog, they promoted the idea that pit bulls were vicious by nature. Shelter workers and animal welfare activists, however well-intentioned, didn't do much to persuade the public otherwise. While they typically mentioned bad breeders as one cause of pit bulls' problems, they also suggested that the dogs were naturally dangerous, which compounded the fear that was cementing itself in the public's mind. At the same time that dogfighting enthusiasts were telling journalists that pit bulls had killing in their blood, animal welfare advocates were telling them that pit bulls were unpredictable, uncontrollable, and more aggressive than other dogs.

In 1979, columnist Jack Roberts asked his *Miami News* readers to consider a pro/con argument on whether "pit bulldogs" were good pets or "a bodily menace."[103] The evidence against the dogs was an incident where two pet pit bulls, leashed and out for a walk, attacked a woman and her dog. The woman required 45 stitches around her eye. The evidence in favor of the dogs was a description of two who Roberts had met while conducting research for the article. They belonged to a member of a local pit bull association and were "as gentle as puppies wanting to be petted." But Roberts gave the final word on the state of the pit bull to Kenneth McGovern, the Executive Director of the Humane Society of Greater Miami: "You can never tell about a pit bull. They were bred to fight. I don't trust them and it isn't the animal's fault." The dogs, he said, were trained to "never let go."

McGovern was one of many experts who would appear in newspapers across the country warning readers about pit bulls. In an article for the *Philadelphia Daily News*, Dr. Alan Beck, a pet-behavior expert at the University of Pennsylvania, compared owning a pit bull to keeping "a lion or wolf in your backyard."[104] Phyllis Wright of the Humane Society of the United States called the dogs as dangerous as "a loaded .45."[105] In 1987, an editorial in the *Los Angeles Times* said that animal-control authorities believed that the pit bull's aggressive nature "can be restrained, but not reliably so." Once a pit bull had "tasted blood," it was "undependable at best, uncontrollable at worst."[106] The director of field services and investigations for the Humane Society in Washington, D.C., said that pit bulls were always "right on the edge" hovering between control and rage.[107]

Animal advocates didn't scare everyone away from wanting to own a pit bull. For some of the public, the dogs' seeming capacity for sudden rage was a positive. After Ethel Tiggs, a 71-year-old Florida woman, was mauled by two of her pit bulls in 1980, one pet shop reported that their phone was ringing off the hook for "the kind of dog that bit the old lady."[108] This local response highlighted the power of the press to shape the dogs' aggressive image but it was also facilitated by pit bulls' shifting geography. As dog-fighting spread from rural areas to cities, it continued to be a source of fast money with little downside.[109] It was also the case that a natural extension of the dogs' skills in the fighting pits was personal protection, particularly in urban areas that felt unsafe. Pit bulls weren't the first to be popular as guard dogs. German Shepherd Dogs, Dobermans and Rottweilers all had their turn, but what made pit bulls different and desirable in high crime

A terrier surveys the street atop a stoop at a row house in Philadelphia. When pit bulls and related breeds made the move from rural areas to cities, their fighting reputations made them popular for personal protection (photo by Carol M. Highsmith. March 12, 2019. Library of Congress).

areas was their size, which made them easier to handle, and widely held misconceptions about their inability to feel pain. Many people also believed that the dogs had extreme loyalty to their owners, however badly they were treated.[110]

Reporting on the rise of pit bulls in economically depressed areas, the press routinely used racialized language and soon, the label "urban dogs" became code for crime and the underclass. In a column titled: "How to Deal with Pit Bull Menace," writer Neal Peirce described out of control dogs from a poor neighborhood in Baltimore. He listed the number of fatalities caused by pit bulls and then sounded a dire warning: "This wave of terror stalking American streets can only worsen. There's an explosion of pit-bull breeding in ghettoes and barrios where idle, embittered youth have chosen the animals as 'macho' status symbols."[111] Pit bulls were the dogs of a disaffected non-white underclass. Worse, Peirce warned, they had "become for many drug dealers the weapon of choice—legal but more terrorizing than guns."

Animal welfare advocates echoed a similar tone in their discussions of pit bulls. A year before Peirce's column, Marilyn Bernstein, Vice President of Humane Law Enforcement for the New York ASPCA, said the pit bull was a popular guard dog among members of the drug underworld and was "becoming a very fashionable, macho dog." The executive director of the Pennsylvania SPCA echoed her comments. Owning a pit bull, he said, "fulfills some kind of macho fantasy."[112] In the *Los Angeles Times*, a letter to the editor said it was "unfortunate that certain undesirable elements of people have adopted the pit bull as the breed to reinforce their antisocial orientation."[113] One study found that every *New York Times* article published between 1987 and 2000 on pit bull owners consistently depicted them as unsympathetic and thuggish.[114] The *Philadelphia Daily News* reported that the dogs were "a common sight in poor black and Hispanic neighborhoods in Philadelphia, Camden and other East Coast cities."[115] In 1987, at the height of pit bull hysteria, *Sports Illustrated* put a snarling pit bull on its cover with the text "Beware of This Dog." The article noted that a pit bull was "the dog of choice for drug dealers and street punks around the country." It was a dog for people who had "insecurities" and needed "macho reinforcement."[116] On the same day, a *Time* magazine article by David Brand called "Time Bombs on Legs," described a pit bull in terms that verged on the supernatural:

> Fire burst from its open mouth, its eyes glowed with a smoldering glare, its muzzle and hackles and dewlap were outlined in flickering flame. Never in the delirious dream of a discorded brain could anything more savage, more appalling, more hellish, be conceived than that dark form and savage face.[117]

Brand then made sure his readers knew who was responsible for the time bombs on four legs. "Violence-prone owners" were "turning pit bulls into killers."[118] The press, with help from animal welfare advocates, told a decade long-story about pit bulls where they were characterized as weapons, extensions of criminality, and status symbols for people potentially at risk for violent behavior. The stage was set for racial fears about crime.[119]

Consistently putting pit bulls together with racialized men in a criminal context, the media normalized the image of the pit bull as a "ghetto" monster. Using this outsider status, hip hop culture co-opted the media representation of the terrifying, unyielding devil dogs and made them stars of music videos and celebrated them as the hardened pets of rappers. Pit bulls, already culturally relegated to the underclass, became a blank slate for disaffected youth. Bronwen Dickey writes:

> In the pit bull, a young man could see whatever version of himself he wanted, from family defender to resourceful hustler to unbowed survivor. Never before had a generation of African-Americans, especially the urban poor, connected with a specific type of dog they felt represented their collective identity.[120]

In this context, the pit bull was less a canine outcast and more an urban street survivor that symbolized a level of control over disorder. Yet, the complex nature of the dogs' meaning to segments of urban populations was lost amid press reports that only sought to vilify them by connecting horrific bite stories with the criminality of their owners.

The media's pit bull narratives, which often created a clear line between evil dogs and evil owners, also gave the public permission to "express the inexpressible."[121] Sociologist Arnold Arluke argues that when people indirectly vent their feelings through animals, "hostility toward human groups may not raise public ridicule because these inappropriate remarks are one step away from us."[122] The media's selective coverage of vicious pit bulls and their criminal owners gave racial anxieties an outlet that appeared acceptable. Arluke describes the impact this way:

> Now, when we think of pit bulls, we think of dogfights and drug traffic, deadly, unprovoked attacks on humans by "vicious" dogs; and owners who threaten mainstream America. Pit bulls—and, importantly, their owners—have become scary and frightening monsters to many Americans. No stereotypical portrayal of an African American, Latino or working-class skinhead gang is complete without a pit bull in the picture.[123]

For pit bulls, the association had deadly results. As killer dog hysteria entered the 1990s, some shelters seized on the idea that pit bulls were only magnets for disreputable and dangerous individuals and implemented drastic measures. The Pennsylvania SPCA (PSPCA) took in almost 4,100 pit bulls in 1999 and put down nearly every one of them.[124] Commenting that there was "a very high percentage of inner-city kids" with pit bulls,[125] Erik Hendricks, Executive Director of the PSPCA, advocated for a breed ban in Philadelphia. He claimed that because there was a "definite racial element" to pit bull ownership, many politicians were "reluctant to take a tough stand."[126]

Hendricks' tough stand wasn't always the organization's policy. In 1984, the PSPCA held the position that a breed ban was not the answer to the problem of dogfighting and emphasized the pit bull's "lovely and affectionate" nature.[127] When the panic over pit bull attacks on humans hit in 1987, the PSPCA's newsletter reported that it had reversed its opposition to banning pit bulls and declared that "terminating the breeding and sale of these dogs may be the only way to stop the incredible suffering the breed has endured."[128] Yet, Hendricks' policy of across-the-board euthanasia 12 years later had more racial undertones than it had concern for the dogs' welfare. Pit bulls may have been incapable of being pets in his view, but the main takeaway was his dismissal of a demographic he believed to be contemptible pet owners.

The connection between race and pit bulls made national headlines in 2007 when NFL quarterback Michael Vick was sent to prison for operating Bad Newz Kennels, an underground dogfighting ring that housed over 50 pit bulls. Investigators found evidence including shallow graves filled with dog body parts and injured and underfed dogs chained to car axles. The indictment stated that Vick (and two associates) "executed approximately 8 dogs that did not perform well in 'testing' sessions ... by various methods including hanging, drowning, and slamming at least one dog's body to the ground." Another dog had been wet down and electrocuted with Vick's knowledge. The dogs' deaths were allegedly seen as funny by Vick and his friends.[129]

Vick was sentenced to 23 months and was tried in state court for felony dogfighting, where he was fined and received a suspended three-year sentence. Coverage surrounding the case typically focused on race, poverty and criminality, with the suggestion that poor racialized neighborhoods desensitized children to violence against animals.[130] In her work on the Vick case and its relationship to race and criminality, Megan Glick argues that "animal abuse is continually represented as somehow endemic to communities of color, while aberrant and psychopathological in the case of whites."[131] It's a position that Vick's lawyers took, arguing that dogfighting was a "culturally based predilection."[132] Years later, Vick would say that watching dog fights as a kid had a huge impact on him. No one, he said, ever told him it was wrong.[133]

Some media pundits placed the blame on the music industry. "Hip-hop culture put Vick in this bind," wrote *Kansas City Star* columnist Jason Whitlock.[134] NBC news quoted Gerald Early, a professor of English and African-American studies, who said that rap and hip-hop music had helped make the pit bull the "tough dog of the day." Early added that football was a macho sport dominated by black men, many of whom had been raised on rap so they were "fired up by the sort of romantic image of being a gangster."[135] Hip hop culture was once again to blame for glorifying the connection between pit bulls, race and crime.

The pit bulls rescued from Bad Newz Kennels had a different battle on their hands after they left Vick's fighting pits. Animal welfare organizations and pit bull rescue groups hotly debated their potential for rehabilitation. People for the Ethical Treatment of Animals called them "ticking time bombs," and the Humane Society, repeating a familiar position, said they should all be euthanized because "temperament testing" was very difficult, and they could "suddenly turn on another animal or child."[136] Pit bull advocacy groups fought for them to be evaluated and matched with owners who understood the challenges of dealing with ex-fighting dogs. Acknowledging the cultural stigma pit bulls faced, one canine trainer noted "If these were German Shepherds, [not saving them] wouldn't even be part of the discussion."[137]

The dogs from Vick's kennel would live to (not) fight another day when the federal government decided that they could be evaluated, rehabilitated, and where possible, placed as pets. The subsequent press stories focused on their transformation from fighters to victims. No longer monsters, individual dogs were described as having "wonderful play manners" and wanting to be "friends with everybody."[138] They were successfully placed in homes with children and cats. No longer the dogs of "thugs," they were free from their vicious reputations.

While the Vick dogs were benefitting from the positive media coverage, other pit bulls were not as lucky. In her qualitative analysis of news articles from three national papers published one year before and one year after the Vick case, Rebecca Pickens found that there were no stories covering the more than 2,190 pit bulls confiscated in dogfighting raids the same year as Vick's arrest.[139] The Humane Society of the United States reported that 54 of those dogs were dead when investigators arrived, with some chained to trees, others with duct tape over their mouths and a few in trash cans.[140] Between April 25, 2007, and April 25, 2008, the raid on Bad Newz Kennels was one of 216 that took place. It was the only one that was covered in the papers Pickens examined. In her study's two-year time frame, 3,383 pit bull dogs were seized in dogfighting raids and nearly all of them were put down. None of these stories were told in the print sources she analyzed. In the case of the Vick pit bulls, fame seems to have played a role in the narrative as strongly as race did.

The rescue and rehabilitation of Vick's dogs triggered a shift in America's relationship with the pit bull that lead to some positive changes. More advocacy groups sprang up to fight the "breed" stigma and popular media joined the effort. *Dog Town*, the first pit bull–focused reality show, was broadcast on National Geographic Channel in 2008 while Animal Planet released *Pit Bulls & Parolees* in 2009, followed by *Pit Boss* in 2010.

How dogs from fighting raids were handled also changed as a result of the Vick case. In 2009, more than 500 pit bulls were taken from multiple fighting operations in a broad cross-state sting operation and the ASPCA performed a behavior evaluation for each of them, in addition to allowing them time to rest and recover.[141] Today, most shelters do not have a strict pit bull euthanasia policy and many municipal governments are repealing pit bull bans. As of 2018, 21 states have some type of anti-breed specific legislation. Seven of these prohibit municipal regulation of dogs by breed while the rest prohibit municipal declaration of dangerous, potentially dangerous or vicious dogs based solely on breed.[142] Despite the positive changes, pit bulls are still euthanized at an alarming rate in American shelters and newspaper stories of pit bull attacks continue to make headlines.[143]

In a 2014 article called, "The State of the American Dog," Tom Junod argued that pit bulls were the center of the national narrative:

> Pit Bulls have become representative…. No other dog as vilified on the evening news, no other dog as defended on television programs, no other dog as mythologized by both its enemies and its advocates, no other dog as discriminated against … no other dog as likely to end up in an animal shelter, no other dog as likely to be rescued, no other dog as likely to be killed.[144]

In the media, particularly during the pit bull hysteria of the 1980s, the most lasting impressions of the dogs came from stories about horrific attacks: The death of two-year-old James Soto, who paramedics said was "unrecognizable as a human being" after being mauled by a neighbor's pit bull, and the spectacle of Florence Crowell, a 33-year-old animal control officer, whose attack was captured on television before making national headlines.[145] There was the 1982 incident of 83-year-old Floridian, Longion Angueira, who "was knocked to the ground and dragged up a driveway" by two pit bulls outside his home.[146] The police officer who arrived at the scene said, "They didn't just bite him. They were trying to eat his flesh…. I've been a cop 17 years, and I never saw animals attack a human being like that." A four-year-old boy was mauled while blowing bubbles in his neighbor's yard. The injury required "massive amounts of plastic surgery."[147] A pregnant woman was attacked near her home, while a six-year-old boy's injuries were graphically catalogued: "His right ear was ripped off, his nostrils flapped loose, and his eyelid and lip were badly lacerated."[148] These attack stories fueled the public's fear but there was another, more socially troubling narrative beneath the headlines.

When pit bulls were coded as "urban dogs," when they were connected to race and criminality, the horrible attacks stoked more than physical fear. Suspicion of the "other" blossomed and grew and what people saw as a strictly human-animal relationship, the fear of a dangerous dog, was actually our troubling relationship with one another, where fear was based in prejudices, stereotypes and racism.

* * *

The discourse surrounding the urban dog is a moral, socioeconomic and racial one that has as much to do with dogs as it does with owners. Wandering dogs of the nineteenth century were framed as rabies-infested monsters that represented a health threat, but beyond the civic panic, was a spiritual one where the very souls of the city's youth were at stake. Participating in cruel capture methods for city-sanctioned payouts, street kids were in moral peril.

When wandering city dogs made their way into more homes and eventually into the urban dog park, canine control became canine management. Owners were expected to demonstrate that their dogs could be docile and master acceptable behaviors. The stakes were high for both. In the contested space of the dog park, biting and aggression were the transgressions of a dangerous urban dog and when these boundaries were crossed, it cast doubt on the ability of owners to be "good citizens."

The era of pit bull owners as good citizens ended when the media reminded the public that "America's dog" was the same one that came out of Kit Burns' fighting pits. Rural dogfighting's migration to urban centers cemented the pit bull's reputation as the dog of the underclass and advanced it as the weapon of thugs and criminals, the macho status symbol of lost boys from the 'hood and the tough dog of hip-hop culture. The fear this association unleashed swept through an already turbulent cultural climate, where it widened the economic and racial divide. The pit bull represents one of the most powerful and enduring constructs of the demon dog but it is merely the latest to hold that status. The next chapter explores working dogs who occupy a space somewhere between human direction and disruption.

CHAPTER THREE

Working

Career Canines

Dogs are multi-dimensional, capable creatures, as anyone who has ever shared a house with one will tell you. Their encounters and time spent living with humans have enabled them to develop a set of social-cognitive skills that facilitate communication with us. They respond to our body language, facial expressions, and voices, and in turn use their own vocalizations and movements to focus our attention on what they want. It is mutual communication that emphasizes how humans and dogs impact each other. While all dogs shape humans on some level, working dogs have far-reaching effects on those they encounter. Some have captured the popular imagination for their ability to perform heroic tasks, like Stubby, a stray who became a decorated World War I hero, or Poncho, a Spanish police dog and Twitter sensation who performed CPR on officers pretending to collapse. There is also Max, a bomb-sniffing dog credited with safely navigating countless men through minefields.[1]

Beyond the anthropocentric descriptions applied to Stubby, Poncho, Max and other working dogs like them, there is some evidence of cognitive ability and purposefulness. In his work on militarized dogs on the Western Front, academic Chris Pearson examined British army reports that attributed impressive feats to messenger dogs. These dogs travelled hundreds of miles over unfamiliar terrain, and one group, having been distracted, returned to the task of delivering information at the "instruction" of the lead dog. The author of the report commented that it was the dogs' sense of duty and responsibility that kept them on task.

Putting aside the unknowable, Pearson argues that the dogs' behavior indicated learning and a level of decision-making. "We cannot be sure why the dogs stopped and then returned to their task.... But it appears that they were capable of making some kind of decision over what to do in that situation and to take the lead from one another."[2] Pearson's research makes an important point about military dogs that is useful to working dogs in general. Their ability to use their senses, their capacity to endure physical hardships, and their response to training commands all allow for a type of agency that works in combination with human intentions, imbuing working dogs with a mixture of human and canine capabilities.[3] When this combination is guided by malign human intentions, the canine rescuers, protectors and battlefield heroes become something more sinister, entering the public consciousness as symbols of racism, dehumanization and death.

Negro Dogs

> *Ranaway Bill; has a scar over one eye; also one on his leg, from the bite of a dog; has a burn on his buttock from a piece of hot iron, in the shape of a T.*
> —*John L. Dillahunty. July 21, 1837. Commercial Bulletin. New Orleans, Louisiana*[4]

Listing a scar from the bite of a dog as one identifying mark for his runaway slave Bill, John Dillahunty's newspaper advertisement revealed a dark reality where dogs were used to intimidate and control slaves, as well as to pursue and capture runaways. The use of so-called "negro dogs" as part of the slave patrol and slave hunting system was introduced to Southern colonies and states after the dogs' association with various wars. Used in the Spanish conquest, the Jamaican Maroon rebellion, the Haitian revolution, and most notably for Southern slave owners, the Seminole War in Florida, Bloodhound-types imported from Cuba earned reputations as particularly aggressive trackers and hunters.[5]

By the 1850s, the use of large dogs to hunt people was a known fact, brought to the public's attention through abolitionist literature and the writings of Frederick Law Olmsted, who documented his journey through seven slave states in 1853. Olmsted, who would be remembered as an eminent landscape architect, also worked as a journalist. He described the training methods slave hunters and Southern planters used:

> No particular breed of dogs is needed for hunting negroes: blood-hounds, fox-hounds, bull-dogs and curs were used, and one white man told me how they were trained for it.... They are shut up when puppies, and never allowed to see a negro except while training to catch him. A negro is made to run from them, and they are encouraged to follow him until he gets into a tree, when meat is given them. Afterwards they learn to follow any particular negro by scent....[6]

While Olmstead noted that breed was less important than training methods, Bloodhounds were the primary choice of slave catchers, as they were

widely considered to be "fierce hunters" who would "tear a man to pieces"
if not constrained.[7]

It wasn't long before slave hunters began to advertise their services across the South, with their dogs prominently mentioned. "Blood
Hounds—I have TWO of the FINEST DOGS FOR CATCHING NEGROES
in the Southwest," declared David Turner, a slave hunter in Tennessee. "They can take the trail TWELVE HOURS after the NEGRO HAS
PASSED and catch him with ease…. I am ready at all times to catch runaway negroes."[8] Like Turner, many dog-owning slave catchers were ready to
accept a job at short notice and often required their fee upfront. J.C. Hardy
of Hillsboro, Mississippi, advertised "a splendid pack of Negro Dogs,"
which he offered to the public at the rate of $15 per day for hunting and
$100 if the slave was caught.[9] Hardy's services didn't come cheap, which
reflected the fine nature of his dogs. Those with less capable canines, like
James Hays, charged $3 per day for hunting and $15 for capture.[10]

Some slave hunters offered advice with their advertised services. A
Missouri-based man, whose Bloodhounds were "in prime training and
ready to attend to all calls" suggested that "any person having a Nigger runaway … send for the Dogs forthwith when the Nigger goes off."[11] Many
slaveholders took his advice, including Louisiana planter David Barrow.
Barrow kept an extensive diary, which included an entry on the "drives" he
and his neighbors participated in. "With the zest of sport," planters, hunters and overseers on horseback would follow a pack of dogs set loose on a
runaway. Summarizing one drive, he wrote: "about a mile, treed him, made
the dogs pull him out of the tree, Bit him badly, think he will stay home a
while."[12]

The role Bloodhounds played in the tracking and capture of runaways
was also compellingly recounted in slave narratives. Former slave Henry
Waldon remembered it this way: "Them hounds would worry you and bite
you and have you bloody as beef…. They would set them on you to see
them bite you. Five or six or seven hounds bitin' you on every side."[13] In
her autobiography, former slave Harriett Jacobs described seeing her son
Benny "covered with blood" after being bitten by a "fierce dog." Harriett
was hidden at the time of Benny's injury and recalled hearing the chill-
ing words of Mrs. Flint, the slaveholder's wife, "I'm glad of it. I wish he
had killed him. It would be good news to send to his mother. Her day will
come. The dogs will grab her yet."[14] Harriet also wrote about a conversation between her grandmother and her uncle Benjamin, who was imprisoned after an escape attempt. With the help of a kind-hearted jailer, Harriet
and her grandmother were allowed to visit Benjamin in the early hours of
the morning. She recalled the sad scene and the powerful words her uncle
spoke to her grandmother:

He told her that when he was captured, he broke away, and was about casting himself into the river, when thoughts of her came over him, and he desisted. She asked if he did not also think of God. I fancied I saw his face grow fierce in the moonlight. He answered, "No, I did not think of him. When a man is hunted like a wild beast he forgets there is a God, a heaven. He forgets every thing in his struggle to get beyond the reach of the bloodhounds."[15]

In slave narratives, some autobiographical, most told to abolitionists, being pursued by dogs left deep emotional scars. For some, it was the sound that haunted them the most. Former slave Solomon Northup described his encounter with "a kind of blood-hound but a far more savage breed than is found in the Northern States." The dogs were trained to "attack a negro at their master's bidding, and cling to him as the common bull-dog will cling to a four footed animal."[16] It was the dogs and the sounds they made, not the men on horseback, that Northup focused on when recalling his escape from Bayou Bouef:

In an instant more, their long, savage yells announced they were on my track.... Fear gave me strength, and I exerted it to the utmost. Every few moments I could hear the yelpings of the dogs. They were gaining upon me. Every howl was nearer and nearer. Each moment I expected they would spring upon my back— expected to feel their long teeth sinking into my flesh. There were so many of them, I knew they would tear me to pieces, that they would worry me, at once, to death.[17]

Other slave accounts echo Northup's fear of being mauled to death by dogs, noting that if the dogs caught them before the men on horseback did, they could inflict severe injuries.[18] At least one plantation owner had the same concern. He wrote his overseer in Alabama with instructions not to use dogs in a slave's recapture, "I wish you to try to get him back, but dont [sic] want dogs to go and Ketch him. It is too dangerous. They may kill a man in a very short time. Last time they had nearly torn him up."[19]

Most planters, however, embraced the use of dogs and slave narratives recorded the results. Former slave James Williams recalled the gruesome fate of a runaway named Little John:

We followed [the dogs] awhile, until we knew by their ceasing to bark that they had found him. We soon met the dogs returning. Their jaws, heads and feet, were bloody.... We found the body of Little John lying in the midst of a thicket of cane. It was nearly naked, and dreadfully mangled and gashed by the teeth of the dogs. They had evidently dragged it some yards through the thicket: blood, tatters of clothes, and even the entrails of the unfortunate man, were clinging to the stubs of the old and broken cane.[20]

Williams, once a favorite slave of a wealthy Virginia family, was sold to an Alabama plantation and forced into the position of "driver" over his fellow slaves, which made him familiar with the hounds used in the hunts. The memory of Little John's death was one he would later recall when he made his own escape. "I thought of the fate of Little John, who had been torn in pieces by the hounds ... escape seemed impossible." Running through the woods, Williams swam across a stream and hid from the dogs. "The woods seemed full of them," he remembered and then a dog named Venus appeared.

> She stopped suddenly, looked up at me, and then came wagging her tail and fawning around me.... I called to [the other dogs] but they did not look up, just came yelling on. I was just about to spring into the tree to avoid them when Venus, the old hound, met them and stopped them.

Shocked, Williams noted his disbelief, "The very creatures whom a moment before I had feared would tear me limb from limb, were now leaping and licking my hands and rolling on the leaves around me." He then took the extraordinary step of continuing his escape with the dogs, "I took courage and started onward once again, taking the dogs with me." Williams would eventually part with the dogs, directing them to pursue a deer. "They went off, yelling on the track and I never saw them again."[21]

James Williams could not read or write. His story, like other slave testimonials of the time, was published and publicized by abolitionists. The anonymous editor of Williams' story began it with an impassioned anti-slavery plea, a regret and an assurance. The editor acknowledged an inability "to present this affecting narrative in the simplicity and vivid freshness with which it fell from the lips of the narrator" but also made sure to note that Williams' "manner and in many instances his precise language"[22] was used. Certainly, the writer of Williams' story had a sense for what would make a compelling tale and likely used descriptive language that would capture the attention of white readers who the writer hoped to enlighten about the realities of slavery as an institution and the humanity of black people as individuals. While this should be taken into account, Williams' story offers a valuable perspective as a historical source.

The editor of James Williams' narrative also added a footnote regarding the training of Bloodhounds: "Blacks are compelled to worry them until they make them their implacable enemies, and it is common to meet with dogs which will take no notice of whites, though entire strangers, but will suffer no blacks beside the house servants to enter the yard."[23] It's a clear reference to the human sources of Bloodhounds' menacing behavior and a suggestion that the dogs were trained to recognize certain people as off limits. The idea that Venus and the pack turned from hunters to companions when they discovered Williams might be due to the fact that, as a driver on a plantation, he was a figure of authority to the dogs.

Not all runaways were immobilized by the fear of Bloodhounds and not all hounds that stopped the chase had a happy ending like Venus. J.D. Green, a Kentucky slave whose story included three escapes, shared his experience encountering a runaway named Geordie and a dog named Fly:

> We were suddenly aroused by the well-known sounds of the hounds. In my fear and surprise I was attempting for a tree, but was unable to mount before they were upon me. In this emergency I called out the name of one of the dogs, who was more familiar with me than the others, called Fly and hit my knee to attract her attention and it had the desired effect. She came fondling towards me, accompanied by another called Jovial. I pulled out my knife and cut the throat of Fly, upon which Jovial made an attempt to lay hold of me…. I made a powerful effort to fling him as far away as possible, and regained my knife; but when I had thrown him there he lay, throttled to death. Not so Fly, who weltered in blood, and rolled about howling terribly, but not killed. The other two hounds caught Geordie, and killed him.[24]

Breaking training, the dogs that chased Green and Williams may have disrupted their image as monstrous beasts, but it was too powerful for a few incidents to dispel it. Bloodhounds were the violent embodiment of a violent system and abolitionists understood the value that image brought to their antislavery message.

Bloodhounds, Abolitionists and Indians

When abolitionists published former slaves' experiences, they were cataloging countless acts of human cruelty in the hope that the horrors of slavery would generate enough moral outrage to pressure politicians to end it. Bloodhounds were an especially arresting image that captured the public imagination because they underscored the violence and inhumanity of slavery and slaves' desire for freedom.[25] The dogs also became a useful symbol for a morally bankrupt South. Abolitionist George Carleton wrote in 1857 that the Bloodhound, an "emblem of cowardly distrust and brutal cupidity," had become "a household word—a 'domestic institution'" in slaveholding parts of the South. To make his point, he listed examples of newspaper advertisements for slave hunting services that all began the same way: "BLOODHOUNDS!"[26]

If "Bloodhound" had become a household word in the South, Carleton and his fellow abolitionists did their part to make sure that it also became one in the households of the North. References to vicious Bloodhounds were numerous in anti-slavery literature. In 1850, it repeatedly appeared in abolitionists' campaigns against the Fugitive Slave Act. They referred to the legislation as "the bloodhound fugitive slave bill," while the supporters of the Act in Ohio were called "Cincinnati bloodhounds" and the northern officials who enforced it were named "blood-hound commissioners."[27] Former slave and acclaimed orator Frederick Douglass wrote "Resistance to Blood-Houndism" as a call to arms against the Fugitive Slave Act[28] while the abolitionist weekly, *Frederick Douglass' Paper*, mentioned Bloodhounds over a hundred times between 1851 and 1855.[29] Massachusetts Senator Charles Sumner talked about bloodhounds in at least two fiery speeches. In one, he named the type as a primary symbol of slavery's brutality, "The blood-hound has become the representative of our barbarism in one of the worst forms."[30] In another, he snidely referred to Senator Andrew Butler from South Carolina as helping to nurture "a whole kennel of Carolina bloodhounds, trained with savage jaw and insatiable scent."[31] The "Crime Against Kansas" speech, which included other derisive comments about Butler, drove Butler's relative, Representative Preston Brooks, to slam a metal-topped cane onto Sumner's head. Sumner recovered from the attack but the image of the Bloodhound as a symbol of slavery's dehumanization only grew.

By the 1880s, the Bloodhound's fierce reputation leapt from the page to the stage. Curious audiences in New York City could pay fifty cents for a ticket to the "Hunting of the Negro," an outdoor performance staged in Shutzen Park, at Union Hill. The handbill explained the show:

> Col. Thomas Butler, of Hamburg, S.C., will illustrate with his highly-trained blood-hounds the exciting scene of slave hunting in the South before the war. Of course the illustration will only be play, but the terror of the fugitives, the rapacity of the blood-hounds that unerringly follow upon their tracks and the escape from the dogs at the last moment climbing beyond their reach, will be portrayed so vividly that it requires no considerable stretch of the imagination to believe the incidents real.[32]

The enterprising Colonel Butler stated that his point was to disabuse the northern public of false notions. The dogs, he claimed, were always under the control of their handler and would obey without question. Their purpose was to strike terror rather than to actually harm. "[Butler] desires to show that there is no cruelty whatever to either man or beast in the pursuit undertaken by these dogs," the *New York Herald* reported.[33] Whatever his intention, Butler recognized the appeal and the economic opportunity in the frightening Bloodhound image. He even participated in the shows himself, playing the role of the slave hunter. As observed by a reporter from *New York World*, Butler mounted a horse, blew a horn and beckoned the dogs to follow. They did but without the ferocity that Colonel Butler's handbill had promised. Rather than "seeking the life-blood of their victim until driven off by the huntsman," the dogs sought food. "They ran here and there about the lot for chicken bones, and generally did everything to help the escape of the flying slave," wrote the bemused reporter.[34]

Colonel Butler's Bloodhounds may not have lived up to their vicious reputation, but others gave more convincing performances. A popular scene in theatrical versions of Harriet Beecher Stowe's 1852 anti-slavery novel, *Uncle Tom's Cabin*,[35] was when Bloodhounds chased the character of Eliza across a frozen river. One reporter quipped that the dogs were such a draw that every production "must have bloodhounds to chase Eliza across the ice with the child in her arms, or the show is bound to be a good deal of a bust."[36] The fact that men, not dogs, chased Eliza in Stowe's compassionate depiction of slaves didn't stop theatre directors from promoting "Tom shows" (as they were called) with images of prominently featured dogs, their mouths open and teeth bared at a horrified Eliza.[37] Some producers even displayed dogs in front of theatres before a performance to drum up business. A review of a show in Nevada described the result, "The street exhibition of the bloodhounds worked people up to the highest pitch, and if some of the people had been compelled to sell some of their already

A lithograph in poster format advertising a theatrical performance of *Uncle Tom's Cabin*, featuring Eliza pursued by bloodhounds. Sensational scenes of angry dogs were often used to promote the show (the Strobridge Lithographing Co., Cincinnati, Ohio. 1881. Library of Congress).

scant wardrobe they would have done so just to see the bloodhounds perform...."[38] Killer Bloodhounds sold tickets.

Whether in abolitionist literature, politician's speeches or stage adap-
tations of Stowe's anti-slavery novel, the image of the Bloodhound was
rhetorically and visually persuasive as a powerful symbol of dehumanization and it began with the dogs' role in war. The American military's use
of Bloodhounds to hunt Seminoles in the Second Seminole War (1835–42)
"preceded and then paved the way for its eventually more pervasive association with southern slavery."[39] It would also earn the conflict an alternative
name: The Bloodhound War.

One of the Bloodhound War's most famous leaders was Zachary Taylor, who would be elected the twelfth U.S. president in 1849. In a letter to
the War Department regarding the importation of Cuban Bloodhounds to
be used in the conflict, he expressed support, writing that he was "decid-
edly in favor of the measure ... as the only means of ridding the country of
the Indians."[40] Yet, he declined to purchase the dogs after receiving the War
Department's authorization and it wasn't until the territorial government of
Florida acquired close to three dozen Bloodhounds and offered them to the
army that he agreed to use a few.

By the spring of 1840, the dogs were relieved of their duties on the battlefield because they failed to track their prey. Taylor believed they were
useless trailing Indians because they were trained in Cuba to track runaway slaves. Pro-dog editorials in Florida newspapers in the 1840s sadly
agreed, with one claiming that "the scent of an Indian is entirely foreign to
[the dogs'] nasal organs."[41] As late as 1895, a Pennsylvania newspaper article
discussing the Second Seminole War noted that "the bloodhounds proved
the flattest sort of failure. They had been taught to trail Africans, but they
turned up their noses when urged to take the track of an Indian and would
not stir."[42] Taylor left his post as commander of the Florida army two years
before the war ended, unable to stop the Seminoles, but his reputation as
an Indian fighter was firmly established. So too was his association with the
Bloodhound.

As Taylor's political star began to rise, those who opposed his presidential nomination wrote scathing editorials in the press that denounced
him for his role in the Seminole campaign. Where Taylor's name was mentioned in these articles, Bloodhounds usually were too. Now part of parti-
san politics, the dogs were used to galvanize the anti–Taylor contingent and
transform him into a dehumanizing figure. In a letter from an Ohio-based
abolitionist named Henry Wright to his friend in Dublin, Wright gave up
referring to Taylor by name and simply dubbed him "the bloodhound." Dismayed that "the Bloodhound will go into the White House and be president," he ended the letter with a suggestion for how Taylor should be drawn

in the weekly British satirical magazine, *Punch*, "Won't it be a spectacle for God, angels and men, to see old Zach seated on his triumphal car, drawn into the Capitol and up to the door of the White House ... by a team of six Cuba bloodhounds, each having Zach's face? Tell PUNCH to give us the picture without fail."[43]

The abolitionists' campaign to stop the use of dogs during the Bloodhound War made an impact, and not just on Taylor's presidential aspirations. One periodical wrote that their efforts had caused "considerable discussion in many parts of the country."[44] Debates in the House and the Senate caught the attention of citizens, with at least one expressing his appreciation that the dog issue crossed party lines.[45] But for anti–Taylor politicians, the heightened attention on the Bloodhounds, courtesy of the abolitionists, was an opportunity to shine a spotlight on the former general. Taylor's run for the presidency especially angered the northern contingent of the Whig party, many of whom were openly hostile to him in the press, and they used Bloodhounds to bring home their point. A full page spread in a Vermont paper printed multiple responses to Taylor's presidential nomination. Throughout the angry editorials, Bloodhounds were mentioned numerous times.[46]

The abolitionists' exploitation of the Bloodhounds of the Second Seminole War as a political symbol rallied those who were opposed to Taylor and generated national debate by highlighting the dehumanizing aspect of hunting people with dogs. It also captured the attention of Southern slaveholders who realized that Bloodhounds would be useful to police slaves and pursue runaways. Historian John Campbell argues that through the Bloodhound War and the political firestorm surrounding it, "slaveholders learned the value of bloodhounds and other comparably trained dogs for controlling slaves and sought to incorporate them into their plantation world."[47]

Before the dogs arrived on Southern plantations, escaping slavery was a different prospect. Former slave Samuel Ward described the difference when recalling his parents' bid for freedom. "I know not their route, but in those days the track of the fugitive was neither so accurately scented nor so hotly pursued by human sagacity, or the scent of kindred bloodhounds, as now, nor was slave-catching so complete and regular a system as it is now."[48] Ward's narrative was published in 1855 and the change he recalled was reflected in the abolitionists' rhetoric. By the 1850s, the abolitionists' previous pro–Indian discourse had shifted slightly and the employment of Bloodhounds against the Seminoles came to symbolize white Americans' bondage of non-whites.[49] The strategy was effective, and critics would continue to use it after the Civil War to express their anger at racial inequality.[50]

While the Bloodhound image continued to be a useful symbol for the mistreatment of non-whites after the Civil War, during the war, Confederate handlers enlisted the dogs to fight black Union soldiers, who they considered "fugitive slaves in arms."[51] The strategy was both psychological and physical; fear would lead to retreat. The request for "negro dogs" was based on the belief that when black soldiers heard the dogs' howl and saw them charge, they would drop their weapons and run.[52]

For one regiment, the dogs' howling and baying did cause anxiety but no one ran. Colonel Thomas Wentworth Higginson of the First South Carolina Volunteers wrote in his field notes, "We marched on through the woods, with no sound but the peeping of the frogs ... and the occasional yelping of a dog.... This yelping always made Corporal Sutton uneasy; dogs are the detective officers of Slavery's police."[53] Higginson went on to describe a rebel attack on black soldiers by a "dog-company," consisting of mounted riflemen with "half a dozen trained bloodhounds." But the familiar encounter had a different outcome now that the men were on the battlefield, "The men met these dogs with their bayonets, killed four or five of their old tormentors with great relish and brought away the carcass of one."[54]

It was a victory worth retelling in 1902, when Charles Fowler dramatically recreated it in his story of the encounter, "The hounds especially dashed against our men with great fierceness, but they were shot down and bayoneted quicker than it takes me to tell the tale with pen and ink. Then the gallant troops held them up aloft for joy on the points of their bayonets and laughed."[55] Yet, the satisfaction of killing a long-hated and feared adversary did little to change the underlying dynamic. Fleeing from the bondages of slavery or wearing the uniforms of Union soldiers, black men were still hunted by dogs that represented an emotional and physical barrier to freedom.

The use of Bloodhounds during the Civil War would become a criminally prosecutable offense but only when they were turned loose on white prisoners of war. In the trial of Henry Wirz, commander of the Confederate prisoners of war camp at Andersonville, Georgia, the charges against him included approving the use of dogs to track escaped prisoners:

> And the said Wirz, still pursuing his evil purpose, did keep and use ferocious and bloodthirsty beasts, dangerous to human life, called bloodhounds, to hunt down prisoners of war aforesaid, who made their escape from his custody, and did then and there willfully and maliciously suffer, incite and encourage the said beasts to seize, tear, mangle, and maim the bodies and limbs of said fugitive prisoners of war....[56]

Eyewitness testimonies corroborated the charges against Wirz: "I have seen prisoners torn by the bloodhounds.... Their legs were torn, and one

"Spot," a Cuban Bloodhound, used for capturing escaped Union prisoners at Andersonville, Georgia (photo by J.W. Turner. 1869. Library of Congress).

SPOT.

Weight, 159 pounds; height, 3 feet; length from tip to tip, 6 feet 4½ inches. This dog is a Cuban Bloodhound; and was one of a pack of thirteen hounds (some of them, however, being the ordinary Southern hounds) used by Capt. Wirtz, at Andersonville Prison, Ga., for the purpose of recapturing Union prisoners who had escaped, and who were frequently killed or badly mutilated by these dogs. Eleven of this pack were killed by Union soldiers who went to Andersonville at about the time the war closed; the remaining two were brought North, and one of them has since died, leaving this dog the only survivor.

Photographed by J. W. TURNER, No. 47 Hanover Street, Boston.

Entered according to Act of Congress, in the year 1869, by W. L. Goss & Co. in the Clerk's Office of the District Court of the District of Massachusetts.

J. W. Turner's original description of his photograph, naming Spot as one of the dogs used by Captain Wirz (Library of Congress).

of them was torn in the arms."[57] With evidence that he had personally murdered prisoners under his care and incited the prison's dogs to kill Federal soldiers, Wirz was found guilty. The judge's strong repudiation, "the guilt of this immeasurable crime is fixed, a guilt so fearfully black and horrible, that the civilized world must be appalled by the spectacle,"[58] was followed by a verdict on each charge. As to the accusation of tracking men with dogs, the judge made his position clear before giving "a most shocking illustration" of the harm the dogs caused two men who tried to escape:

> It was also clearly proved that a part of each pack were ferocious dogs, dangerous to life.... A man overtaken by these beasts, and desiring to surrender, could not, by coming to a stand, save his life; the instinct of the dogs was for human blood, and to surrender to them was death.... Two soldiers had escaped, but were overtaken; the party who captured them returned with but one (who was so mangled that he died) and the chief of the party ... exulted in accounting for the other, stating that they allowed the dogs to tear him in pieces, and left him in the woods.[59]

Wirz was executed by hanging in November 1865. The verdict criminally condemned dog violence against humans, but only as it related to the victimization of white soldiers. As much attention as abolitionists brought to the issue of nonwhite victims of predatory dog practices before, during and after the Civil War, the public outcry would never rise to the level of seeking justice for those victims under the law.

When large dogs were imported to the Americas to track Indians it was as mercenaries meant to regulate "bad" nonwhites. From the conquistadors to slave owners, in the wars against nonwhites and in a system that enslaved them, dog aggression was tied to nonwhite disobedience. Using the dogs' trainable nature, men taught large canines to be a specific threat and in this, both the dogs and nonwhite persons were construed as mutually bad. In slave hunters' hands, Bloodhounds were transformed into devices of control that forced conformity through the threat of violence and death. Police officers would soon replace slave hunters as the dogs' handlers, and Bloodhounds would fade in popularity and be replaced by German Shepherd Dogs, but the stage was set for a battle over the roles and boundaries of animality that would be marked by an enduring association with race.

K-9

> Just as soon as it is generally known that hounds are kept or are coming, crimes seem to almost cease, and for this reason alone it would seem a needed precaution to have hounds at every police station.
> —From The Police Dog in Word and Picture, 1910[60]

Theo Jager was on a mission. The co-author of *The Police Dog in Word and Picture* wrote his instruction and training manual to convince more American police departments to include dogs as part of their detection and protection efforts. How much better the public would be served, he earnestly wrote, if "Mr. Sheriff and Mr. Police Officer," recognized the "sterling qualities of Police dogs."[61] For Jager, dogs' road to the police station was "but a step" from the brave canines of the battlefield who discovered soldiers and saved them from certain death. He made a point to distinguish the police Bloodhound from his human-hunting predecessor, "The Bloodhound that tore his victim limb from limb when discovered, is not the Bloodhound of today, which loses all interest in the trailed party, when discovered."[62] While his manual was primarily intended for law enforcement officers, Jager noted that private citizens could also train their dog to catch criminals. He quoted Mr. George Wallace of Columbus, Georgia, who laid out his training plan for his pet Doberman named Douglas.

Douglas' scent training would start with smoked herring, and then move to the sweaty undershirt, stocking feet, and finally the bare feet of a black man before ending with the scent of a white man.[63] Wallace, who appeared to be concerned about very specific criminal activity, would eventually have Douglas "track and capture the first member of the chain-gang that escapes," which he authoritatively noted, "happens often."[64] Performing as a human police officer would, the pet dog detective may have been useful for making a citizen's arrest but it was as a member of the force that a dog could really make an impact. Well-trained canine units, Jager eagerly wrote, would make a police department "almost invincible."[65]

The enthusiasm that ran through Jager's book was based on the idea that dogs would make police departments more efficient and more cost effective, but it was his firsthand experience that gave him credibility on the subject. A police dog breeder and trainer, his Dobermans were requested at crime scenes in New York state, where they had some success in assisting the police. His activism extended to making the public aware, through the press, of missed opportunities for the use of police dogs. In the case of a young woman's unsolved murder, he published a piece in a New York paper which explained how dogs could have tracked down the killer. It made an impact and local newspaper editorials began to appear supporting the employment of police dogs in the Rochester police department. The *Post Express* offered this assessment on August 13, 1909: "There is no doubt whatever that specially trained dogs should be added to the police department of Rochester. If a Doberman dog had been put on the trail of the murderer of Anna Schumacher before his scent had disappeared he would have been caught."[66] The early marketing of police dogs painted a heroic picture where the dogs' senses, rather than their sharp teeth, would make them dangerous to criminals.

New York City had already begun using trained police dogs and handlers in October 1907, a few months after their counterparts in South Orange, New Jersey, started a small dog unit. Donated by citizens and trained by department personnel, the South Orange dogs were kenneled at the city jail while the New York dogs were housed in Brooklyn.[67] Although neither department broadly used or developed their canine units, criminal activity was noticeably different on the streets of South Orange in 1907. According to Police Committee Chairman Howland D. Perrine's annual report to the Village Board of Trustees, "During the year the entire absence of a certain class of criminals who have heretofore been a trouble and nuisance within our boundaries has been quite significant."[68]

In New York City, where Fourth Deputy Police Commissioner, Arthur Woods, authorized the use of the Brooklyn-based dogs, the new department members were similarly successful; "The police dogs of New York have made good," Woods declared. "They have driven the burglars out of Flatbush."[69] The police dogs, in this case, were Belgian Sheepdogs and an Airedale Terrier. The Bloodhounds that Woods had initially used were reportedly good at tracking but did not impress the officers with their "small show of intelligence" and were quickly replaced.[70]

The Rochester, New York, police department followed Brooklyn's lead and their dog acquisition was praised by a local editorial as a wise choice and a warning to criminals:

> Detective William F. Maguire has purchased a scion of famous German police and military dogs and proposes to train his pet for the trailing and capturing of criminals in this city. Fire bugs, burglars and similar offenders who prowl dark streets ... may take a thought before committing a crime of the possibility of Detective Maguire giving his big sleuth fresh scent and letting him chase them to inevitable and strenuous capture.[71]

While the term police dog could refer to various breeds, "German police dog" was a popular name for the German Shepherd Dog, which had been gaining a solid reputation as part of European police canine units.

By 1911, the press was enthusiastically praising the New York City canine unit. A Boston paper credited the dogs with reducing crime "more than fifty percent" and reported that it was hard to remember a time when burglaries occurred now that the presence of the dogs had made the crime "such a rare occurrence."[72] The news of the dogs' role in lowering the crime rate convinced other city police departments to employ them. Specifically citing their success in the New York City area, the Baltimore Police Department began using police dogs in 1914, announcing the formation of a "dog squad" that would "track down a burglar or marauder in a jiffy."[73]

RAVENOUS POLICE DOGS PROTECT NEW YORK
GIRLS FROM MASHERS
BY NIXOLA GREELEY-SMITH
(Copyright, 1914, by Newspaper Enterprise Association.)
New York, Jan. 19.—New York society girls have found the answer to
The Masher Menace. It is the police dog! Already several of the best
known young women of the social group that likes to call itself "exclusive"

Miss Anne Tracy, niece of J. P. Morgan, with her German police dog, and a picture of how these dogs will "tree" a "masher" who molests his mistress.

An article noting the popularity of "German police dogs" for personal protection among high-society women (*The Day Book*. Chicago, Illinois. January 19, 1914. Chronicling America: Historic American Newspapers. Library of Congress).

Police dogs continued to make it into the pages of newspapers in the 1920s and 1930s as crime fighters who used their senses. A feature article in the *Chicago Tribune* praised Bloodhounds for their excellent service in police departments, noting that some of the famous dogs secured more convictions than human detectives.[74] Their reputation as useful trackers grew and in the tense atmosphere of the Lindbergh child kidnapping, the press even accused the police of falsely claiming that no Bloodhounds were available to employ when the crime took place. One editorial offered a detailed account of how the dogs could have made a difference in the early hours of the crime.[75] Articles also quoted Bloodhound breeders who argued that the breed had been unfairly maligned and its reputation as a "malicious monster with an unconquerable instinct for rapacious assaults upon human beings" was nothing but a legend.[76]

As their media story moved from vicious human hunters literally out for blood to effective members of law enforcement who captured countless criminals with their noses, Bloodhounds shed their frightening reputations and were now admired as dutiful canine detectives. The dogs' tracking abilities, once harnessed to terrorize people, were redirected to keep people safe. In both cases, the Bloodhound's dangerousness (to the innocent or the guilty) was purposefully crafted as something that required control. The difference was how that control was directed, which changed the perception of those doing the controlling. When the dog's tracking was directed in a way that made it a villainous predator hunting slaves, those who harnessed its instincts to that horrific purpose were also, and rightly, villainous. When it was the hero saving police departments time and money through nothing more than its keen scenting abilities, the forward-thinking officers who employed it for that purpose were also heroic. Whichever way the media conceptualized the dog's dangerousness, it was tied in some form to the human in the relationship.

The reimagining of the Bloodhound's image as a crime-fighting tracker interested in using its nose rather than its teeth made room for other breeds to join law enforcement. The German Shepherd Dog, already mentioned in some early press reports about canine cops, became so closely associated with its law enforcement role that it was often simply referred to in the press as the Police Dog. The public also embraced the breed, but its pet status was greeted with some anxiety over a potential for violence.

Feature articles stepped in to explain the dogs' genealogy, their temperament and their suitability for the home. After a New York woman was bitten by her "pet police dog Rolf," controversy erupted over a magistrate's statement that police dogs were savage, originated from wolves, had bitten hundreds of people in New York and should be banned from every city. A lengthy article addressing the subject countered the claims and then weighed in on whether the police dog was "pal or peril," coming down on the side of pal. "The consensus of opinion … is that it is at least a better and safer pal for a pet than any other dog of its size and strength that has yet been bred."[77] The idea was that the German Shepherd Dogs' intelligence and trainability made their dangerousness controllable so that its reported tendency to bite could be directed to ensure the safety of its owners.

More of the public joined the "pal" side of the argument over German Shepherd Dogs when a canine film star named Strongheart won over movie audiences. Originally trained as a police dog in Germany and assigned to its military during World War I, Strongheart was brought to the United States in 1920 and appeared in six movies from 1921 to 1927. One of the most prominent of a group of German Shepherd Dogs to appear on screen in the 1920s, Strongheart, along with Rin Tin Tin, captured the public imagination, and demand for the breed soared. A paper in Vermont reported that at the Strongheart Police Dog Farm, there were always fifty pedigreed, "high class" police dogs on the property to satisfy consumer demand: "Everybody seems to want police-dogs, and they have become a sort of craze or fad."[78] The media-fueled craze meant that all across America "police dogs" were embraced as family pets but the dogs' image would take a hit when they became the Nazis' dog of choice in World War II. Screen hero, family pet, crime fighter, Nazi war dog—all were identities that shaped the German Shepherd Dog, causing the breed's advocates and enemies to spar over its true characteristics. A rising fear of crime and disorder added to the debate.

After World War II, advocates for police canine units became more vocal. One of these voices belonged to Charles Sloane, who was Senior Personnel Technician of the Police Examination Unit of the New York State Department of Civil Service. In 1955, he published an article in the *Journal of Criminal Law and Criminology*, which discussed the value of dogs in military and police work, arguing that law enforcement in the United States needed to embrace new ideas:

> Our national crime record would seem to indicate that many police administrators want to continue fighting crime in the old-fashioned manner and have the idea that what was good enough for the community years ago is good enough now. Certainly, if other countries find an ally in police dogs, we in the police field in the United States could at least take up the idea *and try it.* One police officer saved from severe injury, or possible death, at the hands of the criminal by the use of a police dog would be well worth the effort of adding dogs to the roster of any city police department.[79]

To make his point more convincing, Sloane referenced a high-profile crime that had occurred the previous year in Indianapolis where a gunman had shot eight policemen and his wife before being killed. If the police had sent a well-trained dog into the situation, Sloane wrote, it would have resulted in a "thoroughly cowed individual." This dog, he added, would recognize danger and act with stealth then speed when the time came to strike.[80] In Sloane's example, the police dog was performing its dual role. It would be a hero because it was directed to act as a beast.

The press would follow Sloane's lead in advocating that large dogs, mostly German Shepherd Dogs, would be valuable additions to police departments across the country. A writer for the *Saturday Evening Post* told his readers that a trained police dog was a "four-footed cop, and the next best thing to radar,"[81] as well as an instrument of fear; "No human police-man strikes so much terror in a robber's heart."[82] In a 1956 series on Lon-don's Scotland Yard, *Evening Sun* reporter Martin Millspaugh wrote about the successful use of police dogs in England,[83] which prompted an edito-rial in the Baltimore newspaper a few days later. Along with lowering the crime rate and making up for the manpower shortage, the addition of a dog might increase the police's chance of success when pursuing criminals: "A dog trained to catch and hold a suspect without hurting him might be an improvement on the present system of having patrolmen shooting in the dark at fleeing figures."[84] Baltimore Police Commissioner James Hepbron agreed and announced that two German Shepherd Dogs would walk the beat.[85]

A year later, fourteen dogs were added to the force and Hepbron per-suaded the city council and the mayor to appropriate funds for a perma-nent canine unit. St. Louis followed Baltimore's lead in 1958, implementing the St. Louis Police Canine Section after several officers visited police sta-tions in London to see their dogs in action. By 1960, at least twenty-four departments across the United States had K-9 programs.[86] The growing number of police K-9 units had the support of President Lyndon Johnson's future Assistant Director of Law Enforcement Administration and Justice. Samuel Chapman, who would take up the position in Johnson's adminis-tration in 1965, wrote in his 1960 master's thesis that dogs in law enforce-ment were effective deterrents of criminal activity and disorderly behavior among crowds.

Chapman was writing at a time when fear of crime was on the rise. A 1961 Congressional Quarterly report titled "Control of City Crime," sounded the alarm:

> Mounting violence on the streets of American cities, during the day as well
> as after nightfall, is intensifying the problems of police and other municipal
> authorities and causing alarm among plain citizens. The growing frequency of
> purse snatchings, armed robberies and more serious crimes endangers not only
> pedestrians and others but also law enforcement officers. The spread of street
> crime has been marked by an unprecedented number of attacks on policemen
> by persons resisting arrest and by hostile onlookers. Changing conditions of

urban life are generally blamed for such examples of lack of respect for officers of the law, but they are believed to reflect also lack of adequate financial support of city police departments.[87]

The frequency of violent crime in Washington, D.C., in particular, resulted in a congressional committee hearing in May of 1960. The chairman of the crime subcommittee, James Davis, did not sugarcoat the situation in his opening remarks: "Matters have reached a stage in Washington that decent law-abiding citizens, particularly women and girls, have come to be regarded as fair game for every brute, thug and hoodlum who roams the streets with one purpose in mind: to steal, rob, rape and murder."[88]

As for solutions to the crime problem, one "non-mechanical aid" was mentioned. Police dogs, the Congressional Quarterly report noted, were "particularly useful in handling disorderly crowds," and the fear they aroused in "wrongdoers" made them valuable assets.[89] The idea that a police dog's primary usefulness was broadly understood as bringing order to disorder, rather than being directed at a specific area of criminal activity, gave law enforcement officers wide discretionary powers. When, how and where to employ a dog's "dangerousness" or arouse fear in "wrongdoers," was an individual decision on the part of the dog's police handler. In an effective public relations effort, police departments assured communities that the professional approach of an officer, along with a dog who was expertly trained to only act and attack on that officer's command, meant deterrence more often than violence. An article in a 1963 issue of the magazine *Popular Science* noted that a police dog's main value was to "stop crimes before they happen" because "the sight of an officer and a large shepherd dog strikes terror in the heart of would-be criminals."[90] K-9 units, according to a Baltimore sergeant quoted in the article, were "like guided missiles."[91] In the social unrest of the 1960s, who was guiding the missiles and toward what targets would significantly impact the police dog's place in history.

But first, a missile had to be made. German Shepherd Dogs were considered easy to train because of their intelligence and a belief in their "natural" inclination toward obedience. The transformation from canines to "K-9's," or "the weaponization of the dogs through selection, breeding and training meant the dogs' bodies were taken over by human agents and institutional forces so as to transform them into obedient, disciplined working dogs."[92]

Once trained and on the job, dogs and officers were "teams" but ones where the dogs were entirely under the officers' control. Trainer and Baltimore sergeant Irving Marders emphasized the importance of total submission in his 1960 book, *How to Use Dogs Effectively in Modern Police Work*. The dog, he wrote, "must never be allowed to feel there is anything for him to do but obey."[93] His training method was to nurture the dogs' aggression by agitating and then encouraging them to attack a person (wearing padding) followed by a reward, or a punishment when they failed. He emphasized that the dogs must be taught to stop their attacks on command. Marders' account of police dogs' training constructed them as controlled forms of violence.

The press had picked up on Marders' training ideas a few years earlier. In 1957, a newspaper feature on police dogs' training commented, "On the command of his master, the police dog will spring on a criminal, seize his arm and hold him until ordered to release."[94] A reporter covering police dogs for the *Wall Street Journal* in 1960 wrote, "In a manner of speaking, the dogs are taught to be gentlemen ... until their masters command them to be bounders."[95] A handler of Missouri-based police dogs assured the public that the dogs were only dangerous when commanded to be, "Our dogs are public-safe. They make good companions and will fight only to please their masters."[96] The message was that a police dog's savage side was entirely controlled, and the public had nothing to fear unless a dog's handler decided otherwise.

In the 1950s and early 1960s, it's important to note that the racial makeup of police departments across the country meant that it was typically a white police officer controlling the German Shepherd police dog. In St. Louis, only white, male, married officers were permitted to be K-9 handlers and their wives had to agree because the dog lived with the officers.

Press coverage of K-9 units during this time often included photographs of white male officers with their German Shepherd Dogs. They were depicted together in training sessions, walking the beat, and investigating structures. Usually action shots, the photos promoted camaraderie and discipline while the accompanying story typically celebrated the dogs' role in stopping crime. A 1958 headline in the *St. Louis Post-Dispatch* declared, "Thefts Halted in Areas Worked by Police Dogs."[97] In the article photo, police officer Joseph Beil and his dog Rebel are peering through the storefront window of a gas station. Rebel, with his mouth slightly open, is standing on his hind legs with his front paws on the windowsill. The caption read, "Patrolman Joseph Beil and Police Dog Rebel checking a filling station for prowlers." Curious but not threatening, Rebel appears in the photo as Beil's dedicated partner, responsible for keeping St. Louis neighborhoods safe. The article noted that when Rebel and his fellow police dogs were dispatched to parts of southwest St. Louis, "where daylight burglaries had increased to the point of considerable concern," no robberies or "purse snatchings were reported."[98]

This gendered understanding of criminal threat and domestic protection tasked the police dog with "securing white domesticity."[99] "If we can get these dogs on the street, our women will be safer," said a member of the

St. Louis Board of Police Commissioners. He added, "In many places our women are not safe on the streets at night. I know of no new techniques which can be used to eliminate this situation that would be any better than dogs."[100] St. Louis was not the only city where purse snatching was a special area of concern for police departments. A 1958 article in Baltimore's *Evening Sun* newspaper praising the city's use of police dogs reported that "dozens of imprisoned burglars, yokers, purse snatchers ... would begrudgingly admit that this latest extension of the long arm of the law has been effective."[101] In Ohio, the press featured a "stately German Shepherd" named Bodo who joined the force. His handler praised police dogs for being "especially effective in purse snatching."[102]

Focusing on stories where members of K-9 units stopped a crime associated with white femininity, the press cast and promoted the police dog's role in a racial framework. When the K-9 corps was directed at black demonstrators in Birmingham, Alabama, in 1963, this frame of racialized canine policing grew to include the idea that police dogs brought order to the "disorder" of black "mobs." The decisions in Birmingham created an enduring image of police dogs as a black law enforcement weapon and stirred a national awareness that was often credited with significantly changing the direction of the civil rights movement.

Fear and Loathing in Birmingham

When Martin Luther King, Jr., wanted to make visible the injustice of segregation in 1963, he looked to Birmingham, Alabama, a place he called "the most segregated city in America."[103] The city's history of intense segregation and racial violence made it an effective staging ground for a civil rights campaign. A long list of racist decisions marked Birmingham, including giving up its professional baseball team rather than have the team play in an integrated league, closing at least 68 parks, 38 playgrounds, 6 pools and 4 golf courses rather than abide by federal orders to implement desegregation measures, and refusing to integrate its municipal auditorium, effectively banning opera.[104] Before King's Birmingham campaign, dozens of racially charged bombings and over 50 cross burnings took place in the city. In 1961, President Kennedy sent in federal marshals after Birmingham's police allowed whites to beat Freedom Riders as they were fleeing their burning bus.

In the notorious figure of Birmingham's Commissioner of Public Safety, Eugene "Bull" Connor, the civil rights leaders in the city knew they had a man who would respond with characteristic violence and unnecessary aggression.[105] Connor's reputation as police commissioner was built on strong resistance to desegregation and his anti–Black and anti-communist remarks would frequently make the pages of the *New York Times*. In 1959, the paper labeled Connor "the outspokenly racist police commissioner" who condoned the "intimidation of Negroes and whites who support them."[106] When the Birmingham campaign began on April 7, 1963, with a Palm Sunday civil rights parade and demonstration, Connor released police dogs.

In some press coverage, the dogs were framed as in danger from a criminal crowd rather than a danger to the crowd. A *Miami News* article titled "Birmingham Negroes Sound New Rallying Cry" included a photo of a black protestor on the ground surrounded by two lunging police dogs.[107] The photo caption read, "Negro hurled to ground during Birmingham riot. Police reported he threatened one of police dogs with knife." The article itself used more vivid language, describing a "knife-wielding Negro man" who "tried to slash a police dog." The man was "hurled to the ground" but who or what did the hurling was unclear. What was (allegedly) clear from the picture caption, but not the picture itself, was that the man tried to hurt the dog, and by extension, the police. The caption recast a violent image of two lunging police dogs in attack mode to one of two heroic canines' engaging in self-preservation.

The article noted that when the crowd moved toward the man to protect him, more police with more dogs pushed into the melee. When people began to run and the dogs and officers chased them, Connor reportedly shouted, "Look at that dog go! That's what we train them for—to enforce the law."[108] For Connor, the dog, despite the predator versus prey dynamic implied in chasing people, was a marvel of physicality ("Look at that dog go!"), a fine student who followed training and an upstanding representation of law enforcement. A month later, *Time* and *Life* magazines would set a different meaning for Connor's dogs.

Tension escalated in May when the campaign organizers allowed schoolchildren to join the marches and groups of young people left the Sixteenth Street Baptist Church. Connor gave the order for fire hoses and police dogs to be used to repel them. Captured through the camera lenses of *Life* photographer Charles Moore and Associated Press photographer Bill Hudson, the photographs of police pointing fire hoses and barely restrained snarling dogs at black protestors appeared in newspapers across America and the world. Hudson's photograph of a white police officer holding the shirt of high school student Walter Gadsden with one hand and the leash of a German Shepherd police dog with the other appeared in many mainstream media outlets including the *New York Times* on May 4. In the picture, the dog is straining at its leash and baring teeth at the ribs of Gadsden who seems not to be resisting.[109] The photo caption, "Police dog lunges at a demonstrator during the protest against Segregation in Birmingham,"[110] was noncommittal except for the reference to the dog. "Lunges" conveyed an animal behavior to be feared. The coverage that accompanied the photo told a rather ordinary story with a lead sentence that set the tone, "Fire hoses and police dogs were used here today to disperse Negro students protesting racial segregation."[111]

Despite the neutral sounding account from the *Times*, the photo had an emotional force that reportedly reached the highest levels of government. In his work on the era, Pulitzer Prize–winner and historian Taylor Branch said that "the visual power of the Gadsden photograph was so profound that President Kennedy, like millions of readers, could see nothing else."[112] It also caused a global response, as Congressman Peter Rodino would later remark. When international editions of U.S. papers carried the Birmingham photos, Rodino was on business overseas. He told a July 1963 House judiciary subcommittee hearing on the Kennedy civil rights bill:

> I was attending a conference at Geneva … and the incident of the police dog attacking the Negro in Birmingham was printed all over the world. One of the delegates from one of the nations represented at the conference there showed me the front page of the European edition of the *Times* and he was a little more frank then some of the others, and he asked me, "Is this the way you practice democracy?" And I had no answer.[113]

On the world stage, the power of the photo was its dramatic depiction of brutality within the context of Cold War rhetoric that touted the important connection between racial progress and democracy.[114] American police turning vicious-looking dogs against peaceful black demonstrators was a diplomatic disaster and embarrassing to the nation's image abroad, but the response to the image also came from a psychological association between teeth-baring animals and fear. The German Shepherd Dog's history as a menacing weapon of law enforcement was reinforced with pictures that highlighted the capabilities of the animal inside the canine cop.

At home, the brutality of the photos galvanized sympathy and "struck like lightning in the American mind."[115] A Detroit man wrote a letter to the editor describing his anguish over the "snapping police dogs." "Moved by a deep humane and patriotic anxiety," he wrote, "I consider it my duty to deplore the cruel methods used by the Montgomery and Birmingham Alabama police officers against the Negro population."[116] In a letter to the *Washington Post* Ruth Hemphill expressed her feelings over the Gadsden photo:

> The news photographer who took that picture of a police dog lunging at a human being has shown us in unmistakable terms how low we have sunk and will surely have awakened a feeling of shame in all who have seen that picture,

who have any notion of human dignity. The man being lunged at was not a criminal being tracked down to prevent his murdering other men; he was, and is, a man. If he can have a beast deliberately urged to lunge at him, then so can any man, woman, or child in the United States…. If the United States doesn't stand for some average decent level of human dignity, what does it stand for.[117]

The nation had descended into barbarity by transforming a dog into a monstrous agent of social control. In a story about civil rights and America, the police dog became the villain because the officer holding the leash abused his position of control.

Moore's images, which were printed in a multi-page spread in the May 17 issue of *Life* magazine, became part of the historical memory of the Birmingham civil rights campaign largely due to the mass appeal of the magazine at the time. *Life* reached more people than any television program of the 1960s and was "seen by more than half the adult population of the United States."[118] The photo spread included images of black student demonstrators being cruelly sprayed with fire hoses. One of the most widely shared photos was a young black man trying to run as police dogs ripped his clothes. The dog images captured the national imagination and for Moore, had a profound impact. He remembered it this way:

> The police dogs were what really did it for me. I knew those high-pressure hoses hurt people…. But the sight of snarling dogs, and the possibility of dogs ripping flesh, was revolting to me.[119]

The snarling dogs that so disturbed Moore were captured in four photographs. In one, a dog is on hind legs, ready to strike with a wide-open mouth and bared teeth. The leash in the police officer's hand is tight, suggesting he is barely able to restrain the dog. The other photos show a frame by frame account of dogs tearing a man's pants from his body, revealing his leg. The officers are holding the dogs' leashes, allowing just enough slack to reach the man. One caption read, "With vicious guard dogs the police attacked the marchers…" and noted that Connor ordered his men to let white spectators near, reportedly saying, "I want 'em to see the dogs work. Look at those niggers run."[120] The caption was not ambiguous about the harsh nature of what took place or the attitude of the man in charge. When combined with the article's active descriptions of "vicious guard dogs" and police who "attacked," Connor's racial slur and his desire for white people to watch the "work" of police dogs, which in this context was to scare demonstrators into running like prey, sent a clear message about heroes and villains.

Time's coverage was similarly themed. In its May 10, 1963, issue, the magazine shaped the story around the idea of good versus evil, calling the Birmingham events "a small civil war" with "whites against Negroes, cops against children, dogs against humans."[121] Connor, it said, "roared for his police dogs," but "the Negro children of Birmingham … kept right on marching…."

Much of the press described the Birmingham police dogs in active language that stressed violence. An Associated Press report noted that the "blood-chilling picture of a snarling German shepherd leaping a demonstrator was seen all over the country."[122] Another AP report repeated the term "snarling" to describe the dogs, while the *Chicago Tribune* mentioned "vicious police dogs" and "growling dogs." *Newsweek*'s May 13 issue referred to "snapping, snarling police dogs."[123] Later commentary about Hudson's and Moore's photographs continued to stress the dogs' role as villains. In 1997, historian Glenn Eskew painted a graphic picture of the events, "Snapping at the end of their leashes, the German shepherds lunged at their black victims, burying their snarling teeth in the stomachs of bystanders too slow to get out of the way."[124] Eskew's vivid description highlighted the monstrous image of the police dogs but his reference to their leashes was a reminder that their ferocity was directed and controlled by the police officers who handled them.

The leash, which literally and figuratively tied the Birmingham police dogs to their police handlers, made dogs and humans into a single evil force. "Police Dogs, Police State" read a protestor's sign in a march through downtown Syracuse, New York, several days after the Birmingham demonstrations.[125] An editorial in a Pennsylvania newspaper made a similar connection: "The pictures of the police dog attacking Negro demonstrators in Alabama while being mauled by policemen not only was a vivid picture of the violent things that these dogs can be, but also a vivid picture of brutality in law enforcement."[126] Burned into the national consciousness were violent dogs and a state system responsible for using them against people.

The force of fire hoses toppling people to the ground and ripping their clothes from their bodies was a shocking depiction of inhumanity. But it was images of dogs with teeth pointed at human flesh and the language used to describe them that, for much of the public, recalled a deep-seated fear of animal violence. The photographs made dogs symbols of primitive cruelty in the hands of uniformed representatives of civility who, in turn, became brutal enforcers. The boundaries between the dogs and the police officers collapsed, and one villainous agent emerged.[127] Referring to the beast in the police, Malcolm X suggested that when under attack, "a black man should kill that dog or any two-legged dog who sicks the dog on him."[128] State agents became animalized and the "problem" of the dangerous dog became a problem for police who were publicly condemned as savage.[129] The photos, as a visual representation of startling cruelty, were evidence that those who symbolized civility were capable of barbarism.

The Birmingham images tied the police dog to the terror of southern law enforcement in the nation's collective memory but the use of K-9 units against "disorderly" crowds was not limited to the South. In 1964, an editorial in the *Saturday Evening Post* condemned the use of police dogs at a demonstration in Princess Anne, Maryland, where more than 300 black students from Maryland State College were protesting against segregated restaurants. Commenting that neither side was "entirely right," the editorial argued that dogs had no place at the event and then made a darker connection between police use of them and an old enemy. "Turning dogs and fire hoses on defenseless people (whether they are in Alabama or Maryland) is more like Nazi Germany than a part of the U.S."[130] In 1966, Chicago police were criticized for using dogs against Puerto Ricans who were enraged over the shooting of twenty-year-old Arcelis Cruz by an officer.[131] Dogs were also used in clashes in St. Paul, Boston, St. Louis, Wichita, St. Augustine and Tampa.[132]

The merging of animal violence with police violence was solidifying beyond a southern geography and the rising public anxiety compelled some law enforcement officials to use the press to try and shift the cultural conversation. Repeating a familiar argument in law enforcement, a spokesman for the International Association of Police said that fear of physical contact rather than actual contact was the K-9 officer's goal: "The thinking behind the use of dogs in crowd control is humans' innate fear of them ... the dogs are intended primarily as psychological devices not for attacking."[133] Miami's Assistant Police Chief Glenn Baron supported the idea of a natural apprehension: "Humans have an innate fear of them—that is their greatest value."[134] In the face of visual evidence of handlers allowing police dogs to physically confront crowds, the defense that K-9 units were intended to simply scare people fell flat. The dogs were cast as symbols of uncontrolled police power and would continue to be so decades after the civil rights era.

Taking a Bite Out of Crime

As the iconic symbols of law enforcement brutality, the German Shepherd police dogs of the Civil Rights era were often framed as savage beasts but during a turbulent decade of serial murders, political assassinations and race riots, dogs with imposing images were also seen as useful devices for personal protection. Along with Birmingham's startling photographic evidence that dogs and people could be in relationships based on violence rather than friendship, and faced with growing safety concerns, many Americans sought to own dogs with formidable reputations. By 1969, owners of kennels specializing in guard dogs claimed to have trouble keeping up with demand and the number of German Shepherd puppies registered by the AKC averaged more than 90,000 per year between 1965 and 1975.[135]

The guard dog business was booming but as some of the press reported in 1974, not everyone was happy about it. Dismayed by the number of poorly trained guard dogs used to protect businesses, one rabies control director in Florida compared the dogs to "loaded guns that someday will go off, harming innocent people."[136] If the quote was not alarming enough, the photo accompanying the article featured four German Shepherd Dogs, all baring sharp teeth. By this time, dogs flashing their fangs was practically a stock image of what a "dangerous dog" looked like, and the article's title question, "Guard Dogs: Trained or Abused?" seemed to answer itself.

The story continued toward the "abused" side of the debate, labeling dogs at a particular kennel "a pretty raunchy lot ... malnourished, debilitated and physically incapable of guarding job sites."[137] The kennel owners, according to the Florida rabies control director interviewed for the story, weren't much better. They didn't pay veterinary bills and their businesses were fiscally unsound. The narrative was that dogs were a dangerous problem and so were the people who failed to properly train and care for them. Not unlike the association between police officers and snarling dogs, the relationship between irresponsible kennel owners and vicious guard dogs blurred the boundaries between bad canine and bad human.

In this climate of fear, where police power had been animalized a decade before and guard dogs were all the rage in personal protection, the dog and state authority merged in the form of McGruff the Crime Dog, a rumpled, raspy-voiced cartoon hound who wore a trench coat. The approachable canine crime fighter, with a resemblance to the popular detective character played by Peter Falk in the television series *Columbo*, was created in 1979 after the Ad Council commissioned agency Dancer Fitzgerald Sample to produce an anticrime campaign. Debuting in 1980, McGruff and his tagline, "Take a bite out of crime," became one of the Ad Council's most successful campaigns, spreading the message that crime prevention was everyone's business.

In reimagining police power as a collective responsibility, the McGruff image capitalized on the relationship between dogs, fear and social control—with a twist. Law-abiding citizens were encouraged, like the police, to find their own inner beast to stop crime. The fact that an animated police dog using a tagline that stressed biting became such a successful anti-crime media message suggests that the animalization of authority had become normalized. In the text and images from Birmingham and beyond, media frames had strengthened the idea. Animated or real, the canine cop became a stark example of policing "as a pursuit, a chase, a hunt, transforming humans into prey."[138]

In the 1990s, the animalization of police violence hit the mainstream press again, as reports surfaced of vicious police dog bites. Los Angeles was ground zero and the statistics painted a stark picture. According to a 1992 article in the *Los Angeles Times*, police dogs bit an estimated 1,000 people in Los Angeles County from 1989 to 1991, with 18 dogs from the LAPD unit biting about 900 people and 15 dogs from the Sheriff's Department biting an estimated 150 people.[139] During the same period, Washington, D.C.'s 47 police dogs bit 215 people and in 1991, the 41 dogs of Baltimore's police department bit 30 people. Houston's K-9 unit reported only one bite that same year.[140]

The Los Angeles bites resulted in more bite-related lawsuits than anywhere else in the country. Attorneys Don Cook and Robert Mann, along with the American Civil Liberties Union of Southern California, the NAACP Legal Defense and Educational Fund and a civil rights law firm, co-filed class-action civil-rights suits that accused the LAPD and the Los Angeles County Sheriff's Department of using their dogs through systematic policies in violation of the U.S. Constitution. Cook and Mann claimed the dogs were "instruments of terror." Captain Dan Burt, who oversaw the Sheriff's Department's K-9 unit, conceded at the time that while his K-9 unit officers "could have been doing a better job," he found that there was nothing "going on that was particularly bad."[141] Viewers of the *CBS Evening News* in 1991 saw a different picture.

The video that made the *CBS Evening News* featured Drameco Kindle, who LAPD officers would later say fit the description of a suspect who had jumped out of a stolen car. Kindle was hiding under a couch in a South-Central Los Angeles backyard when a dog from the department's K-9 unit found him and alerted his handler Sergeant Mark Mooring. Mooring, along with three other officers, surrounded the couch. One of them kicked the couch to reveal Kindle, who, with no warning, was attacked by the dog as he lay on the ground. Kindle jumped to his feet screaming as the dog latched on to his leg. Mooring grabbed Kindle by the shirt. The other officers shouted, "Lie down!" and "Shut up!" Kindle screamed over and over, "Get the dog off!" Mooring pushed Kindle to the ground. The dog continued to bite.

Kindle's ordeal was captured in 1989 on tape as part of a short video called "Why Be a Cop." It was a demonstration of the K-9 unit at work and intended to be aired on a public access cable television show called *The Sherry Herst Show*. Instead, it was aired on the *CBS Evening News* in December 1991 after attorney Don Cook subpoenaed it in August from owner Nippon Television International and gave it to a CBS producer. Mooring told the interviewer in the video that it was "one of the greatest experiences ever."[142] Kindle was never charged with a crime.

The tape prompted an editorial by the *Los Angeles Times*, which called for the police commissioner to fully investigate the disturbing allegations about police dog attacks,[143] and a feature story in *Los Angeles Times Magazine* that followed a few months later. In the *Times*' article, retired Sheriff's Deputy Van Bogardus, the first K-9 handler trained in the department in 1980, said of the Kindle video, "That tape is little more than a spectacle for those policemen.... Can you see the terror in that person? ... The dog is consuming him, eating him alive."[144] Bogardus' horrified observations recall what author Tyler Wall calls "the coupling of devourment and the beast of police power."[145] Literally taking a bite out of crime, the police dog as a representative of state power, pursued, captured and began to devour Kindle.

Some of the human representatives of state power saw things differently. In the feature article, Captain Burt of the Los Angeles Sheriff's Department, strongly defended find-and-bite as necessary to keep officers safe from "very serious suspects."[146] Acknowledging that "when a dog bites a human being it causes tearing of the flesh, bleeding," Burt argued in favor of the outcome because it was ultimately better for the officer on the scene. "We don't want the dog to say, 'OK boss, here's the guy, I'm sitting here looking at him and barking at him.'"

Burt went further, explaining that find-and-bark made arrests too risky. A dog attack made a confrontation between a suspect and an officer less violent because the dog was the weapon rather than an officer's gun. "I will take a felon who has been captured with a couple of fang marks in his arm any day over one with shotgun pellets in his heart."[147] By using casual language, "a couple of fang marks," juxtaposed with the more visceral description of bullet fragments in a human heart, Burt framed a police dog who bites as a kinder, gentler alternative to one who barks, despite the disturbing notion of animal teeth sinking into human flesh.

The article would later note that in the LAPD, find-and-bite was referred to as "handler control,"[148] a phrase which emphasized that a human was in charge of all interactions between a criminal suspect and a K-9 unit. For Bogardus, the human in control was the problem. Once a champion of find-and-bite, he became an outspoken critic of the policy after witnessing the bite injuries the dogs under his command inflicted on suspects, most of whom, he admitted, could have been taken into custody without a scratch. At the time, the LAPD statistics proved Bogardus' assertions to be true. Records showed that when the department's K-9 teams were called out, most were arrested on burglary and theft charges and 85 percent of those arrested had no weapon. Sheriff's department records showed a similar pattern. Over a five-year period ending in 1990, 268 of the 272 suspects bitten by the department's dogs were captured unarmed. Proving that Bogardus' concerns were credible was this report from Sheriff Deputy Faulkner on October 21, 1988: "Suspect was motionless and non-combative. Dog stayed with suspect barking and holding suspect. I don't know how to get him to bite. Any suggestions?"[149]

Biting was not a problem for an LAPD dog named Volker. The target was. Volker's case of mistaken identity was described in a 1991 article on the multiple lawsuits facing the department at the time:

> Volker's mission was to find a fleeing gang member who had taken part in a pre-dawn shooting in Hollywood and slipped away. But when Volker, a German shepherd in the Los Angeles Police Department's K-9 unit, emerged from a nearby toolshed, his jaws were locked around the arm of someone other than the gunman.[150]

The person whose arm Volker locked his jaws around was a restaurant dishwasher named Hortencio Torres. His right forearm, the reporter wrote, "had been ripped open." Volker was clearly the villain in the account but so too was the LAPD. The article noted that critics of the department were angered by "the misguided use of force displayed in the incident." Attorney Don Cook remarked on both the dogs and the people commanding them, "These dogs are deadly force, and the cops are using them to terrorize people."[151]

The decisions filed in the police dog-bite lawsuits that flooded Southern California courts in the 1990s were overwhelmingly in favor of the police. By 1995, in four cases that had all started in Southern California, the U.S. Supreme Court had upheld that departments were immune from suits by suspects claiming to have suffered dog related injuries because there was no clearly established law governing dog bites. Former LAPD Chief Daryl Gates reasoned, "It was the animal that imposed the injury, not the human being."[152]

Blaming the animal and not the person commanding the animal, Gates' defense of police officers in the city's K-9 unit spoke to a primal fear of the animal instinct unchecked. Promoting the idea that a police dog was tearing into the flesh of a suspect with no human participation was an attempt to absolve the handler of responsibility, but it also constructed the dog as acting of its own volition. Gates anthropomorphized the dog as an active agent of terror, which made it a bad dog without the accompanying bad human. The problem was that a police dog was already established as a crime-fighting partner to its handler and one that was routinely characterized in the press as existing somewhere between aggressive weapon and obedient pet.

The City of Los Angeles settled the suit brought by Don Cook and others for $3.6 million and agreed to rework its policy for the use of force by dogs in order to minimize future litigation. After the LAPD changed K-9 protocol to "find and bark," the department's bite ratio or the number of bites against the number of suspects located, dropped to 15–25 percent, from an average of 45–55 percent in the early 1990s.[153] The Los Angeles County Sheriff's Department (LASD) however, continued to use "find and bite" or what was later called "Handler Control with an Emphasis on Positive Alert." In 2012, it was reported that the LASD's K-9s bit 50 percent more often than the LAPD's unit.

Los Angeles had a serious police dog-bite problem but it was not the only city facing litigation. In Albuquerque, New Mexico, lawsuits against the Albuquerque Police Department (APD) were reported to have cost the city more than $900,000 from the early 1990s to the early 2000s.[154] In 1991, Broward County police dogs and their handlers made the pages of the Florida press. The *South Florida Sun Sentinel* investigated multiple claims that police in the area were unleashing "one of their most powerful weapons" with little evidence of a crime.[155] In a review of 445 police dog-bite cases reported in Broward from 1988 through 1990, the paper determined that police were "too quick to set their dogs on suspects—and too slow to call them off." Of the 388 cases in which charges could be determined, the paper found that about two-thirds of the people bitten were unarmed and suspected of nonviolent crimes.

The article described several cases in which a police dog severely bit the wrong person, including one involving a woman who was eight months pregnant and another involving a homeless man who was mistaken for a shoplifting suspect. The report also blamed police handlers' unchecked misuse of K-9 units on a lack of state standards for tracking police dog-bites and identifying problems. When a police dog is constructed as a villain, the predicament of its dangerousness is two-fold. A dog's capability to be savage is a problem that needs to be controlled and the state authority (to which the dog is a partner), is a problem for failing to control it.

While lawsuits continued to have mixed results and police departments often defended handlers, a 2001 report issued by the International Association of Chiefs of Police claimed that a significant cause of the dog bite problem resulted from "inappropriate deployment and/or lack of control of canines by their handlers."[156] Over a decade later, "inappropriate deployment" was still an issue for police departments across the country. In 2015, the U.S. Department of Justice (DOJ) released the report from its investigation of the Ferguson (Missouri) Police Department (FPD), which was written a year after an unarmed black teenager named Michael Brown was shot and killed by a white police officer. The DOJ report included its findings on the FPD's use of K-9 units:

A sheriff's department K9 demonstrates his skill by biting the protected arm of his handler (photo by Jason Jarrach. February 20, 2020. unsplash.com https://unsplash.com/photos/eatdp8tvFFs).

FPD engages in a pattern of deploying canines to bite individuals when the articulated facts do not justify this significant use of force. The department's own records demonstrate that, as with other types of force, canine officers use dogs out of proportion to the threat posed by the people they encounter, leaving serious puncture wounds to nonviolent offenders, some of them children.[157]

In 2016, a K-9 officer with the San Diego Police Department gave his dog the command to bite an unarmed, naked man who was under the influence of a controlled substance. Police body cam video showed that the handler allowed the dog to bite the man for over 40 seconds after officers had him pinned to the ground.[158]

The line between property and partial person is blurry in dog-human relationships and for working dogs, both partners and pets, it grows even murkier. As subjects who live in society, dogs have decisions made for them by humans and one of the most important of these is when to show restraint. The decisions made for average pet dogs are primarily about demonstrating control of their less desirable behaviors. The principal and daily decisions made for police dogs are about controlled release of these behaviors: When to bark, when to lunge, when to bite. The timing of these actions results from intense behavioral training, where predictability and obedience are combined with a handler-dog bond of loyalty and trust. Yet, a dog's compliance with human purposes is always unstable. A police dog's compliance is trickier still. From a dog's point of view, biting the wrong suspect or biting the right one is both a form of compliance.

The Good, the Bad and the K-9

Sergeant Michael Goosby is the chief trainer for the K-9 unit operated by the LAPD's Metropolitan Division. He was profiled in the *New York Times* in 2015, partly because his dedication to his work inspired mass market crime novelist Robert Crais to create a primary character in his popular detective novels based on him, and partly because Goosby and his dogs were considered heroic.[159] At the time of the article, Goosby calculated that he personally helped apprehend more than 300 suspects out of roughly 2,000 canine searches, and the number increased by one as the article was being written. After a three-hour search, one of Goosby's 19 dogs found a man hiding under a house. He was suspected of assaulting a police officer with a deadly weapon.

Photojournalism plays an important role in shaping news narratives and the Goosby article had three images. The first picture shows Goosby in uniform posing with a dog in front of a patrol car. Goosby looks straight at the camera. His dog sits at his side, attentive and alert, with an open mouth but no visible teeth. The dog looks off to the right of the frame. The caption is straightforward and neutral, "Sgt. Michael Goosby works with dogs at the Los Angeles Police Department's canine training grounds near the police academy in Elysian Park." Goosby is relaxed. His hands loosely grasp the lead and he is comfortably in control. The theme is more teacher and student than partners, as the dog stares into a distance the viewer cannot see, ever vigilant and ready for Goosby's next command.

In the next photo, a dog is stretched into a lunge with front paws off the ground. Teeth are visible as the dog bites into Goosby's protected arm. Goosby is bent slightly forward at the waist, leaning into the action, signaling a lack of fear. A tight leash is visible but not the person holding it. The picture captures a violent moment of barely restrained rage. The caption reads, "Sgt. Goosby training an LAPD dog in Elysian Park." The third photo features the crime novelist Crais listening intently to Goosby who is pictured side-on in the image's foreground. He gestures, as if in explanation.

Together, the photos created a story where the sergeant was the authority and the dogs, one calm and stately; the other active and biting, were under his strict command. The text of the article made Goosby's attitude toward the dogs clear, "They exist for one reason: hunting bad guys."[160] Goosby and the article framed the dogs as heroic and the accompanying dog images, one calm, one aggressive, told a story that connected a canine with justice and justice with a dog's animal nature. The training photo in particular, made it clear that a police dog is capable of inflicting harm at the handler's command. The narrative theme of the Goosby article was simple and not uncommon: Good policing bad through controlled release of a dog's aggression.

In 2015, police dogs and the handlers in charge of them were framed as good in Los Angeles and as bad in Missouri. This fluid identity is possible because a domesticated dog's status is somewhere between human and the rest of nature but also because the German Shepherd Dog, as a working canine, has long been a conspicuous presence and a valued assistant in the lives of people. Its intelligence, trainability and obedience meant that it was typically the first breed to be employed and remains one of the most broadly employed.[161] As a guardian of homes and businesses, it is still the primary breed that comes to mind when "guard dog" is mentioned.

When military officials were seeking a dog to supplement the work of armies, particularly after World War I, the German Shepherd Dog was the most enlisted. In the early twentieth century it was so widely employed by law enforcement that the press and the public simply called it the "Police Dog." As a police dog, it became a member of the power group it served but dependent on the actions of its handler. When those actions were commendable, when an officer foiled a purse snatcher or a burglary by controlling a police dog's more dangerous skills, press frames celebrated the dog as a steadfast crime fighting partner. When the German Shepherd Dog has been mobilized by state authorities as an enforcer unleashed upon innocent people, press frames typically focused on the dog's viciousness and denounced the officer in charge as a feared agent of social control. The German Shepherd Dog is a valued law enforcement employee, but its performance review depends on the actions of the human presence in charge. Leaving the street to join other breeds on the battlefield, the dogs' association with the nation state elevated them to quasi-human status and in media frames, they often embodied the qualities of the soldiers they served, making them both allies and enemies.

War Dogs

> *That dog was a Marine, by God, and he deserved to be buried in the cemetery with the rest of the Marines.*[162]
> —*Major Richard Tonis, 1944*

The dog that was a Marine was a Doberman named Kurt. In 1944, Kurt was hit by a mortar blast, along with his handler Alan Jacobsen. It was their second day on Guam. Jacobsen was evacuated to a hospital ship while Kurt was left in the care of Lieutenant Putney, platoon commander and veterinarian, who repaired the dog's wound but could not save him from the injury. In his memoir of the Pacific War, Putney wrote that Kurt's burial in the marine cemetery, at the insistence of Major Richard Tonis, was the start of Guam's Marine War Dog Cemetery. Eventually, 24 more Marine dogs killed on Guam would join Kurt.

When Kurt's courage and sacrifice on the battlefield were rewarded with an official burial in a Marine cemetery, he earned the same status as the human Marines who were buried there. In life, his obedient bravery was the ultimate demonstration of canine restraint and soldierly discipline so in death, his status as a partial person was confirmed. Kurt was a working partner, an extension of his human handler's skills, tasked with protecting his unit's safety. Intensive training would have revealed Kurt's unique reactions to stimuli that Jacobsen learned to recognize. He would have instructed Kurt to scout forward of the Marine's lines through difficult terrain, search for enemy soldiers hiding in caves, and use his nose to sniff or point in the direction of danger. Unlike canine cops, war dogs silently alerted their handler to an enemy threat. Not barking, snarling, or attacking often meant the difference between life and death. When the wild, natural side of Kurt displayed itself in the form of superior senses that potentially saved lives rather than savage behavior that potentially lost them, he was temporarily less animal and more human.

While Kurt was "becoming" a Marine in 1944, the Marines had embraced their canine side a few decades earlier. Fighting the Germans at the Battle of Belleau Wood in June 1918, the Marines of the 5th and 6th Regiments were referred to as "Teufel Hunden," or Devil Dogs, so frightening were they to their opponent.[163] The nickname made for good marketing. In one recruitment poster, a cartoon bulldog wearing a marine helmet chased a stressed Dachshund. Research has revealed that the term Devil Dogs was most likely created within the Corps itself during the first few months of World War I rather than by the enemy. When Marines proudly conceptualized themselves as having a degree of animality, it set the stage for the actual dogs that served alongside them to rest eternally among them.

Kurt's symbolic status meant that he was considered more than a weapon of war but his ancestors on the battlefield were considered more machine-like. Throughout history, dogs have followed people in their quest to build empires and militaries have shaped an aggressive role for them as tools used for terror and control. Between 700 BC and the discovery of gunpowder, dogs were present in conflicts in Western Asia, North Africa, Europe and the Americas. The Assyrians, Persians, Greeks, Romans, Gauls, and Celts used dogs as battlefield weapons, equipping them with armored coats of steel plate, mail or leather and collars lined with spikes.[164] In 1495, Christopher Columbus' dogs tormented the indigenous people of Hispaniola when they resisted his men.[165] Benjamin Franklin argued in favor of using dogs to stop Indian raids in 1755, writing in a letter that "they should be large, strong and fierce" and "in case of meeting a party of the enemy, the dogs are all then to be turned loose."[166] During the Civil War, Black Union soldiers faced the psychological terror of Bloodhounds.

Early dogs of war were fierce and dangerous but as gunpowder and more mobile weapons changed warfare, the military role of dogs changed from combatants to tactical support in the field. In World War I, dogs were an asset in locating wounded men. These "mercy dogs" were trained to ignore dead soldiers and seek injured ones. Often, medical supplies and water were attached to dogs that a wounded man could use. The dogs would then return with an item from the soldier, a helmet, cap, bandage or piece of clothing, to inform their handlers that a man had been found.[167]

Another important role for war dogs during this conflict was to navigate the trenches and deliver messages over long distances. The "highest qualities" that needed to be cultivated in messenger dogs, according to Colonel E.H. Richardson, who established the British War Dog School, were "love and duty."[168] Conceptualizing the virtues of the wartime messenger dog in human terms, Richardson created a character equivalence between animal and man that was far from the brutal version of past war dogs who were celebrated for tearing men to pieces on the battlefield. World War I military dogs acted from a place of honor.

The American military was less convinced. Every country involved in World War I, except the United States, considered dogs valuable to their military efforts. Any four-footed soldiers working for the American side were likely borrowed from the French or British.[169] The exception was a pit bull named Stubby. A mascot rather than a trained war dog, Stubby nevertheless accompanied the 102nd Infantry to France, where he participated in seventeen battles. Already popular with those he met in France, his acclaim grew when he returned to the United States with his owner, Robert Conroy. Stubby was celebrated for his devotion to duty, appeared in many parades and met Presidents Harding and Coolidge before dying of old age in 1926. When a new war with different tactics and terrain began, the connection between dogs and duty took on a darker meaning and the metaphorical transformation of canine to soldier became symbolic of authoritarian regimes. Germany led the way.

At the beginning of World War I, Germany had around 6,000 dogs serving as messengers, guardians and sentries. By World War II, the number had increased to more than 200,000.[170] The ranks were overwhelmingly filled by German Shepherd Dogs who were best known for their roles as sheep herders before the passionate intervention of a retired Prussian Calvary captain. In 1899, Max von Stephanitz founded the Verein fur deutsche Schaferhunde, or Society for the German Shepherd Dog, commonly called the SV. Through Stephanitz's superior publicity skills, the society transformed certain groups of local sheepdogs into the "German" Shepherd Dog and promoted the breed as the country's ideal canine. The newly labeled breed was intensely marketed as sharing the same characteristics as the nation's citizens—pure, healthy, strong, loyal and fearless.

Stephanitz's link between the dogs and the Fatherland was heavily promoted in his 1901 book, *The German Shepherd in Word and Picture*. By 1914, the book was republished in more than a dozen editions, and by 1923 it was available in English, followed by a Japanese edition in the mid-1930s. Stephanitz elevated the German Shepherd Dog to immense global popularity but his message was always the same, the dog was "a genuine German withal."[171] As dogs with German characters, Stephanitz sought to militarize them, praising Shepherd Dogs for their bravery and urging police and army units to deploy them domestically and internationally. As historian Aaron Skabelund notes, the photographic evidence from Germany's overseas colonies depicting dogs and handlers, particularly in Africa, suggests that officials followed Stephanitz's lead.[172]

As the Nazis rose to power, Stephanitz's goal to develop the purest race of dogs aligned with Hitler's racial policies, and his idea that the modern German Shepherd Dog was a descendent of an ancient medium-sized wolf spoke to the Nazis' fascination with the animal.[173] Historian Boria Sax writes that "Nazis were constantly invoking dogs and wolves for the qualities they wanted to cultivate: loyalty, fierceness, courage, obedience, and sometimes even cruelty."[174] Stephanitz's zeal perfectly matched many Nazi leaders' adoration for the German Shepherd Dog's supposed wolf-like nature and the breed quickly became the regime's war dog of choice and a symbol of its horror. Deployed as a guard dog in prisoner of war and concentration camps, the GSD was closely identified with the cruelty of the Third Reich. A survivor of Treblinka recalled the terror that resulted from the dogs' systematic integration into the operations of concentration camps: "On their way to die they were beaten by truncheons and gas pipes. Dogs were set upon them; barking, they threw themselves upon the victims. Everyone, eager to escape the blows and the dogs, rushed screaming into the lethal chamber."[175]

The Nazis' pervasive use of German Shepherd Dogs transformed them into enduring symbols of the regime, but other countries saw the dogs as adaptable military instruments prior to the Third Reich's extensive use of them. Encouraged by the achievements of military dogs in World War I, Japanese authorities began to acquire canines and start small training programs. The initial population of dogs were GSDs, which came from Japan's occupation of German-leased territories on China's Shandong Peninsula. By the early 1930s the Shepherd Dog became a symbol of Japanese imperial-military power, and by 1944, the army had around 10,000 military dogs that were used as messengers, sentries, draft animals, trackers and patrollers.[176] While Doberman Pinschers and Airedale Terriers were also used, it is estimated that more than 90 percent of all army dogs were German Shepherds and as in the German context, the Japanese military routinely deployed the dogs to terrorize and subdue. The dogs, like the soldiers who controlled them, were associated with state violence and repressive regimes.

Harnessed to serve the needs of a cruel power group at a particular time and place, a German Shepherd Dog with a Nazi or an Imperial solider holding the leash was terrifying to the enemy because the dog's aggressiveness was inseparable from the human soldier. From a German and Japanese national perspective, the war dog represented the country's best qualities and served with honor. American war dogs experienced a similar nationalistic framing. If their aggression was mentioned at all, it was framed by the press as a trait to be proud of because it helped defeat the enemy.

Dogs for Defense

My Rover, he can hear a mile away
And he can see at night as well as day
I'll get along somehow
If my country needs him now
I'd like to give my dog to Uncle Sam
        —Lyrics from "I'd Like to Give My
        Dog to Uncle Sam" by Red River Dave

The American war dog's military career began with a phone call. In 1942, shortly after the bombing of Pearl Harbor, Alene Erlanger, a well-respected poodle breeder and wealthy socialite from New York, reached out to Arthur Kilbon, a columnist who covered dogs at the *New York Sun* and who wrote under several pseudonyms for other newspapers across the country. With another war on America's doorstep, Erlanger told Kilbon, "The dog game must play a part in this thing."[177] She convinced Kilbon to direct publicity for her new organization, Dogs for Defense, and quickly secured the support of the American Kennel Club.

The War Department was a harder sell. Despite the use of dogs by the British, German and French armies in World War I, the United States military was not convinced that canines were useful in modern warfare but the program's supporters and a growing sense of desperation over the Japanese advance in the South Pacific, convinced them that dogs could serve as sentries and battlefield messengers and potentially save soldiers' lives.

Kilbon's publicity efforts were effective and others in the media began taking the case to the public by stressing the dogs' usefulness. "One well-trained dog is the equivalent of six guards," said the government head of the dog corps, adding that their noses were just as effective as a rifle.[178] Newspapers across the country published information on the program and listed the criteria for enrolling. Advertisements stressed a patriotic angle and asked families to consider a new role for the household pet. A 1942 ad in *The Clearing House*, a journal for middle school and high school teachers and administrators, invited "red-blooded American dogs" to enroll in the program because students "might be interested in a patriotic career for their dogs."[179] Sparton, a precision electrical manufacturer, made a similar appeal in an advertisement with the tagline "Shep will show 'em...." The accompanying photo is a dog poking its face through the slats of a wooden crate that is labeled: "K9 Corps U.S. Army Ft. Hancock N.J." A young boy sadly looks at the camera with his cheek pressed against the dog's face. The text offers words of encouragement, "It is very real, isn't it son—the tug of parting between a boy and his dog? *Pride* fighting down *sorrow*, [italics in original] as you send your 'soldier' away to the wars. We understand. All of us have learned—and are learning—what we must pay as the price of freedom."[180] Soldier was in quotes here, but other ads made a stronger equivalency between man and dog.

"Shep will show 'em..."

It is very real, isn't it, son—the tug of parting between a boy and his dog?

Pride fighting down *sorrow*, as you send your "soldier" away to the wars.

We understand.

All of us have learned—and are learning—what we must pay as the price of freedom.

But while we keep our hearts in the thick of the fight, our eyes are fixed on the hope of the future.

Sparton, now, *is* building nothing but materials of war.

Horns, sirens and warning signals of every type, for motor cars, tanks, trucks, jeeps, planes and ships.

Much highly technical equipment, too, for the Radio Division of the Signal Corps.

A total, in fact, of 14 *major* products for our armed forces!

But what about the future — after Victory?

You may be sure that the "oldest and best name in horns" will again be leading the parade.

You may depend on Sparton for exciting new products for the automotive, marine and aviation fields.

You may expect new and finer Sparton radios—

And other new electrical home products, in tune with the progress of the times.

Better Sparton products, in wider variety — finely engineered as in the past!

Better *values* through improved methods!

These are among the contributions we pledge for the peacetime World of Tomorrow.

Sparton is proud of its continued association—through peace and war — with important manufacturers, a few of whose insignia are shown below!

CURTISS-WRIGHT
Ford
DOUGLAS
BOEING
INTERNATIONAL HARVESTER COMPANY
White
Bendix
BREWSTER
AUTOCAR
Vultee
PACKARD
Lockheed
CONSOLIDATED AIRCRAFT

PLAN AHEAD WITH SPARTON! We invite correspondence with others who are interested in post-war marketing opportunities, in which our 43-year experience in electrical precision manufacture can be invaluable.

SPARTON
PRECISION ELECTRICAL MANUFACTURERS SINCE 1900

THE SPARKS-WITHINGTON COMPANY • JACKSON, MICHIGAN
SPARTON OF CANADA, LIMITED, LONDON, ONTARIO

During World War II, Sparton Manufacturing joined the Dogs for Defense program in encouraging families to do their patriotic duty by shipping their pets to the battlefield. Circa 1942. Division of Political and Military History, National Museum of American History, Smithsonian Institution.

A full-page advertisement from Purina Mills, the maker of the popular dog food, appeared in a 1943 issue of *The Dog News* magazine. The illustration depicts a large dog facing a crudely drawn Japanese prisoner who is standing in shallow water. The prisoner's hands are raised in surrender as he looks at the snarling dog with wide eyes. Behind the dog is a soldier pointing a gun. The text actively dramatizes the events, "ESCAPED! …one Jap prisoner. CAPTURED! …same Jap prisoner. And decorated for the job was 'Prince,' proud member of the U.S. Army K-9 Corps."[181] Prince, according to the ad's text, went through the same soldierly transformation as many American hunters, "Not more than just a year ago hunting ducks was 'Prince's' favorite sport but like so many American sportsmen—today he, too, hunts more dangerous game. He has a job to do!" American men and their dogs had both become hunters of enemy prey.

Several films joined the publicity push, with one specifically addressing the mission of Dogs for Defense in an opening message. *War Dogs*, released in 1942, began this way:

> This picture is dedicated to you loyal citizens who unselfishly are enlisting your "Dogs for Defense." Thanks to the Dogs for Defense organization especially Carl Spitz, who has trained hundreds of dogs. The war dogs you will see in this picture were delivered to the Army immediately after the scenes were photographed. They are doing their part—with you—in our Country's … MARCH TO VICTORY![182]

The film tells the story of a boy named Billy and his German Shepherd Dog named Pal. After Billy ends up in juvenile court for stealing two dollars to get Pal out of the pound, the judge in the case and his social worker girlfriend take an interest in him and his dog. They convince Billy to donate Pal to Dogs for Defense and the dog is assigned as a sentry at a defense plant, where Billy's father also gets a job, thanks to the kind couple. Billy's father sacrifices himself to defend the plant against German saboteurs and Pal captures them. The couple marry and adopt Billy. The film ends with both the judge, who has joined the Marines, and Pal proudly reporting for duty. The movie message was clear: A happy cinematic family and a brave dog have done their part for the war effort, as should the audience. Other films followed *War Dogs* with a similar message connecting children/domesticity and dogs with war. *Sergeant Mike* (1944), *My Pal, Wolf* (1944), and *A Boy, a Girl, and a Dog* (1946) all feature children sending a beloved dog off to fight.

Not every dog made it to the battlefield, but Dogs for Defense had a solution. A contribution to the War Dog Fund enrolled a pet in Home Guard. For $1, a dog would be enlisted as a private or a seaman while $100 would raise the rank to general or admiral. In the press, the fundraising

scheme was promoted, like war bonds and stamps, as an economic contribution to the war effort and it often had a gendered subtext. The participation of women and their dogs in the scheme was praised as honoring
husbands and brothers in service while the dogs were anthropomorphized
to express pride in guarding the home front. A Dayton, Ohio, newspaper
published a six-photo spread of women with their enlisted pets—dogs,
cats and even ducklings, with captions that gave voice to the animals.[183] A
Great Dane named King, seated with his female owner whose husband and
brother were both serving, said, "My picture and the news that I'm in the
Army now, too, are going to both my masters, you may be sure."

Along with "Sergeant King's" photo was an image of two Private First
Class wire-haired terriers named Cranbourne Editor and Cranbourne
Extremist, sitting at the feet of their "mistress" whose husband was the president of the local kennel club. They also expressed their enthusiasm with a
caption that read, "We'll do good home guard duty, too." "Seaman Vicky,"
a dog pictured in a bucolic garden scene with her owner Betty, let readers know that she joined because she was "so proud of Miss Betty's brother
Lt. Rodney Boren, USN." A Dachshund named "Corporal Danny," pictured
with his owner and her new baby, was "proud" to be guarding "his adored
mistress" and his "brand-new baby mistress." Through the dogs' voices, the
silent women became symbols of the patriotic home front.

The high status given war dogs in the press, whether they were publicly celebrated for keeping domesticity safe at home or keeping soldiers
safe overseas, was framed as a source of pride for dog owners and even
some small towns. Beatrice, Nebraska, featured its first enlistee on the front
page of the *Beatrice Daily Sun* on June 4, 1943. "Seaman Poppy Grimes" was
pictured with his owner, nine-year-old Russell Grimes. Appointed the official recruiting officer for the town, Poppy was "doing his part for his brothers at the front."[184] Also doing his part was President Franklin D. Roosevelt's
Scottish Terrier, Fala, who was enrolled in the successful campaign.

With monetary support from the War Dog Fund, Dogs for Defense
recruited approximately 20,000 dogs and the press recounted their courageous activities for readers. As scouts, messengers and sentinels, the dogs
performed human work, but it was their more-than-human abilities that
set them apart. Press reports repeatedly stressed the dogs' military virtues
through stories of their superior senses. Describing them as "Grade A soldiers" an article in the *Birmingham News* gave numerous examples of a war
dog's skills. From being able to lay half a mile of telephone wire in five minutes, to going four or five days without food, to being the perfect silent cap-
tive if caught with a message, the canine soldier was uniquely positioned
to do a job "that only he can do."[185] A *Chicago Tribune* columnist informed
his readers that dogs saved the lives of army messengers because they could

run close to the ground, using vegetation for protection. They could also locate enemy machine gun nests and snipers, "the same way bird dogs find game."[186]

Underlying the dogs' skill set were kind dispositions. Another journalist at the *Chicago Tribune* noted that modern American war dogs, unlike their ancestors who were "clad in armor and spiked collars for attacks," had

Private George E. Sission of Bolivar, N.J., Company B, Military Police, is shown at the Camp Hill stockade, training "Ranger," a Doberman Pinscher sentry dog. The job of war dogs like Ranger was to guard areas around stockades and ammunition dumps. May 10, 1944 (National Archives).

"a background of friendly companionship with the children of its neighborhood."[187] Other press reports confirmed this friendly background but
added a tale of transformation. Before Billy, a Dallas-based dog, arrived at
the Texas recruiting station for Dogs for Defense, he "was considered something of a sissy," wrote Potts Boswell of *The Tampa Tribune*. After six-weeks
of training, he was not. Boswell painted the picture for his readers:

> A white-fanged, snarling dog, 55 pounds of fighting fury, lunged at the
> half-crouched man who menaced him. The dog's mouth was agape, his teeth
> were reaching for the throat of his enemy. Only the tight leash in the tight grasp
> of a soldier held him off. He was a white-furred devil.[188]

Billy's transition from pet to "white-furred devil" suggested that all dogs
had a monster lurking inside them that the right training could control. An
article in an Arizona paper made the case in 1943, "The war dog ... learns
the hardest of all lessons, the Army states, and that is to attack man.... The
difficulty seems to be that a dog, under most circumstances, hates really
to go after a man. It is contrary to instinct and that instinct must be broken down before the war dog will really lay hold of a person."[189] Like human
enlistees, the Army tore down canine military recruits and built them back
up into highly trained soldiers.

   Despite the press story about Billy's transformation into a "white-
furred devil," war dogs did not "really lay hold of a person," at least according to Lieutenant Robert Ruark. In a 1944 piece for *The Saturday Evening
Post*, Lieutenant Ruark set the record straight:

> At the beginning of the war ... a flood of fantastic publicity came close to befog-
> ging what has since turned out to be a sound military proposition. Highly
> colored exaggerations of Rover's niche in the war effort put the poor beast some-
> where between Superman and a werewolf as a potential slayer of the enemy. Sla-
> vering animals, their fangs a thirst for Jap throats, leaped at you from all sides.
> Man's erstwhile fireside companion was transformed, in the public mind, to a
> superanimal deadlier than a machine gun, who could also tend the sick, drive a
> jeep and replace six men on the battlefront.[190]

After mentioning that there was "only one authenticated case of an American war dog actually killing a man with his teeth," Ruark argued that "G.I.
Rover" had "done a good job—within canine limitations." In fact, being a
canine had leveled the playing field, "In a theater where the enemy fights
like a beast, the well-trained beast is an effective counterirritant." For
Ruark, it took an animal to fight an animal but canine soldiers were still
four-footed comrades that "bled and died alongside Yanks in the jungles,
and in many instances ... saved American lives."[191]

   The media celebrated war dogs as scouting heroes and courageous carriers of life-saving messages, dramatically emphasizing bravery in the face

of overwhelming odds. The *Chicago Tribune*'s marine corps combat correspondent, Sergeant Ward Walker, wrote about the dogs on Guam, "There wasn't a marine on the island who didn't speak respectfully of war dogs, for a lot of them owed their lives to the highly trained noses and ears…. In two years of battle in the Pacific the dog heroes have proved that the Japs' fear has a solid basis."[192] In another press report, the part of hero dog belonged to Sandy. A messenger dog sent to the jungles of New Guinea and New Britain, his story was told in the *Birmingham News* on May 7, 1944. When Sandy and his handler Sergeant Brown ran into Japanese pillboxes preventing an advance, a broken radio meant that it was up to Sandy to get the message through for reinforcements. What Sandy did next, was described this way:

> Through a curtain of enemy fire, past bullet-spitting U.S. tanks, through tough kunai grass, across jungle swamps ran Sandy, smack into danger of small arms fire of his own soldiers. Dodging, twisting, Sandy rushed on, leaping small streams, swimming a jungle river until he reached the beach road.[193]

Sandy found his target and the sergeant who received the critical message credited the dog with skills beyond his understanding but consistent with his training. "Don't ask me how he found me. He was trained to find me, that's all. It's part of being a war dog."

Sandy's story was told as an exciting action adventure. He leapt, ran, swam, dodged and twisted his way through bullets to safely deliver a message that saved lives. He was cast as a dog transformed through military training and like his fellow soldiers, he would resume normal life with ease. "Our experience with Army dogs is that once discharged they go right back to their old lives and forget all about Army life…. Just typical GIs, I guess."[194] Through Sandy's story, the press praised war dogs' superior animal senses and abilities while metaphorically transforming them into heroic and adaptable human soldiers.

Sandy joined other canine soldiers who were highlighted in the media for their successes on the battlefield. Newspaper readers in Boston learned about Andy, a Doberman Pinscher and Caesar, a German Shepherd Dog. Both served with Company M of the 3rd Raider Battalion. While Andy led the company to a Japanese road block, alerted his handler to three enemy snipers and a machine gun nest, Caesar made nine round trips, two under fire, for a total of 31 miles, as he carried messages between the raider battalion and a command post.[195] Chips, described as part Border Collie, part German Shepherd Dog and part Eskimo Husky, made headlines for his efforts in Sicily. "With utter disregard for his own safety, he cleaned out an enemy pillbox, captured two Italian gunners, then later the same night assisted in the capture of a column of ten more Italian soldiers," wrote Eileen Callahan in New York's *Daily News*.[196]

Probably the most famous dog of World War II, Chips was given a two-page spread in the *Daily News* that covered his backstory, his war achievements and his happy return to civilian life. Callahan's opening paragraph described Chips this way, "A humble, young, unlettered Army rookie, product of a small American village and the melting pot of mixed ancestry, has emerged a thrice-cited hero from the war, giving proof again that in America everyone has a chance to lead the parade." Chips' story was more than a tale of a dog turned metaphorical soldier. It was an example of the American dream. Chips was awarded the Silver Star and the Purple Heart and met presidents and prime ministers. His press coverage, along with that of Sandy, Andy, Caesar and others like them, was filled with examples of superior canine abilities within a subtext that stressed the very soldierly quality of bravery.

The canines of Dogs for Defense, as members of the American military's first organized animal recruitment effort, were unique because they were primarily recruited pets. The dogs' participation was a patriotic act on the part of their owners and the press made sure that all good citizen dog owners knew that their sacrifice was worth it. Stories consistently emphasized the extensively trained dogs' military value with tales of life-saving feats of heroism. They were a danger to the enemy, but rarely was it the danger of flesh-ripping attack. War dogs, like the human soldiers they had symbolically become, were not monsters but rather highly skilled compatriots. "They lived with us. They shared our rations," said Lieutenant Robert Johnson, in a 1944 newspaper account of war dogs in the jungles of New Britain and New Guinea. "Lots of times, out in the steaming jungle, I've seen a thirsty soldier divide the last bit of water in his canteen with his dog."[197]

The shared physical suffering was also recalled in Marine War Dog Platoon reports on the battle of Peleliu in the Philippines. The harsh coral landscape that badly bruised and cut the dogs' feet also made it impossible for the Marines to bury the dead and human excrement, which resulted in an intolerable amount of stench and decay. The impact of the environmental conditions and the shellshock suffered by many of the 36 dogs of the 4th Marine War Dog Platoon was so bad that the entire unit, or what was left of it, was eventually withdrawn from the island.[198] While this suggested a differentiation—what human soldiers could endure, dog soldiers could not— the Marine dog platoons would go on to invade other islands, including Iwo Jima and Okinawa. And like Marines, they would be sent home with discharge papers if they survived.

The shifting nature of warfare meant that the value of the soldier dogs of World War I and World War II was in the application of their natural sensing skills. The handlers' goal for their dogs was to outwit the enemy rather than physically attack them and because this was often framed in the press as a clever skill, however much it owed to human training, canine soldiers became more than four-footed strategic weapons. Press accounts transformed them with language commonly used to describe human soldiers. The dogs' actions were brave, their achievements were heroic, and their wounds were shared suffering. When it came time to return to civilian life, their reintegration was widely embraced by a public whose admiration had grown with every celebratory account of their wartime achievements.

The Army and Marines, equally respectful of the dogs' service, put time and money toward retraining the dogs for civilian life. At the end of World War II, the surplus dog situation caught the attention of the War Department, which issued a summary of how the dogs would be returned. The author of that summary shared the Department's feelings, "In no event," he stated, "will dogs go to undesirable individuals or to laboratories or institutions."[199] Dogs for Defense, the Quartermaster Corps and Army veterinarians worked together to rehome the dogs, with Dogs for Defense taking the position that a returning canine soldier, like a human one, should receive all the benefits of reintegration into domestic life. A Dogs for Defense spokesman said, "We feel that the place for a K-9 veteran is in a home.... To say that a dog should be kept confined to a kennel, robbed of the pleasure of companionship only to be found in a home, seemed to us just like arguing that the soldier for whom no job is in sight should be kept in uniform indefinitely."[200] There was also some concern that returning military dogs could suffer from battle fatigue or trauma and while this idea was mainly reflected in films, including *Danny Boy* (1946) and *Night Wind* (1948), the dogs in these movies happily recovered.

The public response to the reintegration scheme was overwhelming. Dogs for Defense reported that applications to adopt the returning canine soldiers exceeded 15,000 and would continue to be submitted long after all the returning dogs had been placed.[201] These veteran canines were the lucky ones. After 1945, the American military no longer had a generous policy toward K-9 retraining and rehoming. A war dog's military service would be a lifelong commitment and the media created connection between dogs, home and war that was so successfully mobilized during World War II would not be repeated.

In 1946, the Quartermaster Corps switched from recruiting the public's dogs to acquiring dogs directly from breeders. Dogs for Defense was dissolved and a new program, the Army Dog Association, began but was cut in 1950 due to little or no demand for dogs and a lack of facilities to house the dogs. The responsibility for training K-9 moved from one agency to the next, which resulted in changing methods and overall confusion within the military working dog program. Only one war dog platoon, the 26th Scout Dog Platoon, would be deployed during the Korean conflict.

The platoon received very little attention in the press. When it was mentioned, the coverage noted the high emotional and physical price the K-9 paid.

During this time, one dog did stand out in the press for his successful completion of combat patrols. His name was York and when he led point, no soldier was killed. York participated in over 100 patrols and received the Distinguished Service Award. A platoon commander told a reporter about the dog's devotion, describing it this way: "He never cracked, never froze, never whined. Somehow, he goes on patrol after patrol...."[202] York's fellow war dogs would not see significant action again until 1965, when the army and the air force deployed sentry dogs to Vietnam to provide security for air bases.

Weapons That Save Lives

While the press reports of World War II dogs described their contribution with words like "brave," and "heroic," coverage of war dogs in Vietnam was often written as straightforward summaries of their encounters with the enemy. Typical of the language was this account from a California newspaper: "Airman Second Class Ronald Rutherford, 20, of Atlanta, and his dog Hans chased off probers at the Bien Hoa air base.... Airman Second Class Rick J. Young ... was at Tan Son Nhut.... He and his dog Cowboy helped other sentry dog teams round up 25 persons...."[203] With language this bland, the accomplishments of the early Air Force sentry dogs in Vietnam sounded ordinary in comparison to the feats of World War II dogs. Also different were the references to the dogs' temperaments. In the beginning of the Vietnam conflict, the Air Force's training methods for sentry dogs focused on aggressiveness. The thinking was that a vicious dog served as a psychological and physical threat, but as some recruits discovered, this threat was not always against the enemy. In his history of war dogs, author Michael Lemish describes an incident on the outskirts of Saigon where a sentry dog riding in a jeep "lashed out and mangled the ear of an unfortunate infantryman" in a passing jeep.[204]

The Vietnam War dogs' aggressiveness also meant that new handlers rotating in for service, along with veterinarian technicians, and kennel maintenance workers tasked with the dogs' car, potentially encountered difficult and dangerous animals. By 1968, the Air Force began to focus on less aggressive training methods, but some press reports highlighted the dogs' attack skills. In Minneapolis, the *Star Tribune* described German Shepherd Dogs at an Air Force training facility in South Dakota as "trained to attack anyone who comes near them."[205] An Army scout dog named Murphy was featured in the *Arizona Daily Star* as an aggressive German Shepherd Dog who was surrendered to the Army by his Tucson-based owner, Linda Darnell, because she admittedly trained him to protect her and this "hostility toward everyone but her nearly cost him his life."[206] Warned by rabies control officials that Murphy would be euthanized if he ran into more trouble, Darnell gave him to the Army scout program. It was in Vietnam, the paper reported, that "Murphy's natural aggressiveness and distrust of strangers ... earned him nothing but praise and gratitude." Murphy's aggressiveness was learned rather than natural, as his owner admitted, but it made for a good story in a war where the enemy was elusive, and the losses were mounting.

Aggressiveness was also a theme in the story of a scout dog handler named Michael Lowther who told a reporter that he picked Kentucky, an 85-pound German Shepherd Dog, "because he seemed to be the most aggressive dog in the kennel."[207] According to Lowther, Kentucky, proved him right. "Once, while leading a 25th Infantry Division patrol ... he jumped around and lunged at a North Vietnamese who had popped out of a spider hole and was ready to shoot me in the back. Kentucky tore out his throat." The vicious response endeared Kentucky to his handler who called him "just about the best friend I had in Vietnam." When Lowther and Kentucky were later hit by shrapnel, Lowther was evacuated via helicopter, but Kentucky was left behind. The soldier was told that the dog "died in grief in losing me." The story, reprinted in over 20 newspapers, made Kentucky both a vicious weapon and a grief-filled companion.

Press coverage of Vietnam's war dogs should be viewed within the larger context of how the war was covered in general. Prior to 1964, Vietnam only occasionally made the news and when it did, the reports were a mix of support for brave U.S. soldiers and concern over policies that could put them at risk.[208] As the conflict wore on, President Kennedy and then President Johnson wanted Vietnam downplayed but once Johnson increased combat troops to South Vietnam, he had to gain more public and congressional support for the war. It was a balancing act between keeping the war out of the public mind and managing media coverage to keep the public supportive.[209]

The increased troop numbers meant more television news coverage and troops were typically characterized in heroic terms. In 1966, correspondents on NBC referred to American soldiers as "the greatest men in the world."[210] While the press began to raise some doubts in the editorial pages or deep within articles, television coverage was mainly an image of military success and when it wasn't, as happened when CBS showed footage of Marines destroying the village of Cam Ne, the network was bombarded with calls from angry viewers outraged over the portrayal of American boys as killers.[211]

The 1968 Tet offensive lead to widespread public opposition to the war as journalists reported government optimism more critically. Television news coverage turned equally, if not more, bleak. The shift in media coverage of the Vietnam war and its relationship to public opinion is complex and beyond the scope of this book but the change in how soldiers were described reflects how the military dogs who fought alongside them were discussed. In 1966, media coverage recalled the memory of World War II. American troops were "the greatest men in the world," confident of their mission. A year later, the media painted a different picture and it was one of doubt and confusion. CBS put it this way after the battle for Dak To, which had become the bloodiest of the war so far, "The question every GI asks and cannot answer is, 'Was it all worth it?' No one really knows."[212] The tone of the coverage continued this way during the last phase of the war and grew more personal in some media outlets, including a 1969 edition of *Life* magazine, which printed the names and faces of 242 American soldiers killed during a "typical" week in Vietnam.

It was in this context that Lowther told his story about Kentucky, a dog who was picked for his aggressiveness by a young soldier fighting in an increasingly hopeless war. When Lowther was wounded and the dog who had once saved his life was abandoned and left to die, it was a sad and lonely ending that mirrored the war's devastating physical and emotional toll. Vietnam war dogs, sometimes highlighted for their protective aggressiveness but most notable for their general absence in the press, were, like their handlers, casualties of a battle with no clear winners.

By 1970, criticism over the treatment of Vietnam's war dogs would make its way into media narratives covering the conflict. The *Los Angeles Times* reported on the fate of scout and tracker dogs by noting that American troop withdrawal meant that an estimated surplus of 500 dogs would not be taken back to the United States. They "would have to be 'euthanized,' or turned over to the South Vietnamese army."[213] The officer in charge of assigning war dogs was quoted as saying, "The Army is aware of the problem and I am sure that something will be done."[214] The Army's decision was a weak effort to appease the public, instructing the Veterinary Corps to return only "healthy" dogs, knowing that most carried infectious disease[215] and would therefore not be sent back.

Of the hundreds of dogs in Vietnam, 200 were considered for repatriation and only 120 boarded a transport plane home.[216] Much of the remaining surplus of dogs was turned over to the Army of the Republic of Vietnam (ARVN) but their fate was unclear. As Lemish notes in his work on war dogs, "The general belief is that the dogs became another source of walking protein for ARVN troops."[217] The press promoted a similar theory. In an article on the efforts of a Sacramento-based group called the Animal Protection

Institute of America (API) to get the dogs returned, the API president offered a letter the organization had received from a dog handler in Vietnam. The handler wrote, "I have been offered $20 (military payment certificates) for my dog, because in Vietnam as the offer said, 'Dog is number one, chop, chop.' Our dogs saved American lives. Being cannon fodder is enough to ask of them but being table fodder for the allies, or enemies is too much."[218] In an open letter quoted in numerous papers across the country, another handler wrote, "Under present Army policy not one of our hard-working and much decorated canine friends will return to the U.S.A. alive. Instead we will reward them for a job well done by sentencing them to mass euthanasia."[219]

Other articles focused on handlers' campaigns to bring their dogs home. The *St. Louis Post-Dispatch* reported on its front page that a dog named Prince "after distinguished combat service in Vietnam," would have to "live out his life in exile in that country" despite his handler's pleas to members of congress.[220] Concerned citizens across the country, including Sterling Colthurst, from Huntington Beach, California, responded with letters to the editor, "All animal lovers should be up in arms because of the proposed plan … not to return our military dogs in Vietnam … but to turn them over to the South Vietnamese or to subject them to mass euthanasia. I appeal to animal lovers everywhere to speak up on their behalf."[221] The appeals fell on deaf ears.

The military's reclassification of dogs as equipment in 1949 meant that when dogs were no longer useful, they were assigned to bases to die naturally or be euthanized.[222] For Vietnam's war dogs, this classification was coupled with a complicated logistical and practical problem that the U.S. military was not willing to solve, so the dogs were abandoned. The military also promoted the idea that the dogs were either a health threat or could not be demilitarized and it quickly found its way into the press. An Illinois newspaper article on the dogs' situation said, "None of the animals can be restored to a normal civilian life, as pets…. The well-schooled sentry or tracking dog seldom loses the viciousness acquired during a rigorous four-to-16-week training period."[223] The true war dog, said an article in the *Los Angeles Times*, "cannot be untrained."[224]

Some in the media and government pushed back. A columnist for the *San Francisco Examiner* wrote, "During World War II we had more than 10,000 dogs in our K-9 Corps. But we didn't abandon them. They were brought home…. Perhaps we were a better nation then, with better men making the rules."[225] Congressman John Moss of California introduced a bill to require the military to bring the dogs home, but the proposed legislation never made it out of committee. By 1972, around 130 dogs were under the control of the U.S. and none of them were approved to return home.[226] When the last veterinary hospital closed that year, the eighteen sentry dogs left were given to the ARVN.

After Vietnam, the Army and the Air Force used military working dogs to sniff out narcotics and explosives, skills that would be used in customs operations and later, during Operation Desert Storm. Between the September 11, 2001, terrorist attacks and 2004, dogs participated in seven missions overseas and in over 40 assignments with the Secret Service.[227] When the media paid attention to war dogs during this period, the coverage was less about their missions and more about what happened when they stopped going on them.

A typical theme was the military's callous disregard for handlers who wanted to adopt their dogs after their service ended. A Belgian Malinois named Reno and his Air Force handler, Albert Haines, made the front page of a paper in Oklahoma City in 2000. Haines had been fighting to adopt Reno for two years. "Man and dog formed an incredible bond," wrote the reporter. "Then it ended."[228] Why it ended was attributed to Haines' disillusionment over the military's treatment of its dogs. The reporter laid out the dogs' sad situation for her readers: "They live in kennels and cannot retire like their civilian counterparts. When they are too old to be useful anymore or too sick to go on, the military euthanizes them. They aren't awarded medals for distinguished service. They don't get a funeral when they die."[229] The clear message was that the dogs were unfairly denied the same recognition as human soldiers, a point Haines repeated when he said that Reno "served his country with distinction and deserves to be retired."

A few months later, a columnist for the *Dayton Daily News* told the story of Robby, an 11-year-old Belgian Malinois, "who has a death sentence looming."[230] Robby's handler was a Marine named Shawn Mathey who wanted to adopt him but Robby was "simply not going to be allowed to live." The column inspired an online "Help Save Robby" campaign and the website collected signatures from every state and several countries. Robby's story was such bad publicity that the Military Working Dog Training School at Lackland Air Force Base in Texas posted an "Official Response to the Save Robby Campaign" on its website. Aware of Robby's story, Representative Roscoe Bartlett introduced legislation that President Bill Clinton signed into law in November 2000. The bill allowed trained people, such as handlers, to adopt the dogs and the military would not be held accountable for any damages or injuries the dogs may cause.

Dog-Soldier

In the media story of the war dog, a soldier/handler has been ever present. Whether dogs were reflections of brave World War II Marines or another weapon in Vietnam infantrymen's arsenals, they were members of a unit rather than independent vicious beasts. Military handlers gave war dogs permission to be dangerous and decided when they should stop being so. A few years after the 2000 legislation, military dogs would make headlines again when U.S. handlers at Iraq prison Abu Ghraib gave K-9's permission to act as instruments of torture.

In 2003, the prison complex Abu Ghraib, west of Baghdad, Iraq, became an American military prison. It had been a notorious site under Saddam Hussein, and the U.S. military used it for common criminals, security detainees and "high-value" leaders of the insurgency during the Iraq War. A report by Major General Antonio M. Taguba, which was never meant for public release but obtained by *The New Yorker* in 2004, found that soldiers of the 372nd Military Police Company and members of the U.S. intelligence community had committed "sadistic, blatant, and wanton criminal abuses" against detainees of the prison.[231]

Taguba's report detailed the abuse, including "using military working dogs to frighten and intimidate detainees with threats of attack, and in one instance actually biting a detainee."[232] *The New Yorker* article followed a *60 Minutes II* episode that broke the story and broadcast photographs of the abuse taken by those who had committed it. Several of the pictures showed soldiers using dogs to terrorize detainees.

In one photo, a horrified prisoner is crouched in a corner while a dog snarls close to his face. The handler is straddling the dog and has a tight grip on the leash. In another picture, two dogs, named in the army's Criminal Investigation Command report as Duco and Marko, are facing a naked detainee who is cowering with his knees bent and his hands behind his head in front of a jail cell door. Two handlers control Duco and Marko while a third soldier stands in front of the man. The report labeled the photo as "Two dog handlers have dogs watching detainee," yet the man's posture of surrender makes his extreme fear of the dogs obvious. In a third image, the same prisoner is lying on the ground, naked, with bloody legs. The official caption read "Detainee after dog bite."[233]

Army dog handlers Sergeant Santos Cardona and Sergeant Michael Smith were charged with maltreatment of detainees. The charge primarily focused on the handlers' use of military working dogs to threaten and attack prisoners. It was reported that prosecutors heavily relied on the incident as depicted in the photographs of the men with dogs Duco and Marko.[234] During the handlers' preliminary hearing, evidence was presented that the techniques involving dogs at Abu Ghraib were among approved tactics for use with suspected terrorists held at Guantanamo.

The press coverage of Cardona and Smith's convictions[235] varied in how it described the dogs. Some reports, like the Associated Press version in June 2006, which appeared in papers across the nation, used neutral language for the dogs' actions. The AP article described Cardona as "allow-ing his dog to bark within inches of a prisoner's face."[236] An earlier AP report in March that covered Smith's conviction was less neutral, using the phrase "snarling animal" to describe Smith's dog.[237] Among the articles cov-ering Smith's conviction, a few used the photo of him and his dog from Abu Ghraib, but many more used a file photo of him in his military uniform. The effect was to connect the man with the "snarling animal."

The military working dogs pictured in the Abu Ghraib photographs are forever linked to the torture that took place during the War on Ter-ror, but the idea of dogs as a form of state power was not new when the pic-tures broke. The Birmingham photos of snarling police dogs attacking civil rights protestors had captured a similar concept of brutality decades earlier and as with those images, America's global reputation was damaged. Just as the Birmingham images weakened the credibility of the United States when it pointed to human rights abuses in other countries as a response to charges of discrimination against African Americans, the Abu Ghraib pictures made America's outrage over Arab nations' human right abuses ineffective.

The photos of handlers using dogs at Abu Ghraib to strike fear into people they had power over may have had a startling familiarity, but they also have to be understood within the totality of the images. The Abu Ghraib pictures showed naked Iraqi prisoners stacked into human pyra-mids, men forced to stimulate sexual acts and one where Private Lynndie England held a leash attached to a dog collar that had been placed around the neck of a naked prisoner lying on the ground. The overall impact of the images was one of cruel and aimless authority, of which dogs were an extension. If photographs have the power to mobilize public opinion, as some scholars have argued the Abu Ghraib photos did in terms of global condemnation of U.S. abuse of Arab prisoners,[238] then the images of dogs as part of this abuse were equally powerful in confirming that they were dan-gerous weapons when handled by dangerous people.

Press coverage of Smith and Cardona's trials and convictions high-lighted military dogs as weapons in the hands of non-heroes, making the dogs equally dishonorable, but this image would not last. When SEAL Team Six killed Osama bin Laden in 2011, a dog was there to assist. Later identified as Cairo, a Belgian Malinois, the dog was the only named mem-ber of the raid team and while it was unclear exactly how Cairo was used, the *New York Times* proposed that he "may be the nation's most courageous dog."[239] The story prompted ABC News to praise military dogs in general for their human-like skills: "The dogs are a fighting force on four legs that are able to parachute into action, rappel into combat and swim into a skir-mish."[240] The dog who helped bring down the world's most hated terrorist leader was a valued team member who restored honor to his fellow K-9s and the handlers in charge of them.

Cairo's story is typical of how war dogs are characterized throughout popular media. Countless nonfiction books about war dogs have the word "heroism" in their titles, numerous films have highlighted the bond between military canines and their handlers and decades of press reports have stressed the dogs' bravery, loyalty and sacrifice. Central to these depictions are attributes that make dogs valuable weapons—an extraordinary sense of smell and superior strength and speed, but these are also characteristics that make them dangerous. Yet, war dogs have rarely been discussed in the media as uncontrollable, dangerous dogs in their own right. If their behavior raised debate over the boundaries between the civilized and the barbaric, it has been within the larger context of a dog-human relationship.

In her work on war dogs, journalist Rebecca Frankel notes that there is one phrase a military handler says like a mantra: "Where I go, my dog goes. Where my dog goes, I go."[241] The dog-handler team, and more broadly, the dog-military unit, has been conceptualized as an unbreakable connection, which has lent itself to media frames that humanized the animal and sometimes, animalized the human.

For World War II dogs, this took the form of canines that were patriotic pets, proudly sent to fight for a just and noble cause and warmly welcomed back to civilian life, just like the soldiers who handled them. Vietnam's war dogs were reduced to a talking point by unsympathetic military leaders who often described them in the press as surplus equipment and damaged goods that could not be retrained. The public, disillusioned with a controversial war and navigating a turbulent social climate, put some pressure on the military to change the narrative but these canine soldiers were left to uncertain futures and most probably death sentences on foreign soil.

When dogs reentered the war arena in the Abu Ghraib photos, it was as extensions of soldiers who had become savage tormentors and abusers, humans who had been animalized. As with Birmingham, pictures once again highlighted dogs' roles as instruments of state terror. As Alex Danchev argues in his work on the War on Terror, the abuse was part of a larger system, "Behind the dog is the dog handler. Behind the dog handler is the commander. Behind the commander is the policymaker."[242] The dogs at Abu Ghraib were labeled "savage" in a few press reports, but the military dog/handler bond meant that the real savagery came from the moral breakdown of soldiers and by extension, their leaders.

Some contemporary media accounts of military working dogs have assigned them the ability to communicate the complexities of battle

through the canine-human relationship. Frankel offers a story about Napoleon Bonaparte, who reportedly came upon a dog that had been watching
over his master's corpse after a fierce battle. Upset, the dog ran between the
dead man and Napoleon, alternately licking the man's hand and looking to
Napoleon for assistance. Years later, Napoleon reflected on the encounter:

> Perhaps it was the spirit of the time and the place that affected me. But I assure
> you no occurrence of any of my other battlefields impressed me so keenly....
> This soldier, I realized, must have had friends at home and in his regiment; yet
> he lay there deserted by all except his dog.... Tearless, I had given orders which
> brought death to thousands. Yet, here I was stirred, profoundly stirred, stirred to
> tears.... By the grief of one dog. I am certain that at that instant I felt more ready
> than at any other time to show mercy toward a suppliant foe-man.[243]

Frankel uses this tale of loyalty to demonstrate how a war dog could temporarily change the heart of a ruthless military leader, making him more
human. "To know war dogs is not to know war, but they can help us understand it better ... [by making it] more palatable, but also more tender, and
more human."[244] Perhaps this is why the war dog's media story has more
room for heroic characterizations. The human-canine bond told in a tale of
a brave soldier and a faithful dog is one way to understand the deep impact
of battle.

*   *   *

Stories about slave tracking "negro dogs," crowd controlling police
dogs and combat ready war dogs mediate how we perceive both dogs' and
humans' dangerousness. In the hands of slave catchers, a dog's ability to
hunt people was horrific because it communicated a primal fear of beast
devouring man but also because it made the human commanding the animal equally monstrous. Police dogs that bit criminals (or peaceful protestors) were frightening but so were the men and women who did not prevent
the savagery. American war dogs have been largely spared from this media
frame. Theirs is a story that emphasizes the humane-canine bond almost
mythically, and in this bond, the dog is crafted as a conduit to understanding the human soldier as heroic. Frankel writes, "Knowing the bond
between a handler and his dog, we are able to see the people at the other
end of the leash more clearly."[245] If American war dogs, and by extension
their handlers, found themselves in dishonorable positions, it was typically
shaped in the media as an outlier, the result of disreputable people who had
abused a sacred bond and sometimes as a chain of command gone horribly
wrong. A war dog, a "slave" dog, and a police dog have all been trained to
be dangerous, and when they have been directed to exhibit this aggression,
it is the bond between human and animal that has permitted us to see the
cruelty of the person doing the directing.

From Page to Screen

In the press, dogs that behave badly have played a central role in stories about bad humans. Things aren't much different for the bad dogs that appear on screen. While this book has primarily focused on journalistic accounts to tell the dangerous dog's media story, the popularity of reality television series addressing problem dog behavior means any discussion would be incomplete without exploring a few of these shows. In reality television concerned with correcting troubling canine behavior, man's best friend is a horror to live with, but it's not just the dog that needs rehabilitation.

Screen's bad dogs, however, are just as popular when they're not real, so before investigating how man's misbehaving best friend is represented on television shows, the next chapter takes a brief detour into the fictional side of monster dogs with a look at three horror films.[246] *Cujo, The Pack* and *White Dog* focus on dogs that have gone bad in various ways, from a family pet to a menacing pack to an attack dog trained to relapse into a beastly state. In this animal horror cinema, humans lose control and dogs return to their "natural" state, unleashing their monstrous power before their transgressions against humanity are punished. Each film delivers close-ups of brutal dog-on-people assaults, and while the dogs in these films may be killers, who is the real monster is a more complex question.

Chapter Four

Screen

Dogs in narrative cinema are always meant to be—indeed, are constructed formally to be—about ourselves.[1]

When Animals Attack

While we don't expect to be attacked by insects, gorillas and sharks the size of buildings, film's animal monsters connect us to a very real past. Considering that our prehistoric ancestors were not always successful at evading a predator, whether it was a saber-tooth cat with canine teeth over six inches long or 250-pound wild dogs that could choose to hunt them alone or devour them in packs, "human as prey" is as much a part of the fossil record as is "human as hunter." Modern history has a few alarming examples as well.

In the 1850s, tigers killed 600 people a year in Sumatra and Java, while in India, tigers killed 7,000 people over a five-year period in the 1930s.[2] In 2016, an alligator pulled a two-year-old boy named Lane Graves into a lagoon near a Walt Disney World hotel. His body was found not far from where he was grabbed. Media coverage of the story was widespread and continued into 2017, when Walt Disney World unveiled a statue in his memory, and then into 2018, when his parents announced the birth of another child.[3] There may be lots of choices about what to fear when it comes to being physically or fatally harmed these days, but being on the receiving end of an animal's teeth has not lost its place among them.

Dominic Lennard notes that "fatal animal attacks carry explosive conceptual power," not the least of which is the reminder that we have the potential "to be mere meat for something else."[4] This fear is mixed with fascination. For example, a dangerous carnivore draws crowds at a zoo. Using the work of Paul Trout, Lennard argues that this allure has its evolutionary roots in systems that developed to ensure self-preservation. Trout notes that our ancestors told stories that grew out of encounters with real animals

116

in order to deal with the fear of being hunted, killed and eaten by predators—to basically stay alive, and in a figurative sense, this still takes place.[5]

Part of our interest in the story of a dangerous animal, then, is about observing and judging the levels of threat it represents and this process takes place whether that predator is behind the bars of a cage, tucked into the pages of a book or an image on a screen. From folklore, where a "veritable menagerie" of hungry predators "slither, run, and swoop their way through the mythic landscape in search of human flesh,"[6] to fairy tales to novels to films, animals bite, tear apart and devour people and we pay attention.

With some exceptions, animal horror cinema is typically viewed as low-budget entertainment with little to add to cultural debate, but recent scholarship, including *Animal Horror Cinema: Genre, History and Criticism* (2015) and Dominic Lennard's *Brute Force: Animal Horror Movies* (2019), suggests this is changing. When it comes to animal horror films, Lennard notes that they "allow us to run simulations of hostile encounters" and "show us scenarios, character traits, actions and reactions, some successful and others less so."[7] Whether it's a reptile in *Alligator* (1980), a snake in *Anaconda* (1997, 2004, 2007, 2008) or a series of great white sharks in *Jaws* (1975, 1978, 1983, 1987), the fact that we pay money to see movies where animals eat us suggests that our alpha predator status has done little to soothe our primal fear of being devoured or lessen some deep-seated need to make a mental note of how we might survive it.

While the fear and fascination many of us have with the genre of animal horror movies is to some extent, "ingrained," it is also influenced by any number of environmental and cultural factors.[8] Some animals may be admired, others may elicit disgust. One person's terrifying, man-eating spider is another person's horrifying man-chomping alligator. Both turn people into prey, which is an unwelcome prospect no matter how you feel about spiders versus alligators, but insects and reptiles, for many people, are not beloved pets. The tension in animal horror films typically comes from collapsing boundaries between human and animal, and the stakes are different when that animal is a dog. A dog's identity, being fluid, allows it to be transformed into whatever we want it to be and this is most commonly "man's best friend." It's a cultural frame, present in countless fictional and real stories where dogs are constructed as loyal companions, and one that guides most people's interpretation of them. It also reflects what is for many, a close physical association that includes a mutually beneficial relationship.

The boundary that collapses in animal horror when a dog turns into a beast is less about the fear that humans and dogs no longer exist in separate worlds—the line between these worlds is already blurred—and more about a threatening transformation where a dog's human-like qualities suddenly make it more of an adversary than a friend. The key to man and canine's mutually beneficial relationship is power and when that power belongs to a dog it can be terrifying, but the real horror is often that the canine monster is manmade.

Cujo

IT'S NOT A MONSTER. IT'S JUST A DOGGIE.

Donna Trenton (Dee Wallace) would come to regret that line, and Cujo would go on to become the most famous monster doggie in popular culture. But first, things begin serenely. The 1983 film adaptation of Stephen King's novel about a dog that turns into a killer after being bitten by a bat opens with an idyllic nature scene. Cujo, a Saint Bernard, is frolicking across a field on a bright, sunny day in friendly pursuit of a rabbit. Alternating between Cujo's point of view and the rabbit's, it's a playful scene with the hunted outwitting the hunter. When the rabbit escapes through a hole, Cujo squeezes his face through the opening, disturbing some bats. A rabid one bites him hard on the nose and seals his fate.

Casting a Saint Bernard as a killer dog had its problems, as director Lewis Teague noted in a 2007 documentary on the making of the film. "Saint Bernard's traipse around the Alps with little kegs of rum under their chins to save stranded hikers. They're friendly—named after a saint."[9] Dee Wallace remembered that from the neck up the various dogs that played Cujo looked like they were "going to eat you" but their wagging tails had to be tied down in long shots.[10] Looking back at the film in a 2009 critique, one writer quipped, "Rather than a hellish Baskerville hound, here, a giant St. Bernard with unconvincing shaving foam round its mouth looks like it might lick you to death in a fit of over-zealous friendliness."[11]

Other movie critics weren't so sure. At the time of the film's release, some were less concerned with breed choice and more focused on the brutal nature of the attack scenes. One critic called them "gripping sequences" that were "gruesome and frightening"[12] while another said they were "relentless and breathtaking in their realism."[13] The critic for the *Los Angeles Times* advised readers to "leave the kids at home" because the film contained "grueling and vicious violence."[14] While Cujo kills various characters throughout the film, the real horror takes place in the movie's final section when Donna and her son Tad (Danny Pintauro) are trapped in a broken-down car that the relentless Saint Bernard repeatedly attacks.

The narrative set-up for Donna and Tad's predicament begins with an unhappy household where fear is both imagined and real. Tad is afraid of a monster in his closet, a fear his father Vic (Daniel Hugh-Kelly) tries to calm with a bit of horror movie foreshadowing, "There's no such thing as real monsters. Only in stories." Donna is afraid of growing old and bored in the small Maine town where they live and finds some brief comfort in an affair with a local carpenter. Vic, afraid of losing Donna, also faces the loss of his professional reputation as an advertising executive after his client's cereal brand appears to be making people sick. Donna's unhappiness, Vic's potential loss of financial stability and Tad's anxiety establish a fractured family.

As a character in the story, Cujo is a member of the Camber family. Less prosperous than the Trentons, who live in a large house with a sea view and socialize at a tennis club, the Cambers, Joe (Ed Lauter), his wife Charity (Kaiulani Lee) and their son Brett (Billy Jayne), live on a rural back road in a rundown farmhouse. When Vic, Donna and Tad take Vic's sports car to Joe for a repair, the visual contrast highlights their economic differences. Donna is overdressed in a puffy sleeved outfit with heels while Charity is in a plain housedress, plucking a chicken in the front yard. Cujo runs over to see the Trentons but Donna isn't persuaded by Brett's assurances that he's a friendly dog. A short time later, a close up of Cujo's eyes is cut with a close-up of a loud power tool that Joe is using. The sound disturbs the Saint Bernard, as his disease begins to reveal itself.

The dynamics of the Camber family are played out in a kitchen scene that reveals Cujo's people are as equally troubled as the Trentons. When Joe becomes angry that his wife bought a new hydraulic lift, she soothes him with the news that she paid for it with a small lottery win. Her proposal that Joe allow her to take Brett to visit her sister is met with some resistance until Joe realizes that he can use some of the lottery money on a weekend of "broads, booze and baseball" with his slovenly buddy Gary (Mills Watson). Joe's brutish nature and short-tempered impatience, along with his wife's barely hidden desperation that he agrees to her trip, hints at an emotionally abusive situation.

When he witnesses Joe's initial anger in the kitchen, Cujo reacts uneasily but his change in behavior goes unnoticed until the next day, when Brett encounters him in the fog. Cujo acts aggressively towards him and he shouts, "It's me, Brett!" Recognizing Brett's love for him, or perhaps not yet entirely overtaken by his disease, Cujo retreats.

Later, Brett tells his mother he's worried about the dog and wants to tell his father but she anxiously persuades him to wait and instead call him later, after they've left. Her fear that she will lose her chance to get away from Joe overrides Cujo's needs, so that he is framed, much like the humans of the story, as one more neglected member of a broken household. The scene underscores the idea that Cujo's suffering and eventual descent into violence is easily preventable with treatment, if only the humans in his life would notice.

As Cujo's condition deteriorates, he eventually makes his way to Gary's house, where he finds Gary dumping a mound of beer cans on an already giant pile of trash just beyond his front porch. The attack starts with a growl. Gary pushes Cujo off, runs into his house and grabs a gun as Cujo breaks through the front door. Gary's final moments are shot in close-ups of his face cut with some shots of Cujo's teeth. The camera then moves to a long shot of Gary's legs and the lower half of Cujo, so that Cujo's attack on Gary's chest, neck and face are left to the viewer's imagination—at least until Joe finds him, at which point Gary's injuries are revealed through Joe's point of view. But it is through Cujo's point of view that we witness Joe's death, as the camera angle tilts upward to reveal a terrified and confused Joe. The action cuts to a long shot of Gary's house as Joe is heard screaming "No! No!"

The rest of the film focuses on Donna and Tad's ordeal after Donna takes her broken-down car to the Camber place to be fixed and it dies just as she arrives. With Joe Camber dead, Mrs. Camber and her son out of town and Vic on a business trip, the stage is set for Cujo's final monstrous act. Teague initially brings Cujo into the sequence as Donna is trying to unlatch Tad's seatbelt. The window is halfway down, the music temporarily stops and Cujo runs into the shot, barking and pawing at the window.

After attacking Donna's (Dee Wallace) car multiple times, the titular "Cujo" tries a different approach to get to his prey. 1983. Warner Bros. Pictures. Director: Lewis Teague. moviestillsdb.com.

He disappears, only to suddenly reappear on the car's hood and later at the window as Donna is looking out of it. Teague sets up a moment of false hope when Donna finally gets the car to start. Triumphantly, she yells "Fuck you, dog!" But the car only makes it a few feet before the engine dies one final time.

The extended sequence of Donna's standoff with Cujo takes place over several days. Rapid cuts switch from low angles in the car, to close-ups of Donna's hand straining to keep the door closed against Cujo's attacks, to tight shots of Cujo's face covered in oozing yellow discharge. There is an affective slow zoom out from the car that reveals Donna and Tad's isolation. Shots of the car in the mid-ground, with Cujo in the foreground, set up the idea that the dog is watching and waiting for his next opportunity to strike.

Earlier in her entrapment, Donna spots a discarded baseball bat outside the car. As Tad's panic grows and then turns into physical deterioration, she decides to make a run toward the house. Not knowing where Cujo is, she opens the car door, crouches to check underneath the car ,and not seeing him there, stands up. Cujo attacks her from behind. She dives into the car and Cujo makes it part of the way in. The struggle is an intense series of quick cuts as Donna beats the dog away, but not before he viciously bites her leg. Then the shot slows down to pan from mother to child before making a complete circle that spins faster and faster to simulate Donna's loss of consciousness.

The action cuts to Vic's hotel room, where he wakes up startled, as if from a bad dream. He has not been able to reach Donna on the phone for days, so he cuts his trip short and returns home to an empty house. After Vic alerts the police, one officer goes to the Camber farm to investigate without backup. Cujo attacks and kills him.

Cujo's violation against humans is his transformation from tame family pet (civilized) to wild, uncontrolled killer (nature) and his targets seem to be punished for their mistakes or their misplaced hubris. The police officer's death results from a poor decision. Gary is a slob who fights Cujo off, screaming "I don't give a shit!" before retrieving his gun. Joe is a man who makes his wife afraid. Donna is having an affair. Equating Cujo's transgression with peoples' personal failures temporary collapses the separate worlds of human and animal.

With the police officer dead and Tad's physical condition getting worse, Donna decides to make one last attempt to save herself and her son. Grabbing the bat, she swings at Cujo as the camera shifts to the dog's point of view. The bat breaks, Cujo jumps onto Donna and impales himself on the piece that remains in her hand. Discussing the scene, Teague noted that he "was very careful to never show [Donna] actually hitting the dog"[15] for fear of a backlash. His concern recognizes dogs' relationship to western culture and their more conventional position in cinema, where they are typically framed as susceptible to unscrupulous characters. This extends to horror cinema, where, as Dominic Lennard notes, dogs are often notable as early victims of violent attack. "Much like that of a child, the dog's vulnerability always powerfully enhances the despicability of those who would abuse it."[16]

Donna would appear unlikeable if she was shown beating Cujo, even in his rabies-induced killer state of mind, and likeability was the key to caring about the film's humans. Teague commented that during audience testing for *Cujo*, viewers had less interest in the dog attack scenes when the character-focused scenes were significantly cut. Put another way, it's easier to care about Donna potentially dying if you care about Donna in the first place.

While Teague's direction is careful to avoid physical abuse of Cujo so as not to jeopardize sympathy for Donna, he is also aware that caring too much about Cujo would weaken the film's psychological terror. (This was already challenging considering that Cujo represents a breed known for its helpful qualities, and in some scenes the canine actors appear more playful than menacing.) Yet, the film does depict moments that engage viewers' empathy.

Besides the overall pity that Cujo deserves for his rabies being left untreated, a scene where he repeatedly slams into Donna's car headfirst after he hears the phone ringing in the Camber house is the most direct emotional appeal on the dog's behalf. The suggestion that the sound of the phone (like the sound of the power tool earlier) agitates Cujo to the point that he appears to have hurt himself creates sympathy.[17] His viciousness is somewhat mitigated by the idea that bad luck and a distracted family caused his transformation. The story taps into the fear of a pet suddenly turning on its people but Cujo is more of an accidental attacker than a committed adversary. A disease makes Cujo sick, but it is his family who allows him to become a monster.

The film ends with a limping, blood-covered Donna carrying an unconscious Tad into the Camber house, where she frantically tries to revive him. In one last generic horror film device, the not-quite-dead Cujo crashes through the door and Donna shoots him with the dead police officer's gun. Vic, who earlier decided to head out to the Camber farm after the police officer failed to report back, arrives to find Donna on the porch with Tad in her arms. The family embraces in a final freeze frame. Teague ended it here, he said, because the point of the movie had been made, "If a real lethal fear comes into our life it'll put a lot of our other more, less lethal imaginary fears into perspective."[18] For Teague, the canine monster served human needs as both a manifestation of a family's internal fears and a path to their healing. *Cujo* depicts a typical animal horror trope of the tamed animal rising beyond human control, but the actions of this canine monster are not the product of its choosing.

The Pack

It's a wild dog. That's all. Nothing more.

Jerry Preston's (Joe Don Baker) assurances to his son in the opening scenes of *The Pack* (1977) are, of course, wrong. The scarred and growling mixed-breed dog that they encounter at the local dump is more than wild. He's out for revenge.

The story begins on a popular resort island off New England. A slow pan across a wooded area stops to focus on a horse in the distance, grazing in an open field. The watchers are a pack of dogs and the horse is their next victim. The camera closes in on the panicked animal as the dogs prepare to pounce out of frame.

The scene cuts to a family at the end of their summer vacation packing up to catch the weekly ferry back to the city. A woman impatiently tells her husband to "go take care of that," referring to a dog that their son is sitting with in the backyard. He tries to change her mind, "You don't think we'll find someone to take care of it in the city?" "No! I don't!" she cries. "We'll end up giving it to the pound and they'd end up gassing it which is exactly what would have happened if we hadn't come along." Giving in to his wife's demands, the man tells his son that he'll tie the dog to a tree and "he'll get away if he tries hard enough." Left in the forest, the dog whines and barks and immediately begins to chew the rope.

The summer tourists' cruel abandonment of their temporary pet is expository in that it provides a reason for a pack of dogs to exist in the movie's setting, but it also operates within a frame of pet-keeping that constructs dogs and other animals as disposable. Taken together, this scene and the predatory behavior of the dogs in the opening sequence foreshadow the idea that these abandoned dogs have formed a pack to survive (and eventually get pay back for) the cruel choices of people. The theme is confirmed after Jerry, who encounters the pack's alpha dog a few scenes later, speaks of a more sinister intent.

The island's marine biologist, Jerry is introduced riding in a car with his German Shepherd Dog, Rye, who sits in the front passenger seat. He has deep affection for Rye, chatting with him as if with a friend. After picking up his son and his girlfriend Millie's (Hope Alexander-Willis) son, Jerry, Rye and the boys make a quick stop. Rye is injured when he runs into the forest to chase a rabbit and Jerry, chasing after him, meets the pack leader.

A lobby card featuring a vicious member of "The Pack," a group of abandoned pets who take their revenge on the residents of Seal Island. *The Pack*. 1977. Warner Bros. Pictures. Director: Robert Clouse. moviestillsdb.com

It's a tense standoff and Jerry, rather than the dog, retreats. Back in the car, he tells the boys that the dog is probably starving but nature has taken over and trapping the dog would not work. "He's too far gone. He's too wild," he says. "I've seen it before. It's more than hunger." Jerry's mysterious insight establishes him as an expert and suggests that the dog's irreversible transformation from pet to predator is about more than satisfying a basic need. This alpha dog is angry.

Anthropomorphizing the pack leader makes that particular dog the film's central villain, but the pack itself demonstrates a disturbing level of collective intelligence. Before culminating in a one-on-one fight between Jerry and the pack leader, the action focuses on the pack targeting and killing island residents and members of an off-season tourist group. In one scene, the pack goes after a local blind man at night, in his home. Referred to by his last name, McMinnimee (Delos V. Smith, Jr.) initially scares the dogs off with a shotgun as they try to crash through the front windows, but they change course, seemingly making a collective decision to go to the back of the house and break through a window that McMinnimee is frantically trying to close. The last scene is a close-up of his bloody hands and the dogs' faces as he unsuccessfully fights them off.

Later, the lead dog appears outside Millie's home, seemingly without the pack. She throws a rock to scare him, then scrambles to get inside her convertible. The pack shows up, surrounds the car and attacks it as if each dog has a specific job. Some scratch and claw at the windows, one is on the hood, another rips through the car's soft top. Millie is saved when Jerry arrives, and the pack runs off at the sound of his gun.

After attacking Millie, the pack continues its rampage, chasing one tourist onto a bluff overlooking the ocean. Panicked and cornered, he falls to his death. The dogs then find and kill another tourist when she takes shelter in an abandoned barn. As the film enters its final act, Jerry takes control, instructing everyone who is left to barricade the house where they are hiding. He warns them, "If the dogs got through McMinnimee's house…" before trailing off. Making a reference to the pack's intelligence and motivation, he leaves the consequences of not following his commands to the group's imagination. When the lead dog appears alone at a window, then disappears, a member of the group says, "He seems to know." Repeating his earlier reference to the dog's agency, Jerry replies, "Bastard's survived and he's learned." What the pack has learned is that humans are untrustworthy, but deciding that they are also food upsets the "natural order" of human-animal relations, an idea that the film's tagline—"Last summer they were pets. Now they are predators"—neatly summarizes.

In the climactic scene, Jerry lures the pack into the house with the intention of trapping them and setting the building on fire. In the attic, he struggles to retract a set of stairs, and the pack leader reaches him. When Jerry jumps out of an attic window to escape, the dog follows him and falls to his death. As the pack dies in the burning house, one dog is left outside. It's the abandoned pet from the film's opening sequence. Jerry stops his friend from shooting the dog and offers it food instead. "I won't hurt you," he says. "It's all right." The story ends with a still image of the dog licking Jerry's outstretched hand.

Jerry's actions at the end of *The Pack* highlight the film's emotional and moral structure with a message about responsible pet ownership and the bond between humans and dogs. The abandoned dog from the beginning of the film invites viewer sympathy and when Jerry shows the dog kindness and is repaid with love, that sympathy symbolically extends to the pack itself. Throughout the film, the pack dogs exhibit human inclinations and emotions, which blur the lines between bad dogs and bad people. Callous disregard is the reason for the pack's behavior. The dogs are simply seeking revenge for a grievous wrong. In this horror story about killer dogs, people are the greater hazard.

The film's "lesson" about responsible animal stewardship made its way into press coverage. Karl Miller, the dogs' trainer, commented that those involved with the production "did not set out to give the dog a bad image." The dogs were "not supposed to be man-eaters." Rather the filmmakers were trying to show "that it is criminal to abandon unwanted pets."[19] Paul Heller, a co-producer on the film, tied the anti-cruelty message to real world practices. He told a reporter, "As you know, people pollute with animals. They go off and leave them. They pick up a couple of dogs from the pound or something so they can play with their kids for the summer, then they leave them."[20] In an interview with the *San Francisco Examiner*, Hope Alexander-Willis, who plays Millie, repeated the idea, "The theme is that we have to be responsible for these animals. It's humanity's fault for treating them badly."[21]

The film's good intentions did not persuade critics to embrace it. One reviewer said it "elicits neither fear nor excitement … is insipid, poorly acted and extremely slow-paced."[22] The ending, she argued, was "so ludicrous that if one found any redeeming feature in the previous 90 minutes of the film, it was destroyed by this ultimate sophomoric simplicity."[23] Another offered this assessment, "The dogs are good actors, and so is Baker, good enough to go through this charade as though he might possibly believe it."[24] One critic quipped that "a stern talking-to by a reputable canine, Benji for example, could have turned the whole pack back into law-abiding pets."[25]

Movie critics dismissed the premise, but art was imitating life. In May 1977, months before the film's release, the *Philadelphia Inquirer* reported that a pack of five wild dogs attacked a four-year-old boy "suddenly, for no apparent reason" and noted that "this year, more than ever, people are finding wild dogs roaming in packs."[26] The reason, according to "experts" was that "people who must move, or who can no longer afford to feed their dogs, or who simply tire of them, take them to remote areas … and abandon them."[27] The boy's experience was not the only case in the area. Two weeks prior to the incident, the reporter wrote, a pack of 17 wild dogs chased a 12-year-old up a tree.

The situation was slightly better on the West Coast. In the same month as the *Philadelphia Inquirer* story, the *Los Angeles Times* reported that animal control officers in the city's southeast had broken up numerous packs of roving dogs. Unlike the Philadelphia pack, these dogs were not attacking people, but they seemed to be involved in a recruitment drive. The wild dogs, a city official said, "had attracted other neighborhood dogs to run with them."[28]

Dog packs also made headlines in Florida. The September 16, 1977, edition of the *Tampa Tribune* reported that members of the sheriff's department were hunting for a pack of 12 to 20 dogs that had terrorized area residents. One man recounted a story of meeting a large dog that "kept baring his teeth" and "snarling," and would have torn him apart had he not scared it off with noise.[29] A women in the same area said "a dozen big dogs" appeared in her backyard one night, killed several of her chickens and attacked her German Shepherd Dog, who died a few days later of rabies.[30]

In June 1977, readers of the *Asbury Park Press*, in Asbury Park, New Jersey, learned about Tom Brown, a formidable "dog hunter" who had by his own account "killed close to 1,000 wild dogs since he was 10."[31] The reporter rode along with Brown and his hunting party as they pursued the final eight dogs of a 16-to-18–dog pack that had been attacking livestock. The reporter, who noted that Brown had a necklace fashioned from the vertebrae of a wild dog hanging from his Jeep's rearview mirror, "as a reminder of how dangerous his prey can be," told a suspenseful tale of man-versus-dog pack:

> They could hear the Alpha dog deep in the woods barking and howling. Two men watched the cliff for the inevitable return of the pack.... For the next hour, Alpha continued to bark and howl. Each bark seemed to come a little closer to the edge of the cliff.... Then, from the far left face of the cliff, Alpha appeared, drifting ghost-like onto the flat ground.[32]

"Alpha" was eventually joined by "Beta," the leader's "second in command." After a volley of shotgun fire, Beta was hit and Alpha escaped. Hours later, Alpha and two more dogs from the pack were killed after they returned to the area where the hunters were lying in wait.

While the New Jersey journalist's imaginative account of Tom Brown's encounter with a dangerous pack of dogs would not have been out of place in an animal horror movie script, its appearance in a newspaper, like the other press accounts of scary, roaming dog packs that appeared in 1977, gave the central premise of *The Pack* a foothold in the real world. Social anxieties are often projected onto fiction's animal monsters and in the 1970s, press attention on dog bites, and roaming packs of wild canines, fed the public's fear. As an animal horror movie seeking to attract viewers and make money, *The Pack* certainly took advantage of the media-fueled perception that American dogs were turning on people, but its message was clearly pro-dog/anti–bad owner. One film of the early 1980s would controversially add a racial element to this same theme.

White Dog

THAT AIN'T NO ATTACK DOG YOU GOT. THAT'S A WHITE DOG!

When a cantankerous old man named Carruthers (Burl Ives) tells a young, aspiring actress called Julie Sawyer (Kristy McNichol) just what kind of German Shepherd Dog she has brought to his animal training center in California, she thinks he is stupidly pointing out the obvious. The dog she rescued one dark night after accidentally hitting him with her car is the color white. Carruthers, who had just watched Julie's dog attack a black worker at his facility, sets her straight: "I don't mean his color! He's taught to attack and kill black people!"

Director Sam Fuller's metaphor for racism, *White Dog* was completed in 1982 but shelved for a decade before receiving limited screenings in the United States. Paramount gave into pressure from the National Association for the Advancement of Colored People (NAACP) and the Black Anti-Defamation Coalition, which publicly expressed concern that the film might promote racist activity. In a broader context, the production was caught up in a campaign to increase the number of Hollywood films that appealed to black audiences and were made by African Americans.[33] Robert Price, the executive director of the Black Anti-Defamation Coalition, wrote a letter to the editor of the *Los Angeles Times* in 1982 pointing out the systematic disadvantages that black writers and producers faced before specifically naming the film as compounding the problem: "Meanwhile blacks must suffer such indignities as Paramount's upcoming *White Dog*."[34]

Fuller countered with his own letter to the editor a month later, agreeing with Price that black writers were being denied a fair chance in Hollywood but objecting to his use of the word "indignities" when referring to the film. "One does not have to be black to write the truth about blacks," Fuller wrote. "When he sees *White Dog* he will understand."[35]

Price and most of America would not see *White Dog*, but Paramount was initially behind the production and addressed the concerns of racist content by bringing in two African American consultants midway through the shoot. While one of the consultants did not feel that the movie was racist, the other worried that if black audiences objected to the subject matter, distribution would suffer.[36] The hint at a possible NAACP boycott and Paramount's potential response were made more explicit in an April 1982, *Los Angeles Times* article, which reported that the film was on the NAACP's "white list" of targeted projects that African Americans should consider boycotting.

As for Paramount Pictures, the article noted that the studio was having "second thoughts" and executives were very reluctant to discuss a release plan or even the film itself.[37] By the fall of 1982, Paramount had agreed to preview screenings in Seattle, Denver and a test run in Detroit. Fuller claimed that the Seattle test audience gave the film an "80% good" rating but a Paramount executive disagreed with Fuller's assessment and said that some members of the audience responded negatively to the subject matter.[38] With no clear answer on the film's earnings potential and no upside to further angering the NAACP, Paramount did not release the film in theaters. In 1983, the studio re-edited it for a direct-to-cable sale.

The following year, NBC announced plans to buy the rights to air the film during February sweeps but the earlier campaign against the movie had lost none of its momentum. The executive director of the Beverly Hills–Hollywood branch of the NAACP called the network's decision "unfortunate"[39] and NBC cancelled the broadcast less than two days later, citing concerns over viewer and advertiser backlash. The film premiered in France and England to positive reviews but was not shown in American theaters until it premiered in New York as part of a 1991 retrospective of Fuller's films. In 2008, it debuted on DVD through the Criterion Collection.

White Dog is not, as the studio reportedly hoped it would be early on, "*Jaws* with dogs." It is an allegory on the destructive power of socially indoctrinated racism and true to Fuller's signature style, not subtle in its criticism. Its passionate, in-your-face attack on racially based hate leaves little room for ambiguity. Fuller's approach lacks nuance and for this reason, *White Dog* often seems lurid and sometimes cartoonish, particularly with dialogue like: "Your dog is a four-legged time bomb!"

The film's lesson that racism needs to be unlearned is almost simplistically straightforward: A dog is taught to attack black people and then retrained not to attack them. Man is clearly the enemy here. The white dog, as a trained monster, rather than a natural one, is a victim, but it is also a figure that disrupts how we think about the bonds between people and dogs. In the story of the white dog, loyalty and affection between dog and owner has been perversely twisted to serve dark purposes.

Director Sam Fuller with the star of *White Dog*, named not for his color but rather his racist training. *White Dog* would be Fuller's last American movie. 1982. Paramount Pictures. The Criterion Collection. moviestillsdb.com

Fuller's film is based on the 1970 semiautobiographical novel by Romain Gary, part of which was excerpted for a *Life* magazine cover story. In Gary's book, he and his wife, actress and civil rights activist Jean Seberg, take in a stray German Shepherd Dog they name Batka. Gary quickly discovers that the dog has been taught to attack anyone with black skin and he brings Batka to an animal trainer to be deprogrammed. The trainer turns out to be a Black Muslim, who retrains Batka to attack white people. At the novel's climax, Batka attacks Gary himself.

While the story uses Gary's relationship with Batka to express a critical viewpoint of liberal Hollywood's support of radicalism, the black power movement and Seberg's involvement with the Black Panthers, it was intriguing enough as an animal horror narrative to catch Hollywood's attention. In 1975, film producer Nick Vanoff brought the project to Robert Evans at Paramount. Screenwriter Curtis Hanson was hired to write the screenplay and Roman Polanski was set to direct. When Polanski fled the country to avoid statutory rape charges, the project floated around Hollywood for the next six years with numerous writers, directors and producers involved but it wasn't until the threat of a DGA and WGA strike in 1981 that the film got a green light. Faced with too few films to get through the pending work stoppages, Paramount revived *White Dog* with the support of then–studio president Michael Eisner.[40] Curtis Hanson, who was friends with Fuller, recommended the director for the project, suggesting he could complete the film quickly.

Fuller later recalled in an interview that producer Jon Davison "said he would not make the picture unless I wrote and directed it."[41] Hanson and Fuller worked on the script together, making one major revision. In Gary's book, an angry black Muslim animal trainer directs the dog's aggression toward white people. In the script, Fuller's black animal trainer, Keys (Paul Winfield), is not vengeful but rather a noble anthropologist who believes that racism can be unlearned, and the dog can be cured.

Fuller makes the white dog, which is never given a name in the film (at one point, Julie refers to him as "Mr. Hyde"), more than an animal antagonist. The dog is given human-like status through typical animal horror tropes. Close-ups of white dog's eyes, for example, are a sign of consciousness (rather than consciousness itself) that suggest the dog is a human-like subject. Fuller gives the dog equal screen time, along with point of view shots and at times, places the camera at the animal's level so that the audience is able to move along with him at his height. He also guides the viewer to have positive feelings toward the dog. In scenes with Julie, white dog is depicted as loving and affectionate. She playfully teaches him how to swallow a pill. Early in the film, he saves her from a rapist who breaks into her home at night. Later, she bathes him when he finds his way home after getting lost chasing a rabbit.

The bath scene is important to white dog's framing, as it is meant to elicit mixed emotions from the viewer. Julie does not know that the dog needs a bath because his fur is stained with the blood of an innocent man he attacked and killed, but the audience does. How should viewers feel watching a sweet, bonding moment between a dog and his owner when they know what she's washing away? It's this oscillation between positive and negative feelings for white dog that invites viewers' sympathy. At the same time, the scene blurs the line between the evil human who created him and the canine monster he has become.

Julie experiences white dog's dark side for herself when she brings him to a film set and he attacks a fellow actor in front of her, causing the woman to be hospitalized. Despite being shocked and horrified, she fights for him during a heated argument with her boyfriend Roland (Jameson Parker), who urges her to have the dog put down:

> **ROLAND:** That dog is sick!
> **JULIE:** Then he should be cured.
> **ROLAND:** The people that made him sick, made him permanently sick.
> **JULIE:** Then they should be put to sleep! Not the dog!

The exchange summarizes one of the film's central themes. Who exactly is the monster here? Fuller answers the question in the form of animal trainer Keys, who has agreed to help the dog and tells Julie that the real monster is the "two-legged racist" who turned her pet into a killer.

Keys' retraining experiment becomes problematic after white dog escapes the animal training center and targets a man walking down the street of a nearby town. The man runs into a church to escape but the dog catches him and sinks his teeth into the man's legs. When he falls and starts to crawl between the pews and a wall, the camera does not follow the action. Instead of seeing the man's savage death, Fuller makes the viewer listen to it and then the camera pans up to a stained-glass window of Saint Francis of Assisi looking on with a dog at his feet. Consistent with Fuller's style, it's an in-your-face visual that is as striking as it is outlandish.

The film uses the church death to contemplate and then validate the ethics of Keys' experiment. Julie tells Keys he should kill white dog to prevent more deaths. Keys argues that the experiment serves a larger social purpose "because it's the only way to stop sick people from breeding sick dogs." While Keys' obsessive persistence borders on unhinged—he swears to Julie that if he fails to cure this dog, he'll find another and another until he does—it works to support the film's message. In Fuller's version of animal horror cinema, the monstrous dog is not the most horrific part of the story. White dog merely represents the outcome of a much greater threat—racial hatred.

The scene continues with Keys reasoning that it would be inhumane to stop pursuing the cure while the dog is "on a razor's edge of a mental breakdown." The line reflects one of Fuller's aims, which was to take the audience inside the dog's head as much as possible. He told *Variety*: "You're going to see a dog slowly go insane and then come back to sanity in front of you."[42] This anthropocentric perspective humanizes the dog as a somewhat relatable adversary. He is suffering from a human affliction, with a consciousness similar to the viewers' or at least, able to be understood as similar. A sick animal that needs to be cured, white dog is framed as a protagonist, which makes his role as an adversary more complicated than a predator seeking prey.

While most of the film is about humanizing the monstrous white dog, the second to last scene gives the true monster a human face. White dog's elderly, seemingly polite owner appears on Julie's doorstep with his two granddaughters. He saw one of Julie's lost dog fliers and has come to reclaim his pet. She tricks him into admitting that he created a "white dog" and he adds with pride that the dog was "the best of the bunch." She screams and swears at him, disgusted, then directs her comments to his grandchildren, "He turned that dog into a monster, a killer. Don't you let him turn you into monsters either. Don't listen to a damn word he says about anything!" In Julie's warning, Fuller identifies characteristics of racism that are often overlooked, namely its casual but deliberate passing on of attitudes to children.

In the final scene of the film, Keys faces white dog without protective padding but with a handgun ready in case the dog fails his final test. The tension is depicted through a long shot of the face-off, cut with close-ups of man and dog, as each anticipates the other's move. Carruthers and Julie watch a few steps away. The white dog does not attack Keys, but his moment of triumph is crushed as the dog turns toward Carruthers. Snarling and growling, he charges him as Keys fires the gun, finally ending white dog's life.

Since Keys did not retrain the dog to attack white skin, the scene is open to interpretation. The dog may have finally had the mental breakdown Keys warned about or maybe Carruthers reminded the dog of his cruel owner and he symbolically turned against the master who created him. Fuller offered his take on the scene in a piece he wrote for the journal *Framework* in 1982, shortly after the film was completed. Structured as an "interview" with the white dog, Fuller commented, "That boomerang of the brain was to show the danger of tampering with a sick and tortured brain."[43] The cure for racism was not without its hazards.

Film critic James Hoberman called *White Dog* "one of the most unflinching statements on American racism ever to come out of

Hollywood, something like *Rin Tin Tin Joins the Klan*."[44] Because of Paramount's suppression of the film, this statement would be made years later to a niche audience of Fuller fans rather than the wide viewership Fuller had intended. The studio's decision was an emotional blow to Fuller, who would move to France as a result. He would later write in his memoirs:

> Shelve the film without letting anyone see it? I was dumbfounded. It's difficult to express the hurt of having a finished film locked away in a vault, never to be screened for an audience. It's like someone putting your newborn baby in a goddamned maximum-security prison forever…. Moving to France for a while would alleviate some of the pain and doubt that I had to live with because of *White Dog*.

Recognition for *White Dog* may have been years too late for Fuller but the film's exploration of man's inhumanity to man through the historical figure of the attack dog is notable because it exposes the horrors of racism and the dangers of its nonchalant indoctrination. Because the dog's transition into a beastly state is not natural but due to man's interference, Fuller's metaphor on socially indoctrinated racism is also a commentary on the collapse of the humane into the barbaric. As with all the films in this section, it is a fictional part of the bad dog's media story, but one that expresses a very real cultural anxiety where man, rather than beast, is the monster.

Dog TV

If this show was just about me and the dog, it would be a piece of cake!
                    —Cesar Millan, *Dog Whisperer*

Reality television shows, like celebrity dog trainer Cesar Millan's *Dog Whisperer*, where a bad dog's problem behavior is solved, are useful for thinking about how dogs fit into the category of pet and the ways in which this defines the human-animal domestic relationship. To live in a domestic space with a human-animal, non-human animals must fulfill certain requirements. Particular behaviors are encouraged, and others are punished so the word pet itself has a meaning that suggests dominance and firmly positions a domestic animal as property.

On television, the term pet is used most often (rather than companion animals, for example), which has implications for how we understand the dogs we see on shows like *Dog Whisperer*. Brett Mills argues that "the conventional strategies that define television's representation of animals in the home is one precisely structured around the idea of animals as property."[45] This notion of owning animals has a long history tied to humans' shifting understanding of the natural world and their ability to control it. Mills points to James Serpell's work on the development of pet-keeping in Western cultures, where he suggests that domestic animals were connected to class divisions. Serpell notes that religious and secular authorities encouraged the working class to think of domestic animals as objects, while the dogs of wealthy aristocrats, often included in their portraits, were an expression of their owners' status.[46] Also within these class structures of ownership is a demonstrated ability to train and control domestic animals.[47]

The historical idea of pet equaling property has defined the essence of pet-keeping in Western societies and subsequently informed the televisual representations of domestic animals. While the term companion animal seeks to encourage a more complex understanding of the social and personal value of domestic animals, television shows like *Dog Whisperer* are structured to reaffirm the meaning of pet. In this show, and *Cesar 911*, ownership is the dominant focus and the message is clear. A dog's bad behavior is the result of a human allowing an animal to become too much of a companion. The solution is to restore the person's dominance, which returns the dog's status to pet.

The Rise of El Perrero

As he tells it, Cesar Millan's road to becoming a globally recognized dog trainer began with his grandfather, who he credits with teaching him how to uniquely handle dogs. In charge of herding cattle for the wealthy landowners of their Mexican village, Millan's grandfather would always have a pack of dogs with him and Cesar would walk along, learning how to interact with the pack. The habit and his developing skill soon earned him the nickname "El Perrero" or "the dog boy." By the age of 13, Cesar had a plan that he says was inspired by watching episodes of *Lassie* and *Rin Tin Tin*. He would go to the United States and learn to be a dog trainer.

Eight years later, at the age of 20, Cesar set the plan in motion with help from his father, who gave him his life savings of $100. He used the money to pay a smuggler to get him across the border, and once in the United States he slept on a piece of cardboard under a San Diego freeway doing odd jobs for small amounts of cash. After he walked into a dog grooming salon looking for work, he figured out that the two women who owned the shop were having trouble grooming an aggressive cocker spaniel. He handled the dog with ease, was hired and given the key to the salon once the owners learned that he was homeless. A few weeks later, he had saved enough money for a bus ticket to Los Angeles, where he found work with a dog trainer in Burbank. He was fired, he says, after clients began asking for him to work with their dogs instead of his boss. He started a dog walking business, became known around town as "the Mexican guy who could walk 30 dogs with no trouble," and caught the attention of athletes and celebrities, who started hiring him.[48]

As his business grew, he opened his first Dog Psychology Center in a warehouse in South Central Los Angeles. (It would eventually become a 43-acre ranch based in Santa Clarita Valley.) The press started to pay attention and a *Los Angeles Times* journalist spent three days with him for a profile piece that was published in 2002. The article included several testimonials from satisfied clients. One, whose destructive and mistrustful dog Elvis was completely transformed, said she considered him the Helen Keller of the dog world. "Cesar was able to break through to the Elvis that I knew was inside." Another client, whose dog was aggressive toward strangers and other dogs, commented that Cesar "has a gift" and attributed an almost otherworldly skill to the soon-to-become-famous trainer: "He communicates across species without saying a word."[49]

As Cesar's origin story (which has been recounted to numerous media outlets across the United States and beyond) tells it, the *Los Angeles Times* article sparked the interest of TV producers. *Dog Whisperer with Cesar Millan* (hereafter referred to as *Dog Whisperer*) premiered in September 2004 on the National Geographic Channel. By the time the show ended in 2012, it aired in more than 80 countries. A documentary, *Cesar Millan: The Real Story*, featuring Cesar's rise from illegal immigrant to celebrity dog trainer, was produced in 2012. *Cesar Millan's Leader of the Pack* (2013) brought his methods to unruly dogs across Europe, followed by *Cesar 911* on Nat Geo Wild, which returned the trainer to the US and ran for three seasons, from 2014 to 2016. Also on Nat Geo Wild in 2014 was *Cesar Millan: Love My Pit Bull*, a special that focused on "bully breeds." In 2017, Cesar hit the road with his son and co-host Andre in *Cesar Millan's Dog Nation*.

The Making of the Dog Whisperer

Each of Millan's television series focuses on a signature method that he uses to get clients' unruly dogs under control. While the dogs learn their lessons through Cesar's application of "calm, assertive energy," which often includes physical touch and a stern "tsst" sound, the real students are the humans who need to practice his method or face unwanted canine behavior. He told a *Chicago Tribune* reporter in 2017:

> The formula is: Exercise, discipline, affection. Or Body, mind, heart. But my clients do: Affection, affection, affection. And by doing that, they're focusing on their needs only, and unconsciously they enter into a very selfish fulfillment in that relationship and only one side gets the benefit. So man's best friend becomes a very unstable friend....[50]

In the world of Cesar Millan, the road to recovery for man's unstable best friend begins with restoring a power dynamic and ends with plenty of pop psychology.

On Millan's shows, the solution to every case of problem dog behavior is to first remind the dog that Cesar is the alpha in the room and then to teach the client how to take Cesar's place and become the dominant force in the human-animal relationship. By admonishing his clients' focus on affection or their choice to treat their dog as a creature with needs, desires and agency rather than an owned object to be commanded, Cesar's approach rejects any suggestion of a dog's companion status. Dogs receive little praise and the primary reward for achieving the desired state of calm submission is not being subjected to Millan's submission techniques.

The technique is not without its critics. In a 2006 *New York Times* op-ed piece, Mark Derr called Millan "a charming, one-man wrecking ball directed at 40 years of progress in understanding and shaping dog behavior."[51] Derr, who wrote the book, *A Dog's History of America: How Our Best Friend Explored, Conquered and Settled a Continent*, denounced Millan's method for ignoring the success of nonpunitive reward-based training programs "which have led to seeing each dog as an individual, to understand what motivates it, what frightens it and what its talents and limitations are." Derr's support for long-term training methods based on a companion-centered framework of human/dog relations is deeply at odds with Millan's self-taught, quick fix, dominance approach.

Yet, Millan's immense popularity, as demonstrated by the ratings for his numerous television programs, his multiple best-selling books, his packed live stage shows, his business ventures (from supplements, to training products, to pet insurance, to entering the CBD pet market), and his more than nine million Facebook followers, not to mention the glowing testimonials from happy clients, suggest that his formula is impactful. In the case of Millan's client, Sandy, and her French bulldog–Boston terrier mix, Simon, the effusive praise the trainer is used to receiving from happy owners—Sandy said Cesar gave Simon "a brand new life" and "made all the difference"[52]—was even more impactful than usual because it came as a response to an animal cruelty investigation launched by Los Angeles County Animal Control.

Sandy sought Millan's help because Simon could not get along with her potbellied pigs. When footage from her 2016 episode of *Cesar 911* showed Simon nipping the ear of a large farm pig, causing it to bleed, multiple viewer complaints led to the investigation. Sandy vigorously defended Millan and noted that within an hour of the biting incident, the pig and Simon were walking peacefully together, a happy outcome that was depicted later in the episode.

Millan's response to the investigation was that he does not use animals as bait, and it was necessary to put Simon in a situation with a pig in order to correct his behavior. He then stressed his broader message, repeating his belief about the central role that humans play in a dog's misbehavior, "My main goal is to educate human kind so we don't end up euthanizing dogs with the mistakes we make."[53] No charges were filed in the investigation but the press coverage put Millan and his approach in the spotlight again, a decade after Derr's critical editorial.

Training people. Rehabilitating dogs.

The opening voiceover to Cesar Millan's flagship television show, *Dog Whisperer*, makes an important distinction that disrupts a typical understanding of the human-dog relationship. After the narrator says, "When good dogs go bad, there's one man who's their best friend—Cesar Millan." Millan adds, "I rehabilitate dogs. I train people." The concept of training or teaching a particular type of behavior is typically applied to dogs so when Millan attaches it to people and rejects dog training in favor of dog "rehab," he makes dogs offenders who need to be restored to health by people who need to be taught how to make that happen.

Each episode follows a pattern. Footage shows dogs' bad behavior, the pets' owners comment on the situation to camera then Cesar arrives to diagnose the problem. As the expert, he demonstrates his mastery over the dogs, typically stopping the disruptive behavior within minutes. The bulk of the episode focuses on Cesar training people to act differently with their dogs in order to achieve his results. From a narrative point of view, dogs are relatively and surprisingly scarce because the show is fundamentally about training people.[54] If these people learn their lessons, which are centered on how they control their "energy" and emotions, their dogs' rehabilitation will follow.

Millan's focus on pet owners' emotions is a running theme on *Dog Whisperer*, and in many interactions, Cesar plays the role of therapist. On an episode called "Family Feud," he speaks to Christine about her Chihua-hua, Chico, which has been biting her. Chico has also been attacking her mother Pauline's Chihuahua, Peanut. Christine had originally adopted Pea-nut but when he formed a bond with Pauline rather than her, she got Chico, so she would have a dog that "liked" her. Millan asks Christine to define their relationship: "So, Chico. So he represents what to you?" She replies hesitantly, "Um, he's my pet?" "Is he?" Cesar counters before asking her if she humanizes the dog. Christine thinks for a minute and then agrees with Millan's observation. "Well, I guess I treat him like a human too much." Cesar then stresses the importance of recognizing the difference. "You're looking for a permanent solution, so it has to be a permanent belief. So if you believe, saying 'He's a pet,' but in reality treat him like this—" Christine interrupts, slightly defeated, "I spoil him."

At this point Millan turns to Pauline to ask how she treats Peanut. She directs her response to Christine, "I don't know if I treat him like a human. How do I treat him?" Much to Pauline's embarrassment and surprise, Christine says that her mother definitely spoils Peanut. With nervous laughter, Pauline eventually admits that she does not think of Peanut as a dog but like a "little person, a person with a tail." Footage cuts to Christine and Pauline picking up their dogs and showering them with affection. As the interview continues, Chico, who is now at Christine's arm while she sits on a couch, starts to lick her. Millan stops and asks if that behavior is ok. "It's ok!" Pauline immediately says and calls Chico to her but then Cesar challenges her, "That's ok? The licking?" Pauline looks alarmed. "Oh! Isn't it? Oh. I don't know!" Cesar tells her the behavior is ok if it is invited. Pauline admits that she usually lets Peanut lick her and now she's starting to "look like a real pushover."

Pauline's self-conscious assessment leads to the segment's most therapeutic moment as Cesar turns to Christine and asks her if Pauline was a pushover when Christine was a child. After she says yes, Pauline explains her parenting philosophy, adding that she is a psychology professor. "I was kind of like live and let live and no restraints. Like each person will find their own boundaries." "On their own?" Millan asks. "Yeah," Pauline responds. Cesar simply says, "Wow."

At this point, Pauline, feeling a need to defend and explain herself to a mildly disapproving dog behavior expert, lays out her professional experience as a professor who teaches graduate students to become school psychologists. "But see, that's my counseling approach. It's very much, you know, let people find what their limits are. You know. (And here she turns toward Christine who has Chico in her lap.) Let dogs find what their limits are. I have a thing against—about, being the disciplinarian, I guess. I don't like that role." She tells Millan that to her, discipline means being "aggressive and stern," something she is capable of in her professional life but in her personal life, she "let's things go the way they go." "Wow," he says again before giving a lesson in "dog psychology," in which he explains that dogs are not rational and cannot seek help. Then he clearly identifies the problem for the women and the viewer, "This is the challenge, right here. How can I help the human to understand that a simple concept is not harmful, that it's actually helpful?"

Millan observes the two dogs' behavior and when Chico signals that he is going to attack Peanut, he effortlessly prevents the confrontation, and uses it as a teaching moment for Christine. When it's her turn to calm the situation, Chico launches across her lap, lunging for Peanut, and bites her in the process. The bite is startling and unexpected, and Christine is visibly shaken. Millan jumps in, scoops Chico up, and pins the dog on its side on the floor.

The action then cuts to Cesar in a first-person interview explaining that the bite was regrettable but "it needed to happen so we could see a different Christine." Back in the living room scene, Christine's anger pushes her to reclaim her position at the top of the canine-human power dynamic, "He thinks he can bite me and get away with it." Sensing that his student is starting to absorb the lesson, Cesar agrees, "What he did was the ultimate disrespect...."

Moments later, it's Christine's turn to try the exercise again. This time, she successfully prevents Chico from attacking her mother's dog. Millan tells her the difference is that now, she is demonstrating strong leadership. With Christine's training successful, she gives her end of episode testimonial, "For Cesar to be here and tell me, 'Ok, now you have this energy, use it this way.' It was great. It worked amazingly." Pauline adds her evaluation, noting the universality of Millan's approach. "I realized that with the strategies I've seen on TV, that it wasn't specific to that dog and that it was about the presence of the individual.... The family made Chico the way he is."

With the training of the humans complete, Cesar ends the episode with a question, "Who's happier? The dog who's treated as human, which is not a human. Or the dog who's been treated as dog, which is a dog?" The answer is that neither version of this dog is more content because the episode's happy resolution is for the humans. Millan's punitive approach to Chico's bad behavior teaches Christine to find her inner leader. Accepting blame for her part, Pauline is transformed into a true believer.

Jaime was already a true believer. She was also a dedicated dog owner. Learning that her adopted Border Collie/Boxer/Greyhound mix, Chloe, was prone to nipping, she immediately enrolled in dog obedience class. The pair excelled and Chloe was a star, "trained to do everything" Jaime asked of her. It all came crashing down within six months of the adoption when Chloe and another dog got into a vicious fight. After that, Chloe was highly reactive to every dog she encountered and when Jaime's hold on the leash would prevent her from reaching her targets, she would often take her frustration out on Jaime. The physical toll was steep. Jaime had scars on her hands and all over her legs. The marks prompted her mother to ask if someone was beating her.

Determined to help Chloe, Jaime took her to two sets of group obedience classes, then hired a private trainer. When all that failed, she went to a trainer to evaluate Chloe's aggressiveness. The trainer said the dog had no chance. Jaime then took Chloe to an animal behaviorist who told her that the dog's only hope was to be constantly medicated. Blaming "bad genes," both experts mentioned euthanasia and a broken-hearted Jaime scheduled the procedure.

With one week left before Chloe was to be put down, Jaime made a final effort to save her dog. She searched the Internet and found out that *Dog Whisperer* was holding auditions in Los Angeles. Her friends took up a collection for the plane ticket. Jaime and Chloe flew from Boston and Jaime arrived at the audition hours before the doors opened to make sure she was the first in line.

Jaime and Chloe's story is part of the October 14, 2010, episode, "Gotti's Honor." In an atypical move for the show, the producer who first heard Jaime's case at the Los Angeles' audition appears on the episode and talks about how Jaime's earnestness and willingness to do anything to save her dog was the deciding factor on her being accepted for the show. The commentary, along with the details about Jaime's work with multiple expert trainers, establishes Jaime as a responsible animal steward. The fact that all of these efforts failed sets up Cesar as Jaime and Chloe's miracle worker and following the show's usual narrative pattern, Millan performs the miracle on the human rather than the dog. During filming, the cameraman asks Cesar if Chloe is a hard case. "Strong," he says matter-of-factly. "Hard case is the human. Strong is the dog."

Chloe's strong state of mind, of course, is no match for Millan and within a few minutes, he has her running and playing with his pack at his training center as Julie watches in amazement. When Chloe shows signs of not listening to him, he talks about matching her stubbornness with patience and the effort pays off. Jaime's attempt to repeat Cesar's success leads to Chloe reverting to bad behavior and he steps in and stops it before it escalates. He tells Jaime that her anxious response to Chloe not listening to her caused the problem and Jaime fully accepts the blame:

> It's me. It's not her. It's me.... He's working with me. He's not working with Chloe. It's actually really how it is. Like you see it on the show. Like he trains people, but he really does. It's kind of intimidating to be like, "Oh. It's really me that has the problem...." I have a lot more work than she does cut out for me.

Moments later, Jaime has mastered the lesson and Chloe plays happily with the other dogs. She leaves the training center with no doubt that she will succeed without Cesar because he has given her all the tools she needs to change herself.

In the case of Adrianna and her exuberant, large-breed dog Madison, the problem is diagnosed before Cesar arrives. During her one on one interview on the "Gotti's Honor" episode, she describes Madison's habit of jumping on people, and adds, "I need to be the calm, assertive one and really, I think I've turned into the calm, submissive one." Already familiar with the language of Millan's approach, she is primed for his brand of self-transformation and it's not too long before she begins to explore her personal background for reasons why her dog is not listening to her.

When Millan begins the lesson by telling her a dog displays happiness by respecting human's personal space, Adrianna reflects on how, as a twin, she has never embraced her self-identity and is not "very confident in her space." He then asks Adrianna to think about an accomplishment that makes her proud and when she begins to talk about how she felt after sky diving, he connects it to the familiar notion of being calm and assertive. The scene cuts to Adrianna talking directly to camera and as she says the following commentary, the scene cuts back to Cesar talking to her, but all the viewer hears is her words:

> Just having him, sort of, almost, reach into my soul and bring out the awareness and the energy and the strength and the experience, it was powerful. He saw that in me and it really helped make the point that I've got it in me.

The sequence frames Millan as a caring counselor who has enabled an emotional and spiritual breakthrough without him saying anything more than the phrase "calm and assertive."

Millan eventually shows Adrianna how to express her calm, assertive energy so that Madison understands boundaries and limitations. Quick to show submissiveness, Madison exhibits little to no resistance and quickly responds to Adrianna's gentle commands. The dog's behavioral change is barely the point in this segment, as Adrianna's ending testimonial suggests, "I learned that I need to take more charge and more confidence in myself and the way I approach my dog and the way I approach life generally." Millan agrees, "You can transform your life as long as you really want to."

Not every problem dog Millan rehabilitates is a scary dog, as Madison, the bumbling gentle giant demonstrates, but most are framed that way with "before" footage featuring attacks and fights and animals physically overpowering their helpless owners. Close-ups of bite marks and snarling teeth are not uncommon. The images help lay the foundation for Cesar's expertise and set the stage for his always successful intervention, which is based on a lesson that never changes: Behind every bad dog is a bad owner. The lesson also comes with an instruction.

Every episode of *Dog Whisperer* warns, "Do not attempt the techniques you are about to see without consulting a professional." Of course, the success of Cesar's brand is based on the idea that he is the professional the viewer is virtually consulting, as they watch the show (or read his books or attend his road shows) and then try to apply his techniques to their particular bad dog situation. At times, a case will remind viewers of Millan's elevated status among dog trainers, as happens in the episode featuring Chloe, where the viewer learns that the dog's owner, Jaime, had consulted multiple experts before Cesar stepped in.[55] Failure on Millan's shows rarely happens, and if it does, it is framed as a temporary setback on the clients' part, rather than a weakness in his method.

While the canine behavioral changes on *Dog Whisperer* are visually effective as a form of before and after makeover television—undisciplined dogs and their exasperated owners are peacefully co-existing by the end— the narrative of the dogs' physical change is inseparable from the humans' self-reflection. Cesar makes dog owners personally responsible for their pets' bad behaviors and then leads them through a treatment program that requires them to engage in self-analysis and initiate inner change with his expert advice and coaching. Millan may say he is "just a guy who knows dogs,"[56] but *Dog Whisperer's* narrative structure, training humans to reha- bilitate their dogs, makes the show about people. As Brett Mills argues, the program is "about the 'whisperer' and the humans he 'whispers' to. The pets are simply resources that humans can draw on in order to evidence the development of their own self worth."[57]

Millan gives viewers a specific way to understand dogs that has very little to do with dogs as subjects. Rather, dogs are framed as objects that allow pet owners to demonstrate successful self-actualization. When he trains people to recognize that their emotional states affect their dogs' behavior, he puts dogs' lives at the mercy of those emotional states.[58] This is problematic to a more complete understanding of the canine-human rela- tionship and it advances the idea that dogs will behave in unacceptable or dangerous ways, if not properly controlled by a human. But achieving this means reshaping the self. It's a theme that runs through the storylines of all his behavior programs.

On an episode of *Cesar 911*, which is a slight variation of *Dog Whis- perer* where concerned friends and family, rather than pet owners them- selves, contact Cesar for help, he tells viewers, "How the people react, is for me, the most important part."[59] The episode features the owners of Junior, an aggressive Great Dane who has bitten several people, and Cesar leaves little doubt as to who is to blame: "Junior is aggressive because the owners are showing weakness and they lack in confidence." A dog's dangerousness always begins and ends with a person and the road to pack leader is marked by therapeutic signposts that stress the language of personal growth and responsibility.

The idea that bad owners create bad dogs is not unique to Millan. It's a theme that runs throughout the media story of the dangerous dog but his popularity, and the general appeal of reality television programs that encourage success through self-examination, have created a public space for willing pet owners to dig deep, and following Millan's guidance, rec-ognize their capacity for emotional strength. Only then are they ready to use this new-found confidence to control their dog. On his shows, every human gets a happy ending and central to their satisfaction is the realiza-tion that they are capable of personal change.

Millan Meets the "Most Aggressive Breeds"

Millan's philosophy rejects categorizing specific dog breeds as natural-born killers because it normalizes the idea that all domestic dogs, even those that belong to breeds with a bad public image, are potentially problematic until they learn to be submissive to emotionally strong humans. He tackles the subject directly in a special episode of *Dog Whisperer* called "Most Aggressive Breeds."

Described by the narrator as "an eye-opening look at the breeds Americans think of as our most dangerous canines," the March 4, 2010, episode begins with a menacing soundtrack that accompanies news foot-age of dog bite victims and dog attacks. Horrific newspaper headlines float across the screen: "Dog attacks toddler." "Doberman is sought after attack-ing two-year old." A desperate woman is heard pleading with a 911 opera-tor: "Please help. Pit bulls are attacking me!" A broadcast news clip shows a woman telling a reporter that the dogs that attacked her ripped every-thing out of her hands that she was trying to use to defend herself before cutting to her gruesome injuries. The action then shifts to an official stand-ing behind a podium addressing journalists at a press briefing, where he says, "These are land sharks." In the opening montage of alarming video and audio, dogs play the starring role of monstrous beasts.

The format of the episode is structured around an online poll in which viewers of *Dog Whisperer* were asked to name the most dangerous dog breed. The top three finalists are revealed one by one, starting with Rottweiler at the third spot. After a short history of the breed, the narra-tor mentions the breed's role in the *Omen* films and points out that more than 30 people died during the 1990s as a result of Rottweiler attacks. Cesar appears and pleasantly counters the alarming statistic: "A properly raised and socialized 'Rottie' can be the most loyal, loving companion ever. All it takes is patience, hard work and the right human."

To demonstrate, he presents the case of Apollo, a Rottweiler on death row at the Orange County Humane Society. Considered unadoptable after biting two people, he is scheduled to be euthanized the next day, so two caring shelter volunteers take him to a local pet store where *Dog Whis-perer* is holding open auditions. Bree, a sixteen-year-old volunteer who has developed a bond with Apollo but is unable to adopt him, tearfully asks the producer to help, telling her that he is a loving and playful dog. The other volunteer adds that Apollo is very aggressive toward some, but not all, men. Footage of Bree and Apollo calmly walking together suggest he can be gentle. Then he meets Cesar for the first time.

With his leash secure, Apollo greets Millan with bared teeth and an intimidating high-pitched bark. Millan avoids eye contact and takes several small steps toward Apollo until Apollo lunges at him. Millan jumps back then slowly takes a few steps forward. In a voiceover to the scene, he explains that fearful dogs typically want to run away from a person rather than bite them and that the dog's aggressive state will not last. "After the storm is calm, always." The screen flashes an elapsed time of three minutes. The storm has passed, and Millan addresses the camera directly while holding Apollo's leash, "Who knows how this was created but this was created by a human."

Apollo's rehabilitation takes place at Millan's dog psychology center, where he leashes him to a puppy who walks the Rottweiler around an area full of dogs and people, acting as a kind of gentle guide into this new world. A beaming Cesar watches them. The soundtrack swells and he says, "The magic is about to happen." Apollo, now on his own, is calm and content. The narrator lets the viewer know that the Rottweiler spends a few weeks at the center, and time at Millan's home, but the footage only shows a scene of the dog at Cesar's home, happily playing with his son Andre.

Without seeing the hard work of Apollo's actual rehabilitation, and only watching an idyllic shot of a boy and a dog playing together, the storyline is reduced to a simple before-and-after dog makeover. But this is a show about people more than dogs and without an owner, there is an anonymous human to blame (as Cesar notes in the beginning of the case) but no human to train, until Bree visits Apollo a few weeks into his rehab.

Sitting on the ground with Cesar, Bree pets Apollo while he is lying on his side. Cesar encourages Bree to change her touch to a more kneading motion and when she does, Apollo jumps up and gives a loud squeal/bark. Bree is startled and has tears in her eyes. Millan tells her that her emotional reaction is a "soft state" and "weak" and the remedy is to take a deep breath, calm down and only resume showing him affection after he goes back to his "old self." The dog reacted to a sensitive spot in a way that did not meet human demands and Bree's emotions failed to control the situation. She listens and nods, eager to correct her mistakes. Apollo's case ends with Millan surprising his son Andre with news that he is allowed to adopt the dog. Andre's reward for learning and applying his father's lessons is a dog he has bonded with but it's also a very personal confirmation that Cesar's method works.

German Shepherd Dogs get the number two spot on the viewer poll and are again introduced with a brief breed history, including stock footage and photos of the dogs' role in war. Cesar gives his assessment, "In the hands of a calm, decisive owner, a German Shepherd can be the most amazing companion ever, but the lack of leadership has led many of the German Shepherds we have come across into seriously aggressive behavior." A dog named Troy is the example case. Troy attacked his housemate Dottie, a Poodle/Maltese mix, and almost killed her. Troy's owners, Edie and Neal, describe his behavior around Dottie as a "state of frenzy that is uncontrollable." Cesar interacts with Troy and the couple's other two dogs and Edie recognizes Millan's strategy immediately, "You're showing him who's boss."

Later, Millan and Edie do an exercise where a glass door separates Troy and Dottie, and Millan explains that the viewer could try this at home, correcting their dog when needed. Edie and Neal have success with the door exercise but not on walks, so Millan takes Troy to an obedience school run by another trainer who focuses the dog's energy using games. The scene's purpose is to show Edie and Neal that Troy is smart and needs more mental stimulation, but it does not solve Troy's problems at home. Only Millan does that, and as the action returns to the couple's house, he stops a muzzled Troy attacking Dottie again. Undeterred, Millan stresses the upside, "When I see an attack, I see an opportunity to rehabilitate. I see an opportunity to help dogs to see each other in a different form, which is a more social way." Troy is on his side in the next scene, panting and submissive and Cesar tells Edie and Neal that "this is what happens" if Troy attacks Dottie. Edie understands, "So he's learning that this is unacceptable."

Troy's learning is through physical domination and Millan, uncharacteristically, does not stress the usual personal growth work that Edie and Neal need to do, but a comment from Edie implies that she and her husband have not quite achieved it. There is no footage of them practicing Cesar's techniques and Edie's announcement that Troy is still "a work in progress" suggests that they have not yet mastered Millan's lessons. She gives him a glowing testimonial all the same, "We're a living example that if you do what Cesar tells you to do and you keep working with the dogs, it works!"

The episode's breed winner for most aggressive dog is pit bull and the introductory segment focuses on the dogs' fighting history, attacks that made headlines and the bans that some communities have put in place. The action cuts to Millan, pictured with his pit bull Junior. "Anyone who knows me, knows I love pit bulls!" He adds that "when raised correctly," they make loving and loyal pets. He demonstrates with the separate cases of Buddy and Trinity, two highly aggressive dogs. Buddy, abandoned and abused, is taken in by Sherry and Lee. He attacks Millan several times and when it's Sherry's turn to control him, she talks about her lack of trust and what she needs to do: "I just have to get rid of my frustration with him." As Millan's brand has grown, his clients/fans often know the therapeutic strategies expected of them and express their weaknesses before he identifies them. The case is edited to get to the "after" makeover moment quickly and Buddy is another success story.

The second pit bull case features Trinity, who was abused before her current situation with caring owner Monica. A vicious fighter, Trinity has drawn blood from Monica's other dog, as well as Monica herself, who has broken up multiple fights between her two dogs. As Monica discusses her efforts to help Trinity, the camera pans over a table full of training devices she has used. Three weeks with a dog trainer was also unsuccessful. Cesar is her last hope. In his conversation with Monica, Millan says he has "a very deadly, silence feeling" from Trinity and immediately proposes that he take Trinity to his dog center for at least two months. He classifies her as an "intense case" that needs around-the-clock attention. She becomes part of Millan's TV family, accompanying him on several *Dog Whisperer* cases, and footage shows her spending time at his home.

Things are looking up for Trinity until Monica visits her at Millan's center. A few minutes into their off leash walk, Trinity gets into a vicious fight with another dog in the pack. It's a dramatic moment, with center staff and the show's crew members jumping in to pry Trinity's mouth off another dog's face. Millan points out that Monica's panicked reaction to the situation had a ripple effect but the only footage the viewer sees of Monica during the fight is her picking up a small dog that was near the action.

The next time she is on screen, she calmly says, "I wasn't not expecting that to happen. I mean I've seen the show before and it seems like a lot of times, everything will be great until the owners come." Monica's awareness of how the show's narrative unfolds suggests that she is already a student of Cesar's method and accepted her role in her dangerous dog's behavior before she was ever a client. Yet, Millan does not try to train Monica. After the fight, he makes her an offer. He will give her a lower energy dog from his pack and in exchange, he will keep Trinity.

As the scene cuts to the interior of an RV, where Monica is talking to Cesar about what to do, one of the pack dogs comes too close to Monica, Trinity attacks, and again has to be physically pried off the other dog. It's a surprising moment because the shot does not include Trinity until the fight erupts. Monica tearfully agrees that Cesar should keep Trinity but one month later decides that she will do whatever it takes to bring Trinity home. Millan praises her for confronting her fears.

The action shifts to Monica's home, where Cesar has brought Trinity. In the backyard, he tells Monica to walk and mentally "see the reaction" that she wants from Trinity as they stroll together around the yard. It is a calm, easy walk with one simple verbal correction from Monica at the end. In the next shot, Monica is walking Trinity and her other dog Sandy off leash in the countryside near her home. The narrator says the dogs "are best friends again." Millan adds, "To see a dog being rehabilitated is beautiful but to see humans to [sic] really stepping up to the plate, to see people practicing calm, assertive energy, to see people totally moving forward. It's a beautiful thing."

Monica may have moved forward, but the editing choices show very little of her journey. What makes the segment satisfying is the focus on the before and after of Trinity's behavioral change. The fight scenes are loud and savage and the shots of Trinity afterward, with blood around her mouth, frame her as a monster. Juxtaposed with later scenes of her acting friendly and calm, she appears completely transformed. Edited to focus on Millan's success with the pit bull, more than her owner's training, the case elevates his expertise. The scene with Monica and Trinity walking in the backyard as Millan serenely watches is further confirmation that in his presence, all is peaceful.

Millan's method relies on a pet owner performing the emotional work of changing their energy from weak to strong, but Monica's work is largely absent. In its place are recognizable themes—despair, hope, resignation, determination, success, which seem to make her journey to becoming a better dog owner less about Cesar's talk therapy and more about basic storytelling tropes. Yet, his abrupt offer of exchanging dogs clearly communicates that the problem lies with Monica, and she reluctantly accepts that her "energy" means that Trinity is probably "too much dog" for her to handle. When Millan celebrates Monica's change of heart, calling her "brave" and describing her as "somebody who really wants to live life to the fullest," he ties Monica's decision about her dog to a positive life choice.

The episode ends with Millan's pick of the most dangerous breed from the top three viewer choices. "None of the above!" he says, citing his successful rehabilitation of German Shepherd Dogs, Rottweilers and pit bulls throughout his career. Then he makes a suggestion to the viewer, "The next time you hear about a dog attack please don't just blame the dog or its breed. Let's all make sure everyone understands why the dog became that way—because of the human in that dog's life."

The case studies on "Most Aggressive Breeds" confirm that Rottweilers and German Shepherd Dogs and pit bulls are scary but also that they are not, at least not after Millan gets involved. When considered as a stand-alone episode, the focus on Millan and the dogs rather than the owners' training (as is the case in most episodes of *Dog Whisperer*), appears to do little more than confirm Millan's skill as a really good dog trainer. But considered within the context of his well-recognized approach of "training humans" in order to "rehabilitate dogs," the episode follows the series' over-all narrative message, because one does not happen without the other. Its condensed narrative arc highlights the drama, raises suspense and favors emotional reactions, but a human's story is still told, however subtly, along-side a dog's story.

Millan's advice at the conclusion of "Most Aggressive Breeds" goes a long way in the fight against attitudes that lead to breed bans. When the "Dog Whisperer," whose methods always work and lead to a happy ending, says there are no bad dogs, it's difficult to disagree. His clients are convincing examples that a human in a dog's life who embraces his or her position at the top of the human-canine relationship results in a good dog. Anxious, fearful or otherwise emotionally weak dog owners are not leaders and the remedy is a dominance-based approach to dog behavior that rejects physical punishment of an animal in favor of personal growth. On this episode and all the others in Millan's television series, pleasure is found in the before and after or the behavior makeover of dogs, but the deeper satisfaction lies in watching the humans in those dogs' lives improve themselves.

Dog: Impossible

> I let the dog decide. Do you stay uncomfortable and stuck in
> life? Or do you relax and get free?
>   —Matt Beisner, Dog: Impossible[60]

In the opening narration to the series *Dog: Impossible*, trainer Matt Beisner says his goal is to "take the dogs other people don't want to touch and rehabilitate them with respect, trust and love" because he knows "there are no bad dogs." It's a philosophy that echoes Cesar Millan's but with a key difference. Where Millan's path to canine good behavior begins and ends with humans improving themselves in order to exercise power over dogs, Beisner's "respect, trust and love" ethos positions dogs and people as play-ers on the same rehab team, working together for the transformational win. But pet owners are not free from blame.

Like Millan, Beisner believes that owner behavior is a contribut-ing factor to problem dog behaviors—he consistently refers to unhealthy "co-dependency" and tells owners that they will see success if they "do the work" of reinforcing his training lessons—but this work is typically sim-plified to reducing the amount of affection they show their dogs. While Millan's clients must learn to demonstrate dominance through emo-tional strength, pet owners on *Dog: Impossible* engage in what amounts to self-control. If they participate in a more intense effort to transform themselves in order to change their dogs' behavior, it is largely absent from the cameras, so the show is about caring but clueless owners who have disadvantaged their dogs by setting them up to fail.

Beisner's primary role on the show is to step in and give aggressive dogs the tools to heal themselves. He explains his approach in the second episode of the series:

> The way we work with dogs is different in that we don't use any conventional training methods. We're not using treats, shock collars, choke chains, prong collars, commands. Everything is designed for the dog to think for itself because the dog that can think for itself is not going to be reactive.

Where Millan "trains people" to embrace their inner alpha, which eventually leads to their dogs' rehabilitation, Beisner assigns most of the hard work to dogs and his method teaches them how to self-soothe.

In his use of therapeutic language directed at dogs, and his attention to dogs' interior lives, Beisner sets up canine well-being as his ultimate goal, with their owners' subtle transformations framed as a secondary win. His successful dog clients are sent home to delighted pet owners who marvel at their no longer "impossible" dogs' surprising makeovers. In his telling of the (not so) bad dog story, dangerousness is temporary and entirely in dogs' power to change, if only they choose to do so. Beisner's show is primarily a canine empowerment narrative. While it recognizes the part that pet owners play in their dogs' behavioral failures, it gives them one main task: Root for their canine best friends as they take the necessary steps to heal themselves.

Each episode of the series follows a pattern. Matt meets clients and their dogs at the clients' homes to observe the dogs' behavior around their owners and strangers. The dogs lunge or bark or try to bite.[61] Matt quietly watches and then tells owners their first mistake, which is their failure to practice "respectful detachment" or only showing affection when their dogs behave calmly. Then he asks that the dogs be brought to his training center to undergo dog and/or human socialization. Similar to Millan's shows, the dogs are framed in a before and after context, emphasizing behavioral transformation.

To the aggressive dogs who respond anxiously to his presence, Beisner assures them directly, "I promise you. I'm not going to hurt you."[62] To the viewer, he offers a diagnosis. In the case of a pit bull mix named Pax, who has a history of biting, it is a lack of coping mechanisms, "Clearly Pax has some stunted development that has left him crippled with fear and left him no skills to deal with that stress."[63] For a Rhodesian Ridgeback mix called Honey, who was rescued from an abusive situation and is now "insanely codependent," it's a case of the dog not knowing "how to have her own healthy, independent experience."[64] Agedashi, a Blue Heeler mix with a tendency to lunge at anyone who comes to his owners' home, has to understand how to "choose calm."[65] Longtime canine client Ollie, a Boston Terrier mix that attacked and killed another dog, must learn that "surrendering his fear will lead to his freedom" and that it is okay "to give in and choose peace."[66] Beisner's canine talk therapy anthropomorphizes each animal as a damaged patient who must choose their recovery.

Beisner's facility is called "The Zen Dog," and once dogs enter the "Zen yard," their treatment begins with a little help from (their soon to be) canine friends. At the center, dogs teach dogs, a process Matt describes this way:

> What's different about what we do at the facility is we have dogs to help us teach. Dogs get to be with dogs that are good role models [to learn] that they can be trustworthy. It's fundamental to their experience in being alive that they get to be a dog and know what that's like.[67]

In an almost hands-off process, Matt and his fellow trainers narrate the action when the dogs meet in the fenced yard areas. It's a technique that positions the viewer as a fellow animal behaviorist, observing along with professional trainers, but the use of anthropomorphic language also brings the audience into the mind of the dog. When Honey meets one of Matt's dogs in order to learn socialization skills, he and trainer Stef DiOrio talk through the encounter, voicing the dogs' feelings:

> **STEF:** It doesn't feel like "Oh. I'm happy to see you!" It feels like a little bit more of a fixation. It doesn't look, on my end, like "I want to play with you."
> **MATT:** He's not giving her eye contact.
> **STEF:** But she's got hard eyes on him. It's like she's working through something.[68]

Stef combines professional assessment (no eye contact) with what she imagines Honey is thinking and feeling so that Honey is observed as both a dog and more than a dog, capable of complex mental processes.

For Beisner, treating dogs with "respect, trust and love" often means speaking to them conversationally. In the premiere episode of season one, "Don't Fear the Collar," he introduces himself to Lou, an aggressive Jindo mix with a history of abuse.[69] Lou reacts violently to having a collar placed on him and he is in danger of being put down by animal control. If his new owner Corazon is unable to collar and leash him and he is picked up again, he will not be returned to her. After telling the viewer that the first step to helping Lou is "to earn his trust," Beisner sits cross-legged on the floor and begins quietly speaking to the dog:

> Hi Lou. Very good to meet you. I've heard so much about you, that you went through something really terrible here. But you know what? You've gotta get a collar on you so that you actually get to stay alive and go out in this amazing, amazing world that's out there.

He lets Lou walk him to his favorite park and then sits next to the dog on the grass. The camera is behind them. "This is a beautiful park you have here Lou," he says. Later in the episode, Lou fiercely resists a collar but eventually relents after Matt, Stef, and two crew members perform a synchronized maneuver to get one around his neck. The scene is intense and after the collar is on, Beisner shouts, "You belong in this world Lou!" Getting a collar on Lou is not simply about dog trainers engaged in a successful team effort. It is life affirming and framed as Lou's triumphant choice.

Beisner's conversational tone and positive reinforcement continues in another episode where the canine client is an aggressive Bulldog. By way of introduction, he gets on all fours and walks beside him, gently speaking, "We're going to see about getting out in this world together, ok?"[70] Matt's chatty approach extends to his own dogs, which are recruited to help at the Zen yard. When he wants his dog Nama to work with a dog named Monkey, he tells her what to expect, "Ok, treasure, Monkey's going to come say hi. He's probably going to be like a boy at a junior high dance, ok? Like I was, awkward, right? Practicing dance moves—."[71]

Matt's warm and caring tone makes him relatable to many pet owners who talk to their dogs in the same affable way, but it also sets up a contrast that again, emphasizes canine choice. In each episode, the makeover aspect is depicted as dogs snarling or snapping at him and then quietly listening to him. The behavior shift demonstrates that his conversational approach is effective and because it is based in the language of therapy, it suggests that the dogs have not only listened but have also decided to participate in their own recovery.

Beisner's consistent use of therapeutic language when talking to highly aggressive dogs privileges the dogs' personal growth over their owners' transformation but he offers people advice too, though the focus is quickly brought back to the dogs. When Honey's owner Jessica, whose relationship with her dog is affecting her marriage to new husband Joe, tells Matt that Honey is her best friend (before awkwardly adding "Well, besides Joe."), he temporarily steps into the role of therapist. "Ok. I know that she's special to you. And she can be your best dog friend. She doesn't have to fill something that you need elsewhere."[72] His advice is well received by a teary-eyed Jessica who nods in agreement but then his focus turns back to Honey, "Ok. We're going to help bring her into life. She doesn't know that she has a lot to contribute."

To camera, he assures the viewer that Jessica is unaware that she was taking care of her dog in a way that was going to make her dangerous to other people. Later, he repeats the theme in a scene where Jessica is learning to walk Honey without transmitting her "anxious energy" to the dog. He again reassures her and the viewer that she is not really to blame, "You're not on the hook for it because you didn't know what you didn't know." His language suggests that Honey has lost her way because of her addiction to her owner, who he then frames as a loving, if misguided enabler.

The situation is similar in an episode where Matt works with recently widowed Jasmine. Her Australian Shepherd Dog, Grayson, bites people and is so aggressive that she is unable to have friends visit her home. After Matt meets Grayson, who is muzzled and violently thrashes and lunges on the leash that he is holding, he says, "Grayson's life has gotten very small."[73] In voiceover, he adds that the dog's behavior is "also constricting Jasmine's world making it impossible for friends to support her when she needs it most."[74]

Matt's professional assessment focuses on the dog's behavior first, which is not unusual for an animal behaviorist asked to treat an aggressive dog, but his comment about Grayson's life being "small" as a result of his behavior, shape the story around the dog's self-limiting choices. Grayson, rather than his owner, has made his life small. Matt acknowledges that Jasmine's life is affected too, but as a secondary comment made in voiceover, it's less impactful. The treatment recommendation follows the familiar plan. Grayson rehabs at the Zen yard and Jasmine learns how to practice respectful detachment so that Grayson will feel calm and secure.

While Grayson is shown multiple times working with trainer Carlos, Jasmine's lesson on how to handle her dog is limited to one scene where she walks Grayson while Matt gives her advice on how to release the tension she has on the leash. Yet, what she says during this scene reveals a significant aspect of Matt's training philosophy. She tells him, "Maybe I have to do something about me too,"[75] and in voiceover, he points out the significance of the admission. "That realization is the turning point. When an owner begins to understand the impact they have on a dog's behavior and commits to changing themselves, then the dog and the human are better off." Despite his laser focus on his canine clients' inner monologues, Beisner believes in a direct connection between a dog's behavior and an owner's ability to engage in personal growth.

Matt's philosophy of dog training was borne out of his own rehabilitation experience. During the series, he explains to camera that he began working with a roommate's aggressive dog while trying to get sober. Then he helped other friends' dogs and realized it was having a profound impact on his life. "In helping these dogs, in putting their needs first, I had changed in ways that I had never been able to change. I had become more considerate. I had become more trustworthy.... I wouldn't be here if it weren't for the dogs. They rehabilitated me."[76] In Beisner's backstory, dangerous dogs are agents for positive human change, rather than the reason for human suffering. His personal transformation then informed his training philosophy:

> I say that there are no bad dogs because I was that dog. When I started this whole journey, I was detoxing. I grew up making all kinds of choices that put my life and other people's lives in danger. I was given a second chance, so I look at the dogs as a reflection of my own experience.[77]

Sharing this history with the viewer, Beisner is free of judgment. Damaged people and damaged dogs are similar and both, if offered the tools to change, are capable of rebirth.

Throughout the first season of *Dog: Impossible*, Beisner gently acknowledges the role that people play in the creation of aggressive canine behavior by pointing out that their mistakes are more selfish choices than deep personal failures. The owners who appear on screen are guilty of putting their need for affection before their dogs' desire for it. What little is asked of them is easy to achieve, and they are applauded for putting their dogs on the road to recovery. That road leads straight to the Zen yard, as it did for Pax, an aggressive pit bull mix.

In the episode featuring Pax, Matt praises his owners for their contributions to his recovery ("You're making all this possible for him!"), even though their primary on-camera training work is ignoring the dog until he is calm. As for Pax, he is celebrated for taking all the right steps toward self-healing. Observing the dog at his center, Beisner says:

> This is all part of a more mature Pax. A dog that is not only practicing consistently good impulse control but is making decisions that are about not engaging, about self-soothing, about being deferential…. He's clearly moving into sustainable change.[78]

He continues to camera, describing Pax as "crippled and underprivileged" before telling the viewer that his ultimate hope for the dog is that "he can be safe in this world, that he's not a bad dog." For Pax and all of Beisner's canine clients, it's a judgment-free zone of therapeutic healing where pet owners play a part in their dogs' misbehavior but as not so bad people creating not really bad dogs. On *Dog: Impossible*, the narrative of dangerous dogs and their dangerous owners shifts from monster to misunderstood.

Pit Bulls & Parolees

> *Contrary to what a lot of rescuers and people think, not every dog can be saved. I mean there are such things as dangerous dogs.*[79]
>
> —Tia Torres, Founder of Villalobos Rescue Center

Before there was the Animal Planet television show *Pit Bulls & Parolees*, there was a wolf/wolf hybrid rescue founded by Tia Torres in California. A former contracted dog trainer for the City of Los Angeles Animal Services, where she worked for 11 years, Torres named her organization Villalobos Rescue Center and soon expanded it to focus on pit bulls. The center began employing parolees in 2006. Three years later, Animal Planet picked up the show after producer Michael Dinco, who had been a student in one of Torres' pit bull training classes, visited Villalobos and filmed a TV pitch.

Dinco and the network's interest came at just the right time. Torres' attempt at creative financing to cover the rescue's high running costs was a brothel that burned down. She joked at the time that had that not happened, the show would have been called *Pit Bulls, Parolees and Prostitutes*.[80] Dinco's feeling that Torres and her parolees would make good TV, with or without prostitutes, paid off. The popular show is now in its fifteenth season and has been branded into a retail shop and restaurant in New Orleans (where the rescue relocated in 2011). Tia has even reached a level of celebrity, that, according to the rescue's website, has people showing up at the facility in the middle of the night "yelling and screaming" for her.[81]

While the show's focus on rescue and adoption rather than rehabilitation and training means that it does not directly address the relationship between bad dog behavior and the person holding the leash, it is briefly examined here because the premise of ex-cons who take care of pit bulls plays on the cultural association of the dogs with criminality, even as it aims to disrupt it. Torres says of her employees, "We call them the baddest good guys in town. They are polite, thankful. They are two-legged versions of the dogs we take in."[82] Her direct comparison is a consistent theme throughout the show, where dogs and parolees are bound together in the language of personal growth. It's an ethos that extends to Torres' team. When her daughter, Mariah, invites parolee Spencer to join her on a home check, which is the final step before a dog is given to a potential adopter, she describes his resiliency and praises his positive attitude before adding that he "deserves" to do the check.

Mariah's comments suggest that Spencer's behavior and approach to life have earned him the opportunity to hand a dog off to a promising future and Spencer appears to agree. He describes his feelings after dropping off the dog, "I feel more committed to keep myself on track to like make sure these dogs get homes and you know help myself in the process. It's a win, win for both of us."[83]

The sentiment is similar for a parolee named Robert, who Tia recalls had a violent past and a "tough exterior" when he came to the rescue center but now, the positive change in his behavior is "pouring off onto the dogs."[84]

The exchange goes both ways, as Robert points out when he talks about a dog named Trejo, "He helped me help myself." The men and the dogs are both characters in the show's redemption plot, deserving of a chance to be seen as something more than monsters.

Part of the show's drama derives from the parolees' history as bad guys, and over fifteen seasons, some of the featured dogs are depicted as dangerous, but the main action is full of heartwarming rescues, sweet dogs and happy endings. Tia and her team save pit bulls from hard lives on the streets and in the fighting pits, severe cases of heart worm and infections, and shelters that would otherwise euthanize them. The dogs find caring adopters, who are featured in every episode, welcoming another Villalobos pit bull into neighborhoods across America.

It is these potential new dog owners who form the secondary narrative to the show's primary association between misunderstood dogs and unfairly maligned men. During the adoption segments of the show, they participate in an audition of sorts, as Tia or her staff sit down with them to discuss their lifestyles and what they are looking for in a dog. The staff play matchmaker, instructing a parolee to walk out several prospective dogs one at a time to meet adopters. Depending on how much attention a dog shows them, the adopters will typically comment on an animal's behavior as either an impressive ability or a disappointing inability to "put on a show."

The adoption interview routine is repeated in each episode, which makes the dogs seem as if they are aware of the high stakes, while the "which one will they pick?" format adds a little drama before the happy ending reveal. All of this adds up to a picture of good dogs going to good owners. The evaluation of the adopters' worthiness, at least on screen, is rooted in how nice they seem and typically, how nice their home is.

Off screen, the adopters would have probably filled out the extensive questionnaire on the rescue's website. It's also likely they read the page that describes the pit bull's general temperament toward people and other dogs. Under the "precautions" section, there is a warning:

> Two dogs may be best friends for years, sleep together, cuddle, play and even eat from the same bowl. Then one day something triggers one of them and BOOM! Often the dogs act like best friends as soon as the fight is over. They might even lick each other's wounds. You have been warned though. They will do it again and get better at it every time.[85]

The section notes that pit bulls may have an "urge" to fight another dog, which has been "bred into the breed for many generations," and it continues by suggesting that "any canine can fight," but pit bulls "were bred specifically for it...."

The website's information page ends with a recommendation that a potential adopter conduct research and make a "wise" decision because "serious pit bull owners would rather the 'bleeding hearts' not take one of these dogs on merely for the fact that they might find that they've 'bitten off more than they can chew.'" The rescue takes a clear position on the nature of pit bulls that casts a shadow on its admirable attempts to place the dogs with loving families and to change public perceptions about them. By suggesting that good pit bull stewardship involves knowledge, respect, and taking precautions to keep the dogs safe from their inherent tendencies, the rescue's viewpoint seems to be that pit bulls have the natural potential to become dangerous, which a competent owner recognizes and knows how to control.

A future owner of a Villalobos pit bull should be emotionally strong and morally upstanding. As the website material states, no "bleeding hearts" or those seeking to profit from the breed's "remarkable fighting abilities" need apply. But for those who appear on the show to adopt a dog, previous ownership of a pit bull or a strong love for the type is the defining criteria. Some share touching stories, as single mother Sharon does when she gives an interview to camera empathizing with a dog's history of abuse:

> His story just melted my heart. I understand what it's like to be abused.... You learn not to trust people and you think less of yourself and you know, you start making bad decisions. All it takes is that one or two people that make that difference. Had he not been found that day, where would he be now? And like with me. If a few people hadn't given me a chance and loved me, where would I be?

Sharon's emotional confession is compelling television and the nature of reality TV means that watching adopters fill out questionnaires is not, so it makes sense that the suitability of potential pit bull owners is simplified on the show. But taken together with the rescue's stated philosophy on the dogs' naturally aggressive tendencies, pit bulls are framed as scary if not in the right hands. It's a complicated position that on the one hand acknowledges the association between bad owners and bad dogs but on the other, suggests that there is a reason for the dogs' sometimes violent behavior that exists somewhere deep inside them, independent of a pet owner.

Adding to the confusion is environment, as an owner's suitability to adopt a dog often appears to be related to their neighborhood. Tia and her staff often comment on adopters' "nice" homes when going on a home check and while this could be attributed to polite small talk, the idea of someone being a good pit bull owner because they live in a nice neighborhood and therefore do not fit a stereotype nevertheless promotes that stereotype. Tia makes the point more directly in an episode that features a group of four pit bulls that attacked a 17-year-old boy in Auburn, California.[86] Her involvement in the case, and the choice to feature it on the show, gives a national platform to a familiar pit bull debate—the dogs are capable of monstrous attacks—and Tia takes an interesting position. She becomes a champion for one of the dogs and suggests that the aggressive behavior of the others may be due to breeding. As for the owner of the dogs, Tia has only good things to say, and one of the first is that he has a nice home.

The Curious Case of the Dogs in the Parking Lot

The months long saga of the Auburn four (Ronin, Sherman, Maui and Otis) began in the early evening of September 16, 2009. Joseph "JoJo" Kerschner, seventeen years old, was attacked by four pit bulls in a parking lot as he was walking from his car to meet his parents and grandparents at a restaurant in downtown Auburn, California. The dogs, he said, approached him in a friendly manner at first, but when he took a step back, one of the pit bulls lunged at him and bit him and the others followed. He was knocked to the ground twice and tried to push the dogs away, but they did not stop attacking.[87]

Kerschner, it turns out, was not the dogs' first victim. Another witness said that the dogs came after him too, but he locked himself inside a car and sounded the vehicle's alarm to scare them off.[88] Kerschner was not as lucky. While two people helped by pulling him into a car, with one fighting the dogs off with a wrench until they backed away, he was left with over 20 puncture wounds and bites to his body, including a bite to his ankle that was deep enough to expose bone. He ended up with more than 30 stitches.[89]

The initial investigation found that the dogs' owner, Daniel Coverston, was not present at the scene but that the dogs came from his residence. It was later determined that they dug their way out from under a chain link fence in his backyard, which had access to the parking lot where the attack took place.

At an administrative hearing in September, Auburn Police Chief John Ruffcorn reported that the dogs were released into Daniel's mother, Patricia's care the evening of the attack, with strict instructions that she secure them in the house. When Daniel returned from a trip the next day, officers arrived at his home to take the dogs to the Placer County Animal Shelter, until the investigation was complete. Ruffcorn observed at the time that the pit bulls "were not aggressive but it was clear that Daniel did not have control of the dogs."[90] Daniel disagreed with Ruffcorn's claim and told the press that the dogs were "very kind" and listened to him "very well."[91] He believed that had he been home, the attack "probably wouldn't have happened" and said he built a new fence the next day. His attorney Dean Starks described his client and his family as "very nice people." The dogs, he said, had never been aggressive before and some neighbors would let their children play with them. Further investigation discovered that there was a history of five calls to police dispatch regarding the pit bulls on Coverston's property.[92] The administrative hearing ordered that the dogs remain in the custody of the Auburn Police Department and they were quarantined at the Placer County SPCA.

The attack lead to a steady stream of articles, opinion pieces and letters to the editor published in the *Auburn Journal* from September 2009 to June 2010.[93] While some residents expressed opinions that Coverston's dogs should not be scapegoats for the larger problem of bad dog ownership, most Auburn letter writers were not on the dogs' side.

Barbara Lacy, whose residence was within 100 yards of the dogs, said she feared walking around town and hoped that the city will remove them.[94] Marilyn Carter asked that officials "not return these animals to their owner, and make our city safe."[95] Ron Paitich wrote that pit bulls "are the most dangerous breed around," wondered why, considering their viciousness, Coverston would own four, and said that his dogs "don't deserve a second chance."[96] Dan Lucas was more direct, suggesting that pit bulls that attack people or animals "should be instantly euthanized."[97] Some offered their experience putting their own dogs down after a biting incident. Tony Hazarian, the publisher of the *Auburn Journal*, wrote about his dog Kona, who he euthanized after the Labrador mix acted aggressively toward friends and family and snapped and growled at him during a routine exam at the vet. He said the incidents made him realize that he was not the dog owner he thought he was, implying that Coverston was probably not either. "If my experience is any indication, this was not the first time these dogs acted in a violent manner toward a human being."[98]

Matt Green, the director of operations at the Placer SPCA participated in a special "pro and con" article to lay out some facts about pit bulls and the owner-dependent factors that may contribute to dog bites in any type of dog.[99] He ended it by inviting residents to a free educational class on the pit bull, hosted by the SPCA. The counter article followed with a list of pit bull bite incidents in Auburn and surrounding communities as evidence that the pit bull "earned its reputation one attack at a time." By December, it was all too much for one newspaper reader, who wrote that her fellow residents were upset about pit bulls when they should be concerned that millions of dollars were potentially funding a new jail when the money should be invested into local schools.[100]

The interest in the case prompted the *Auburn Journal's* editorial board to criticize city leaders for their failure to implement plans to prevent dog attacks and to suggest that the members of the city council consider limiting the number of dogs allowed per household and require fenced yards with properly functioning gates.[101] At least one council member agreed. About two weeks after the article was published, councilman Kevin Hanley wrote a memo asking the city manager and the police chief to consider a pit bull ordinance to be placed on a future city agenda. Among his ideas were to ban pit bulls and other fighting breeds from the city limits and to put specific restrictions on those types of dogs, while listing them on a dangerous dog registry.[102] (California state law allows for regulating specific breeds only through spay/neuter or breeding programs. It prohibits outlawing specific breeds.)

The editorial repeated details that were revealed during the September administrative hearing, which planted some doubts about Coverston's earlier claims that his dogs were gentle and sweet. Daniel had told police that when his dogs ran together, "they have a pack mentality" and that he "gives them anti-aggression shots."[103] At a court hearing in October, Coverston testified that his veterinarian told him that his dogs would receive anti-aggression shots as part of their "puppy plan" and he did not administer the shots himself. One of the veterinarians at the clinic wrote in a letter, which was read in court, that she had never heard of anti-aggression shots.[104] Coverston responded that he was "very surprised" to hear this.

The purpose of the October hearing was to determine if the dogs would be labeled vicious or potentially dangerous. It was a significant distinction because a vicious label meant a dog may be euthanized. On November 5, 2009, Judge Joseph O'Flaherty issued a four-page decision, which stated that all four dogs were "vicious," and the City of Auburn must decide their fates. He wrote that "Mr. Coverston seemed clueless as to the danger and damage he had unleashed on the community" and his efforts to reinforce his backyard were "woefully short of the mark." He added, "To securely house such powerful, aggressive animals there should be walls and fences of a big city zoo."[105] The police chief said that euthanizing the animals was necessary to ensure the public's safety. In December, Coverston filed an appeal and his attorney Dean Starks said that a judge had approved his motion to have Tia Torres of Villalobos Rescue Center come to Auburn to assess whether she could retrain the dogs.

The second trial was held on January 28, 2010, and the press reported that Tia was scheduled to testify.[106] She did so by phone and said that Otis was the only dog she would consider trying to rehabilitate based on his submissive behavior. Judge Richard Couzens upheld the ruling that all four dogs were vicious but decided to spare Otis' life partly because there was no direct evidence that he bit Kerschner. During the trial, new information was presented that Coverston offered a $10,000 bribe to the program manager for Placer County Animal Services to get the dogs back.[107] The manager also testified that while in the quarantine area of the shelter, the

dogs' aggressive and anxious behavior caused staff to administer tranquil-
izer drugs twice a day for two months and one of the dogs lunged at a staff
worker's face and torso, ripping her shirt. As she tried to back out of the
cage, the dog grabbed her pants and tried to pull her back in but her pant
leg ripped and she was able to free herself.

Tia would later tell the *Auburn Journal* that she knew she would not
take the other dogs, even before meeting them. "I was told that one dog
jumped on the car [during the attack] and kept coming. Right there, I
said I'm not even going to mess with that dog."[108] She said that during a
brief visit with the other dogs, one tried to bite her on the hand, and their
behavior of constant barking, growling and lunging at their cage doors
was enough to confirm her earlier decision not to take them. On February 26, 2010, Ronin, Sherman and Maui were euthanized. The city of
Auburn continued to debate pit bull regulations until June, when council members voted three to two to delete regulations regarding mandatory spay and neuter of pit bulls from the city's animal ordinance and
directed staff to support a new educational and assistance program for
dog owners.[109]

Saving Otis

Pit Bulls & Parolees introduced Otis' story with Tia taking a phone call
from attorney Dean Starks. While he briefly explains the case, the scene
cuts from her on the phone in her office to broadcast news footage of the
attack, which features close-ups of the victim's bloody wounds. It then shifts
to headlines floating across the screen, "Pit bulls locked up," and "Hearing
on track in pit bull attack." Tia says in voiceover that her first reaction to
hearing about a pit bull who has attacked a child is that the dog "needs to be
put down" if dangerous.

Tia's second reaction was to "become like a CSI," and research every
aspect of the case, from looking at police reports, to reading blogs and
newspaper articles. She waves a handful of printed news articles at her
daughter Tania and says that they have painted a dark picture of Daniel as a
dog owner. "From what I've read, they've made this guy out to be the beast,
like he's trained these dogs to attack humans." Combined with the shots of
the victim's bloody wounds, Tia's comments establish narrative suspense. Is
she going to meet a sadistic pit bull owner in Auburn? Or has the press sensationalized the story? The drama deepens when she arrives at the house
and she says in voiceover, "As I'm walking up to this door. I'm actually nervous and not much scares me."

If Tia was nervous, she doesn't show it when Daniel opens the door.
Dressed in black, he is tall and thin, with close-cropped hair and the edges

of a tattoo just visible on each side of his neck. His mother is behind him, dressed stylishly conservative and pleasantly smiling. They welcome Tia and Tania into a cozy living area with a fire burning in the brick framed fireplace. The scene cuts to Tia recalling the moment in a to-camera shot. "When I met Mrs. Coverston and Daniel, I just, I had to take a step back. You know, here was this woman and her son who was very quiet and…." Here, she searches for the right word, "gentle."

Tia's surprise at not finding whatever stereotype she expects at the Coverston residence is not actually that surprising because she foreshadows their normalness when she and Tania arrive in Auburn. Driving through the historic town, Tania says, "This is amazing," and Tia responds, "Yeah, it's like lost in time." To camera she tells the viewer,

> The first thing I notice is what a cute, quaint little town. It's like out of a story-book and I thought you know how could something so horrific happen here? So when I pull up to the Coverston's house I have to double check. I have to look at my piece of paper and say you know, is this the right address because this does not look like the house of killer dog owners.

The Coverston house is not a run-down shack in a seedy neighbor in an economically depressed town, and Daniel is apparently not a "killer dog owner" because he is soft-spoken. If she asks him anything about how or if the dogs have been trained or socialized, it is not on-camera.

During a short conversation, where she hopes to understand the "mystery" of the case, Tia listens as Daniel says he suspects the dogs dug out of his yard and then describes Otis as "kind of shy, very sweet, very snuggly." She then sympathizes with the Coverston's loss and reassures them, "I don't see what everybody else is trying to portray you guys to be. This was just a horrible accident for everybody involved. Everybody, the dogs, your family." Tia's comment is prompted by a visibly upset Patricia who angrily says, "The newspaper has been absolutely relentless. We have been portrayed as this monstrous family, who's raising fighting dogs and aggressive dogs."

As Patricia says this, the scene cuts to a headline that reads "Pit Bulls' Owner Called Into Question," and then it cuts again to cute pictures of Patricia with the dogs when they were puppies. Because Tia has already made her point of view clear, the juxtaposition of the headline and the photos creates an impression that the press had unfairly condemned the family as irresponsible pet owners. In researching the case, I found the article that the show uses in the graphic, but under a different headline that reads "Pitbull Trial Reveals Alleged $10,000 Bribe."[110] It is an objective account of the proceedings of the second and final trial in the case of *Daniel Coverston vs. Auburn Police Capt. John Ruffcorn*. It quotes the testimony of

Mike Winters, the program manager for Placer County Animal Services, in which he called the dogs "aggressive" before describing the incident where Maui lunged at a shelter worker. Nowhere in this article was Daniel or his family portrayed as monstrous or raising fighting dogs.

The episode's editing frames Daniel and Patricia as victims of a press smear campaign by the *Auburn Journal* but Jenifer Gee's reporting, which covered the case extensively for the paper, and was examined as part of this research, did not portray Daniel in a negative light. As for the public reaction, the majority of the letters to the editor did not mention the Coverstons. Some discussed dog ownership but only within the context of limiting the number of dogs one person should have. A few writers said that Daniel was negligent in securing his property. Only one person suggested that "the owner of these dogs ... could be raising them to fight."[111] One commented that the "dog owners are at fault,"[112] and a male Auburn resident raised questions about Daniel's suitability to be a pet owner because his "judgement is seriously in doubt."[113] However, the majority of the Auburn public who weighed in on the case consistently referred to the dogs as harmful. There was no running theme that depicted the Coverston family as "monstrous."

In the episode however, Tia defends the family and blames the press, "The Coverston family did not meet the criteria for a stereotypical bad pit bull owner. I couldn't believe that this was the family that was being portrayed as nothing short of the Mansons." The press is the enemy and the idea of the Coverstons being bad dog owners is dismissed as quickly as it is introduced. The rest of the episode turns its focus and sympathy from the family to Otis. "Dogs follow other dogs," Tia assures the Coverstons. "Just because he was there doesn't mean anything…. I'm glad one of them can be saved."

Well, maybe. Despite Tia's sunny optimism to the family, she summarizes her meeting this way in a to-camera shot:

> After talking to the Coverstons for a little bit you know, I thought, ok, these are nice people but you know, I still have to base any decisions that I make after meeting Otis. If Otis does turn out to be aggressive and not salvageable in my opinion you know I'm going to have to put in a recommendation to the judge to have him euthanized.

For Tia, Daniel and Patricia are good owners because they are "nice people" and her no-nonsense, unsentimental approach to the very real possibility that she will recommend putting Otis down (with no serious investigation on camera of how he was actually trained), sets up the problematic idea that the dog's dangerous behavior is a natural trait.

Luckily for Otis, Tia assesses him to be a "big doe-eyed, shy dog," who was just a "follower" the day of the attack and she decides to take him to Villalobos. She sums up the events in Auburn as a strange mystery:

> This story will forever have me stumped. I mean, we have four dogs that were apparently raised by a very loving home and they got out and they attacked a kid and we'll probably never know what happened in Auburn that day.

Yet, Tia's framing of what happened in Auburn that day, from the straw man depiction of the Coverstons (who go from scary owners to loving owners in a matter of one scene) to the subtle suggestion that some pit bulls are inherently vicious, tells a clear story.

On March 5, 2010, Jennifer Gee interviewed Tia about Otis' progress at the rescue center. She said via phone that Otis had "gotten better and better and better" since arriving and was "a gentleman" who stayed inside her house and did not bother her cats.[114] She saw "good things in his future" and would not hesitate to adopt him to another family, if the judge would allow it. As for what went wrong, she told Gee that she told Daniel it was "a combination of things" including environment, "Having four large, powerful dogs in this little town—Auburn just wasn't the kind of town where you have four big pit bulls." Considering the connections that she made on her show between the Coverston family's apparent responsible pet stewardship and the environment in which they live, it's unclear what she meant here.

Gee's article ends with Tia suggesting for the first time that there may have been more to the attack than naturally bad dogs, "Everything pointed to a perfect dog, so what happened? What aren't we knowing? Something is missing." The fact that she posed the question with little interest in answering it is perhaps due to her focus on dog rescue rather than dog behavior. Yet, the mystery of the Auburn attack was solved as far as the TV episode was concerned, and the eight months between the interview with Gee and the episode's broadcast date, would mean that most viewers would be unaware of her cryptic remark. As for Otis, his time at Villalobos was edited to a scene where Tia introduced him to the staff, who joked about their common predicament. By order of the court, Otis had to wear a GPS collar, essentially making him a parolee.

Pit Bulls & Parolees' focus on both a type of canine many people fear and ex-convicts who may produce similar feelings aligns dangerous dogs with dangerous men. The show, by design, is all about second chances, but this concept is more grounded in rebranding the poor reputation of pit bulls and parolees than it is about rehabilitating canine and human behavior so the narrative format favors a subtle personal growth theme over the more obvious makeover aesthetic of the bad owner/bad dog dynamic found in *Dog Whisperer* and *Dog: Impossible*.

The show's plot structure of happy adoptions and testimonials from parolees who praise the dogs for helping them change their lives is an impactful way of disrupting the perception that pit bulls are scary, but Tia's attitude toward dogs she deems unsalvageable problematizes the program's overall message that pit bulls are "the world's most misunderstood breed." If, as the Otis episode demonstrates, owners are judged to be good simply on the basis of their appearance and economic status, and dogs who attack are judged to be bad because of natural viciousness or an unknowable mystery, then the audience is encouraged to respond to pit bulls as being capable of becoming unpredictable monsters independent of human involvement. On *Pit Bulls & Parolees*, dogs are loved but in some circumstances they also appear to be disposable.

*   *   *

The examples discussed in this chapter, from animal horror cinema to dog behavior television series to a rescue show featuring one of America's most feared canine types, feature scary dogs but not without a scary human or two at their side. On the big screen, one of the narrative functions of a dangerous dog is to shine a light on humans' callous disregard and cruel treatment of man's best friend and then to teach them a lesson about responsible animal stewardship. The small screen gets more personal, highlighting dog owners' failure to achieve transformational growth as a reason for their canines' disruptive behavior. The lesson is to be better in order to have a better dog. The reality show pit bulls examined here exist somewhere in between. Rescued from terrible circumstances, the horror of their owners is implied. But when the dogs transgress, human responsibility is sometimes cast as a shadowy mystery and the dogs are deemed naturally, and irreparably damaged, making the teachable moment of second chances harder to learn.

Endings

Like most things involving Max's health, his cataract surgery wasn't a simple undertaking. We had to take a short flight to his veterinary ophthalmologist and find rental accommodation for four days—not easy with an 85-pound dog. Eventually, we found a place to stay and rented an SUV to shuttle Max back and forth to the doctor's office for his pre-op checks. Post-op, Max was fitted with an e-collar that could not be removed for two weeks. The collar didn't allow him to turn around in his travel crate so flying home the way we came, on a commercial plane, wasn't an option. Neither was staying. Our best choice was to hire a small plane that allowed him to fly without being in a crate, so Max got a prime spot next to the window on a six-seater. With his eyes now clear of milky film, he quietly spent the bumpy flight curiously looking at the passing clouds.

I later shared this story with an older friend who had grown up in India and he marveled at our willingness to undertake it. The dogs of his childhood were tolerated vagrants. It was unthinkable that they would be treated for a medical condition. In fact, it was unthinkable for most people in his town to have any surgery, so economically out of reach was the prospect. It occurred to me that it was unthinkable that Max not have his eyes fixed. Who would let their family member eventually go blind if they could afford not to let it happen?

My bond with Max and my friend's bewilderment over it is part of a complicated interspecies connection between people and dogs that encompasses love, hate, companionship and exploitation. The writer Jon Katz suggests that dogs "seem a blank canvas on which we can paint anything we want."[1] We have painted the blank canvas with dogs that are best friends and dogs that are real and mythical monsters, with those that seem to understand and share our pain and those that are capable of causing it. Our attachment and revulsion to dogs means that some are buried and mourned like people while others are mistreated and discarded as pests.

Overall, however, our cultural view of dogs elevates them. James Serpell writes that we have made the dog into a "paragon of canine

165

A happy Max with his favorite ball. July 2020 (photo by Alan Crawley).

virtue … our loyal and faithful servant and companion; a sort of amiable culture-hero whose friendship is proverbially better than that of our fellow humans."[2] When a dog's behavior upsets this conception and our "devoted and trusted admirer" unexpectedly turns on one of us, it feels like a disloyal, betrayal of trust.[3] Beyond the betrayal is fear.

When my faithful friend Max broke my trust with his uncivilized moment toward Bonnie, it was fear that I felt. Fear for the dog he charged, for him and for me, but mostly for me. The attack meant that the story I tell myself about Max isn't necessarily true; the one where he is incapable of turning into a demon dog, however temporary. The reality is that Max, like all dogs, exists somewhere between civilized and wild with an identity that is fluid, complex and created. Whether dogs are represented as feeling members of our family, as a source of social support, as a product of commercial value, as an object of art, as a subject of scientific study, as an animal to avoid, or some combination of these, they are what we say they are.

And what we say they are is part of a complicated national conversation that reaches even the highest officeholders. When the Navy SEAL squadron commander gave his account of the operation that killed Osama bin Laden in 2011, President Obama reportedly interrupted him when he mentioned the role of a K-9 named Cairo. "There was a dog?" Obama asked. "I want to meet that dog."[4] When President Trump announced that Abu Bakr al-Baghdadi, the Islamic State leader, was killed in a raid in 2019, he made it a point to mention the dog that assisted the soldiers, "Our 'K-9,' as they call it. I call it a dog. A beautiful dog—a talented dog—was injured and brought back."[5]

Trump's reference to the dog was on a Sunday. On Monday, he shared the dog's photograph on Twitter with the caption, "We have declassified a picture of the wonderful dog (name not declassified) that did such a GREAT JOB in capturing and killing the Leader of ISIS, Abu Bakr al-Baghdadi!"[6] On Wednesday, Trump tweeted an altered photograph of himself placing a medal around the neck of the dog with the words "AMERICAN HERO!" above the picture. He followed this up with another tweet thanking the original source of the photo mashup and announcing that the "live" version of the dog, whose name was revealed to be Conan in a *Newsweek* article, would be visiting the White House soon.[7]

Conan arrived at the White House on November 25, 2019. He stood near Trump in the Rose Garden, as the president praised him. "The dog is incredible," Trump said. "We spent some good time with it. So brilliant, so smart."[8] He went on to say that Conan was "a tough cookie" and called him "the ultimate fighter."[9] The president's admiration for Conan was somewhat confusing in light of the language he used in his announcement of al-Baghdadi's death. "He died like a dog," he said of al-Baghdadi. "He died like a coward."[10] Earlier that same year during a rally in El Paso, Trump told the crowd, "You do love your dogs, don't you?" before adding, "I wouldn't mind having one, honestly, but I don't have any time. How would I look walking a dog on the White House lawn?"[11]

Trump's complicated relationship with dogs didn't go unnoticed. Keith

Olbermann, who hosts the GQ video series *The Closer with Keith Olbermann*, noted the president's contradictory attitude in an episode titled, "WTF! Why Is Trump Such a Weirdo About Dogs?" In the episode, Olbermann goes through various tweets by the president where he refers to people getting fired "like a dog," one person begging for money "like a dog," a celebrity cheating on her boyfriend "like a dog," and Senator Marco Rubio sweating "like a dog." In one tweet that Olbermann puts on the screen, Trump says Mitt Romney "choked like a dog" during his presidential run.[12]

Olbermann wasn't alone in his criticism of the president's "like a dog" slurs. A dog-loving freelance journalist wrote that Trump's reference to "dying like a dog" during the al-Baghdadi announcement was a step too far:

> This, in the president's mindset, is a pathetic, humiliating, degrading cowardly way to go. Among the outrages of our times, one would be tempted to consign this to the whatever pile, but to one who has been blessed to love and be loved by a dog, to one who mourns a dog he or she has lost, it is absolutely infuriating.[13]

The media attention that President Trump received for his confusing relationship to dogs is not surprising considering how integrated America's cultural life is with man's best friend.

Consider social media, where, thanks to Instagram, hundreds of strangers find Max appealing. His Instagram account, which my husband started as a way to chronicle his TPLO surgery, had 1,000 followers in eight weeks, and the number increases every day. Many of these people are dog owners who post photos of their own four-legged companions but some of Max's fans are recovering from the human equivalent of his surgery. They cheer his progress and sympathize with his setbacks. As they heal, they seek connection and find it in a goofy, lovable German Shepherd Dog they will never meet. As the old journalistic adage says, everybody loves a dog story.[14]

Yet, American culture's deep interest in and love for dogs exists within a paradox that leads to an uncomfortable statistic. Yi-Fu Tuan writes that in affluent nations of the Western world pets "receive, as we all know, lavish care…. On the other hand, pets exist for human pleasure and convenience. Fond as owners are of their animals, they do not hesitate to get rid of them when they prove inconvenient."[15] Take my friend, for example, who once told me about a dog she owned when her children were young. She recalled the dog with genuine affection and talked about his sweet and loving nature. I nodded along in sympathy, expecting the story to end with a wistful comment about his sad death at an old age. Instead, she told me it was a shame that she had to get rid of him, but she was just so tired of walking him, especially in bad weather. She currently owns a cat whom she raves about to anyone who asks.

The ASPCA estimates that approximately 670,000 dogs[16] are eutha-nized in shelters each year and nearly half of dogs are surrendered because of "pet problems." According to their survey, these problems fall into sev-eral categories: "problematic behaviors, aggressive behaviors, and health problems an owner could not handle." There were also enough people who were apparently surprised by their dogs' growth spurt to create a fourth cat-egory of: "size bigger than expected."[17]

For dogs, the specter of disposability lurks in the shadows of their relationships with people and media plays a part. Our appetite for stories about dogs, in print, on screen and across social media platforms, reflects the high status we assign them, but popular media is more than a delivery system that satisfies our appetite for all things dog. It also shapes how we categorize their behavior, which has consequences for both canines and people.

When media communicates what it means to be a good dog and a bad one, this messaging reflects our expectations about canine behavior. In the dog-human dynamic, nature must give way to culture or it causes conflict. Dogs must learn to master their instincts, or they risk being rejected and considered unworthy of our care. Academic Karla Armbruster argues that the classic dog narrative initially represents dogs as hostile to the norms and expectations of human culture, which taps into a sense that domesti-cated dogs still have a powerful wild side. In order to prove themselves to be good dogs, as defined by the humans who look after them, they must "conclusively demonstrate loyalty to culture over nature."[18]

Good dogs are ones who either repress their wild side or only use it under the complete control and in the service of people. Bad dogs reveal their wildness, which in its mild form, results in annoying behavior and in its extreme form, causes physical harm. But dogs, tied as they are to us, are not good and bad in a vacuum. Their success or failure to master their instincts is inseparable from our intervention. A good dog means that we have triumphed over nature. A bad dog means that nature has triumphed. In the media story of the dangerous dog, a win for nature is a loss for both canine and human. As bad dogs roamed across urban settings, were con-fined to fighting pits, menaced peaceful protestors, and appeared to be nightmares on screen, it was not just their transgressions that the media covered.

When stray dogs in nineteenth-century cities caused frustrated mem-bers of the community to express their fear of rabies to the press, it came along with a deep dissatisfaction with municipal policymakers. When changing attitudes toward pets strengthened the campaign against the mis-managed business of canine control—a system designed to economically reward those who caught dogs, no matter how cruelly they did so—the

ensuing outcry increased mistrust of dog catchers, who were declared disreputable for their corrupting influence on the moral character of a city's
disadvantaged youth. Journalists wrote about "nuisance" dogs but not without mentioning the surly men tasked with their disposal. When city-based
dogs left the fear of rabies behind them and were eventually rewarded with
their own parks, four-legged behavioral transgressions spilled over into
two-legged decrees on what constituted good pet ownership.

Pit bulls never really made it into the dog parks, one of several setbacks they have faced in their long fight against negative public perception. As they struggled to shake off the legacy of the fighting pits, press
hysteria created an enduring image of demon dogs that attacked without
provocation, wreaking havoc just because they felt like it while their owners were characterized as somewhere between disreputable and irresponsible. It's a hard reputation to shake for both dogs and people and has led
municipalities to implement breed bans and shelters to perform high rates
of euthanasia.

Despite the heartwarming and headline-making press stories of pit
bulls lucky enough to find loving homes after being freed from a star ath-
lete's cruel fighting kennel or cared for by parolees on the grounds of a
reality TV star's rescue center, they are generally not winning hearts and
minds. It took 30 years for Denver to end its ban on pit bull ownership with
a city council vote of 7–4.[19] The pit bulls of Prince George's County, Maryland, who have been banned for 22 years, weren't as lucky. The vote in their
jurisdiction was 7–4 in favor of keeping the ban in place.[20] Council member Sydney Harrison told colleagues that they were "all lying to each other"
if they said pit bulls did not exist in the county. A few weeks before the decision, the jurisdiction's number of euthanized pit bulls stood at more than
250.[21]

Pit bulls enjoy a large measure of good will in my county but at least
one, described as a "black and white Pitbull [sic]" made headlines on my
local edition of the social networking platform *Nextdoor*. The post was
titled: "Killer Dogs Prowling Lahaina Again" and the writer urged people
to "please be on the lookout for at least 2 killer dogs." Despite a complaint
from one user about the term "killer dogs," most commentators supported
the language and added their pleas and observations. One user warned
everyone that the dogs "kill for sport."

A pit bull called Kiah would disagree. Kiah was hit in the head with a
hammer shortly before she arrived at a Texas' shelter. She was offered a rare
opportunity to change the public's negative perception of pit bulls when she
was rescued in order to be trained for a law enforcement job. She landed a
position with the City of Poughkeepsie Police Department as a narcotics
and missing persons detection dog. In 2016, she received the ASPCA Public

Service Award in New York City as the first pit bull police dog in the state of New York.[22] Times change for the pit bull and they stay the same.

Beyond being a pit bull, Kiah was a celebrated dog with a job. She joins a long line of working dogs that have made the pages of newspapers for their bravery, loyalty and smarts. Journalists have reported on the extraordinary physical abilities of canine patriots on the battlefield who saved men from certain death while editors have featured steadfast law enforcement dogs in photospreads. But like any employee, not all dogs received good performance reviews and when things went wrong, the press turned to the dogs' co-workers for an explanation. Working dogs, after all, are not independent contractors. They are a mixture of human and canine capabilities and when handlers/soldiers/police officers with malign intentions command working dogs to use their skills to achieve sinister goals, the boundary between the human and the animal collapses.

The results of this collapse have been recorded in the personal accounts of slaves as told to abolitionists, in newspaper stories detailing the silencing of protestors and in photos of abuse that shocked people around the world. When scent dogs were repurposed to hunt people, army dogs were directed to terrorize captives and police dogs were ordered to subdue peaceful crowds, the dogs became objects of fear but so too did the men and women who commanded them. Through "negro dogs," contempt for slave owners grew into condemnation for a morally bankrupt South. Birmingham's police dogs became inseparable from the brutality of representatives of the state and the dogs of Abu Ghraib demonstrated that those who proudly served our country during that time were also capable of shameful acts. The media story of working dogs has recognized that aggressive behavior is an integral part of their skill set but it has also reminded us that abuse of those skills has consequences for the handlers as much as it does for the dogs.

The television and film industries put dogs on the payroll too but not every screen dog could be Lassie. Some had to settle for the part of Cujo. The big bad screen dogs covered in these pages, whether they were an A-list St. Bernard whose name has become a cultural touchstone for monster dogs, an art house German Shepherd Dog who will be remembered for his color as much as for his performance or a pack of rogue horror hounds who had to settle for B-movie respectability, all belonged to society, until they didn't. In this break from culture, they challenged audiences to confront their expectations of canine behavior and imagined a world where the intersection of dog and human lives had dark consequences for humans when they chose mistreatment over care.

On television, the problem is similar, if not similarly solved through brute force. For the human clients of reality TV's most famous dog behaviorist, bad dogs are a reflection of failed personal growth. In Cesar Millan's onscreen world of canine rehab, there are no bad dogs, only bad dog owners and canine behavior modification is possible if human companions are willing to change. The behaviorist on *Dog: Impossible* offers a more Zen approach and gives dogs the tools to self-correct. In Matt Beisner's world, bad dogs are not really bad, just simply unaware that they have the power to choose peace over conflict and confidence over fear. A critical look at the show uncovers the human-dog connection when it comes to bad behavior, even if its approach prefers to name it "confused dog-misguided owner."

For television's most well-known pit bull rescuer, Tia Torres, dangerous dogs absolutely exist, and some cannot be saved. While her show's focus is adoption rather than behavioral modification, it highlights how pit bull narratives still rely on the dogs' monster reputation and alignment with dangerous men in order to dispel both associations. Despite the show's overall promotion of positive pit bull images, these dogs' narratives continue to hint at darker themes.

There is no surprise ending to the dangerous dog's media story. No last-minute twist or turn. Media continues to overlook that dogs have a limited degree of agency,[23] which means that a bite or attack is rarely reported as a purposeful communication from dogs in response to a fear-provoking or agonistic behavior from people. Labeling that communication malicious or a "breed trait," as the public, municipal governments and even animal welfare advocates have done in the popular press, not only ignores the complicated factors that may lead dogs to respond aggressively but also makes it easy to reduce dogs to one-dimensional objects.

With sensitivity given to degrees of harm, from disruptive to physically damaging, dogs' bad behavior exists within the complicated dynamic of our deeply personal relationship to them as pets, our desire to bend nature to our will through domestication, and our unease at knowing that a complete triumph over nature is not possible. The transactional—we take care of dogs' needs and in exchange they adjust their behavior to fit into our lives—and the emotional—love, loyalty—are intertwined. When we encounter dogs' resistance to conform to our behavioral expectations, in the form of unruliness or biting or attack, it is a harsh reminder of our vulnerability, a demonstration of our failure to control nature and a disappointing betrayal of the implied contract between dogs and humans. When the media talks about dogs, the representations communicate something about us and when those dogs are scary, the message is clear. The most frightening aspect of monster dogs is that they do not exist without us.

Chapter Notes

Preface

1. A cranial cruciate ligament or CCL rupture (anterior cruciate ligament, or ACL, in humans) is typically degenerative rather than the result of a traumatic injury.

2. The term pit bull is a subjective one that can mean different things to different people, often becoming a catchall phrase for a generalized shape of dog. Throughout this book, it will be applied to breeds such as American and Staffordshire bull terriers, American Staffordshire and American Pit Bull Terriers, as well as mixes of these.

3. Bonnie has since moved to a new life in Northern California.

4. Animal Legal and Historical Center, Michigan State University, Animallaw. info, September 22, 2018, https://www. animallaw.info/topic/state-dangerous-dog-laws.

Beginnings

1. Nathan Robinson, "Police Shooting of Dogs Can Be Curbed With Better Training," *Washington Post*, reprinted in *Chicago Tribune*, November 15, 2015, https://www.chicagotribune.com/news/opinion/commentary/ct-police-shooting-dogs-20151115-story.html.

2. Jennifer Sullivan, "Des Moines to Pay $51,000 Over Fatal Shooting of Dog," *Seattle Times*, February 20, 2013, https://www.seattletimes.com/seattle-news/des-moines-to-pay-51000-over-fatal-shooting-of-dog/.

3. The case file is found at: https://-s3-us-west-2.amazonaws.com/docs.puppycidedb.com/DeirdreWright_etal-v-CityofDesMoines_etal.pdf. Accessed December 18, 2018.

4. David Grimm, *Citizen Canine: Our Evolving Relationship with Cats and Dogs* (New York: Public Affairs, 2014), 12. 12.

5. Donna Haraway, *The Companion Species Manifesto: Dogs, People and Significant Otherness* (Chicago: Prickly Paradigm Press, 2003), 5.

Chapter One

1. American Pet Products Association, "2017–2018 APPA National Pet Owner Survey," https://americanpetproducts.org.

2. Keith Thomas quoted in Katherine Grier, *Pets in America: A History* (Chapel Hill: University of North Carolina Press, 2006),7.

3. *Ibid.*, 8.

4. James Serpell, "Anthropomorphism and Anthropomorphic Selection-Beyond the 'Cute Response,'" *Society & Animals* 10: 4 (2002): 438.

5. Nicholas Humphrey, *Consciousness Regained* (Oxford: Oxford University Press, 1983).

6. Steven Mithen. "The Hunter-Gatherer Prehistory of Human-Animal Interactions," in Linda Kalof, Amy Fitzgerald, eds, *The Animals Reader* (Oxford: Berg, 2007), 117–128.)

7. Serpell, "Anthropomorphism," 440.

8. Kerry Lengyel, "American Pet Spending Reaches New High," *Veterinarian's Money Digest*, March 24, 2018, https://www.vmdtoday.com/news/american-pet-spending-reaches-new-high.

9. Lengyel, *Ibid.*

10. John Archer, "Why Do People Love Their Pets?" *Evolution and Human Behavior* 18 (1997): 237–259.

11. Archer, "Why Do People Love Their

Pets?" See also Stephen Budiansky, *The Truth About Dogs: An Inquiry Into the Ancestry, Social Conventions, Mental Habits and Moral Fiber of Canis Familiaris* (New York: Viking, 2000), John Archer John and Soraya Monton, "Preferences for Infant Facial Features in Pet Dogs and Cats," *Ethology* 117:3 (March 2011): 217–226..

12. Edward Wilson, "Biophilia and the Conservation Ethics," in Stephen Kellert, Edward Wilson, eds, *The Biophilia Hypothesis* (Washington, D.C.: Island Press, 1993): 31–41.

13. Catherine Amiot, Brock Bastian, Pim Martens, "People and Companion Animals: It Takes Two to Tango," *BioScience* 66: 7 (July 2016): 553.

14. Grier, *Pets in America*, 154.

15. KM Keddie, "Pathological Mourning After the Death of a Domestic Pet," *British Journal of Psychiatry* 131 (July 1977): 21–25.

16. Julie A. Luiz-Adrian, Aimee N. Deliramich, and B. Christopher Frueh, "Complicated Grief and Posttraumatic Stress Disorder in Humans' Response to the Death of Pets/Animals," *Bulletin of the Menninger Clinic* 73 (September, 2009):176–187.

17. In two studies, this number reached approximately 90%. See Steven Cohen, "Can pets Function as Family Members?" *Western Journal of Nursing Research* 24 (2002): 621–638. Pamela Carlise-Frank, Jean-Michael Frank, "Owners, Guardians, and Owner-Guardians: Differing Relationships with Pets," *Anthrozoos* 19 (2006): 225–242.

18. Thomas Garrity and Lorron Stallones, "Effects of Pet Contact on Human Well-Being: Review of Recent Research," in Cindy Wilson and Dennis Turner (eds), *Companion Animals in Human Health* (New York: Sage, 1998), 3–22; Erika Friedman, Sue Thomas, Timothy Eddy, "Companion Animals and Human Health: Physical and Cardiovascular Influences," in Anthony Podberscek, Elizabeth Paul and James Serpell (eds), *Companion Animals and Us* (Cambridge: Cambridge University Press, 2000), 125–142.

19. JM Siegel, "Stressful Life Events and Use of Physician Services Among the Elderly: The Moderating Role of Pet Ownership," *Journal of Personality and Social Psychology*, 58: 6 (June 1990): 1081–1086.

20. R.C. Budge, J. Spicer, B. Jones, and R. St. George, R., "Health Correlates of Compatibility and Attachment in Human-Companion Animal Relationships," *Society & Animals: Journal of Human-Animal Studies* 6:3 (1998): 219–234.

21. Molly Cook and Sydney Busch, "Health Benefits of Pet Ownership for Older Adults," *Grace Peterson Nursing Research Colloquium* (2018), https://www.semanticscholar.org/paper/Health-Benefits-of-Pet-Ownership-for-Older-Adults-Cook-Busch/73d928fbea1db4b9305394fcf572132b4c20d1e2.

22. Rachel Pruchno, Allison Heid and Maureen Wilson-Genderson, "Successful Aging, Social Support and Ownership of a Companion Animal," *Anthrozoos*, 31:1 (2018):23–39.

23. G. B. Parker, A. Gayed, C.A. Owen, M.P. Hyett, T. M. Hilton and G.A. Heruc, "Survival Following an Actue Coronary Syndrome: A Pet Theory Put to the Test," *Acta Psychiatrica Scandinavica* 121 (2010): 65–70.

24. Judith Siegel, "Pet Ownership and Health," in C. Blazina, G. Boyraz and D. Shen-Miller (eds) *The Psychology of the Human-Animal Bond* (New York: Springer, 2011): 167–177.

25. S. Cobb, "Social Support as a Moderator of Life Stress," *Psychosomatic Medicine*, 38 (1976): 300–314.

26. Serpell, *Anthropomorphism*, 443.

27. G. F. Melson, "Child Development and the Human-Companion Animal Bond," *Animal Behavioral Scientist* 47:1 (2003): 31–39.

28. Karen Allen, "Coping with Life Changes and Transitions: The Role of Pets," *Interactions* 13:3 (1995): 5–8; A. Cain, "Pets as Family Members," in M. Sussman (ed.), *Pets and the Family* (New York: Haworth Press, 1985):5–10.

29. Mark Doty, *Dog Years* (New York: HarperCollins, 2007).

30. Allen, *Interactions*, 5–8.

31. Karen Allen, Jim Blascovich, Wendy Mendes, "Cardiovascular Reactivity and the Presence of Pets, Friends, and Spouses: The Truth About Cats and Dogs," *Psychosomatic Medicine* 64:5 (September-October 2002): 727–739

32. Ann Cain, "A Study of Pets in the Family System," in A. Katcher and A. Beck (eds.), *New Perspectives on our Lives with Companion Animals* (Philadelphia, PA:

University of Pennsylvania Press, 1983): 72–81.

33. L. Powell, D. Chia, P. McGreevy, A. Podberscek, KM Edwards, et al. (2018) "Expectations for Dog Ownership: Perceived Physical, Mental and Psychosocial Health Consequences Among Prospective Adopters," *PLOS ONE* 13:7 (2018).

34. S. Bonas, J. McNicholas and G. M. Collis, G. M. "Pets in the Network of Family Relationships: An Empirical Study," in A Podberscek, E. S. Paul, and J. A. Serpell (eds.), *Companion Animals and Us: Exploring the Relationships Between People and Pets* (pp. (New York: Cambridge University Press, 2000): 209–236.

35. Serpell, *Anthropomorphism*, 445.

36. *Ibid.*

37. Stephen Kellert, *The Value of Life: Biological Diversity and Human Society* (Washington: Island Press, 1996).

38. See Stephen Kellert, "Public Perceptions of Predators, Particularly the Wolf and Coyote," *Biological Conservation* 31: 2 (1985): 167–189 and Stephen Kellert, "Values and Perceptions of Invertebrates," *Conservation Biology* 7 (1993): 845–855.

39. Timothy Eddy, Gordon Galllup, Jr., and Daniel Povinelli, "Attribution of Cognitive States to Animals: Anthropomorphism in Comparative Perspective," *Journal of Social Issues* 49:1 (Spring 1993): 87–101.

40. Scott Plous, "Psychological Mechanisms in the Human Use of Animals," *Journal of Social Issues* 49: 1 (Spring 1993): 11–52. See also Sarah Blatt, "Human Attitudes Towards Animals in Relation to Species Similarity to Humans: A Multivariate Approach," *Bioscience Horizons* 2:2 (June 2009):187. Blatt's study investigating participants' perceptions of 40 species does not include dogs or cats but it does determine that "liking is strongly dependent on similarity."

41. Stephen Kellert, 1993. "Values and Perceptions of Invertebrates," *Conservation Biology* 7 (1993): 845–855; Sarah Batt, *ibid.*, 180–190.

42. Ernest Becker, *The Denial of Death* (New York: Free Press, 1973): 159.

43. J. Goldenberg, T. Pyszczynski, J. Greenberg and S. Solomon, S. "Fleeing the Body: A Terror Management Perspective on the Problem of Human Corporeality," *Personality and Social Psychology Review* 4 (2000): 200–218.

44. Ruth Beatson and Michael Halloran, "'Humans Rule!' The Effects of Creatureliness Reminders, Mortality Salience and Self-Esteem on Attitudes Towards Animals," *British Journal of Social Psychology* 46 (2007): 619–632.

45. The association between thoughts of creatureliness and attitudes toward animals in this study was moderated by self-esteem, which is similar with previous Terror Management research. See: E. Harmon-Jones, L. Simon, J. Greenberg, T. Pyszczynski, S. Solomon, and H. McGregor, "Terror Management Theory and Self-Esteem: Evidence that Increased Self-Esteem Reduces Mortality Salience Effects," *Journal of Personality and Social Psychology* 72 (1997): 24–36.

46. David Berreby, *Us and Them: The Science of Identity* (Chicago: University of Chicago Press, 2008).

47. Richard Bulliet, *Hunters, Herders, and Hamburgers: The Past and Future of Human-Animal Relationships* (New York: Columbia University Press, 2007): 3. This shift also raises the ambiguous nature of dogs' tame versus wild status. If dogs that were once pets lose this identity and live on the fringes of society, do they take on the status of rats and other unwanted vermin? Forced to scavenge for food, were they ever really tame?

48. National Safety Council, "Lifetime Odds of Death for Selected Causes, United States, 2016," https://www.nsc.org/work-safety/tools-resources/injury-facts/chart. Numbers 24 and 25 are railway passenger and airplane passenger, respectively.

49. Janis Bradley, *Dogs Bite: But Balloons and Slippers Are More Dangerous* (Berkeley, CA: James & Kenneth Publishers, 2005: 15. On page 39 of her book, Bradley cites a UK study that notes bedroom slippers cause significantly more medically treated injuries than dogs do. See: Royal Society for the Prevention of Accidents, "Home and Leisure Accident Surveillance System," Annual Report. 2000–2002.

50. J.J. Sacks, M.J. Kresnow, and B. Houston, B., "Dog Bites: How Big a Problem?" *Injury Prevention* 2 (1996): 52–54. J. Gilchrist, J.J. Sacks, D. White and M. J. Kresnow (2008). "Dog Bites: Still a Problem?" *Injury Prevention* 14:5 (2008): 296–301.

51. Janis Bradley, *Ibid.*, 34.

52. See: https://webappa.cdc.gov/sasweb/ncipc/nfirates2001.html.

53. Quoted in Scott Nolen, "The Dangerous Dog Debate," *Journal of the American Veterinary Medical Association* (November 1, 2017) https://www.avma.org/news/javmanews/pages/171115a.aspx.

54. Quoted in Browen Dickey, *Pit Bull: The Battle Over an American Icon* (New York: Vintage Books, 2017), 121.

55. Gary J. Patronek, Jeffrey J. Sacks, Karen M. Delise, Donald V. Cleary, Amy R. Marder, "Co-Occurrence of Potentially Preventable Factors in 256 Dog Bite–Related Fatalities in the United States (2000–2009)," *Journal of the American Veterinary Medical Association* 243: 12 (December 15, 2013): 1726–1736.

56. CDC, "Dog Bite Related Fatalities, United States." *The Morbidity and Mortality Weekly Report (MMWR)*, 46: 21 (May 30, 1997): 463–466. https://www.cdc.gov/mmwr/preview/mmwrhtml/00047723.htm.

57. The study noted that one of the report's limitations was the difficulty in computing accurate breed-specific bite rates because these statistics need good data for both the numerator (number of bites attributed to a particular breed) and the denominator (number of animals in that breed).

58. See also C.L. Hoffman, N. Harrison, L. Wolff, and C. Westgarth, C. (2014). "Is that Dog a Pit Bull? A Cross-Country Comparison of Perceptions of Shelter Workers Regarding Breed Identification, "*Journal of Applied Animal Welfare Science: JAAWS*" 17: 4 (2014): 322–339 and R.J. Simpson, K. Simpson and L. VanKavage, L. "Rethinking Dog Breed Identification in Veterinary Practice," *Journal of the American Veterinary Medical Association* 241:9 (2012): 1163–1166.

59. See V. Voith, E. Ingram, K. Mitsouras, K. Irizarry, "Comparison of Adoption Agency Breed Identification and DNA Breed Identification of Dogs," *Journal of Applied Animal Welfare Science* 12 (2009): 253–262, and V. Voith, et al. "Comparison of Visual And DNA Breed Identification of Dogs and Interobserver Reliability," *American Journal of Sociology Research* 3:2 (2013): 1729.

60. K. Olson, J. Levy, B. Norby, et al., "Pit bull-Type Dog Identification in Animal Shelters," *Fourth Annual Maddie's Shelter Medicine Conference*, 2011. Cited in Lisa Gunter, et. al., "What's in a Name? Effect of Breed Perceptions & Labeling on Attractiveness, Adoptions & Length of Stay for Pit-Bull-Type Dogs," *PLoS One* 11:3 (2016). https://doi.org/10.1371/journal.pone.0146857.

61. A.M. Beck, H. Loring and R. Lockwood, "The Ecology of Dog Bite Injury in St. Louis, Missouri," *Public Health Reports* 90:3 (1975): 262–267.

62. Lisa Gunter, Rebecca Barber and Clive Wynne, "What's in a Name? Effect of Breed Perceptions & Labeling on Attractiveness, Adoptions and Length of Stay for Pit Bull-Type Dogs," *PLoS ONE* 11: 3 (March 23, 2016) https://doi.org/10.1371/journal.pone.0146857.

63. DogsBite.org. "13-Year U.S. Dog Bite Fatality Chart 2005–2017," https://www.dogsbite.org/pdf/13-year-dog-bite-fatality-chart-dogsbiteorg.pdf.

64. Dickey, *ibid.*, 215–216.

65. *Ibid.*, 215.

66. See Haley Bemiller, "'Not Just a Breed Issue': Wrightstown Pit Bull Owners Fight Vicious Dog Ordinance," *Green Bay Press Gazette*, December 20, 2018, https://www.greenbaypressgazette.com/story/news/2018/12/20/pit-bulls-wrightstown-owners-push-back-against-vicious-dog-policy/2339842002/

67. National Canine Research Council, "Medically Attended Dog Bites," https://www.nationalcanineresearchcouncil.com/-injurious-dog-bites/medically-attended-dog-bites.

68. See J. Matthias, M. Templin, M.M. Jordan and D. Stanek, "Cause, Setting and Ownership Analysis of Dog Bites in Bay County, Florida from 2009 to 2010," *Zoonoses and Public Health*, 62 (2015): 38–43 and J.J. Sacks, M. Kresnow, and B. Houston, "Dog Bites: How Big a Problem?" *Injury Prevention: Journal of The International Society For Child And Adolescent Injury Prevention*, 2: 1 (1996): 52–54.

69. See M. Kikuchi, J. Oxley, T. Hogue and D. Mills, "The Representation of Aggressive Behavior of Dogs in the Popular Media in the UK and Japan," *Journal of Veterinary Behavior* 9:6 (2014) and Anthony Podberscek, "Dog on a Tightrope: The Position of the Dog in British Society as Influenced by Press Reports on Dog Attacks (1988 to 1992)," *Anthrozoos* 7:4 (1994): 232–241.

70. Justin Murphy, "Astonishing Recovery by Dog Bite Victim," *Democrat and*

Chronicle (Rochester, New York), March 3, 2020, B1.

71. Ruth Brown and Chadd Cripe, "Nampa Police Release Video of Officer Shooting a Dog," *The Idaho Statesman*, February 26, 2020, 4A.

72. Katherine Rosenberg-Douglas, "Man Dies After Being Mauled by Pit Bull," *Chicago Tribune*, February 12, 2020, 9.

73. Carrie St. Michael, "Bred for Trouble," *Good Housekeeping*, October 2002.

74. Se Eun Kim, Boaz Arzi, Tanya Garcia, Frank Verstraete, "Bite Forces and Their Measurement in Dogs and Cats," *Frontiers in Veterinary Science* 5 (2018): 76.

75. In late 19th century press accounts of dog attacks, reports often included what may have contributed to the event, including details on the care and (mis)treatment dogs received from their owners. See Karen Delise, *The Pit Bull Placebo: The Media, Myths and Politics of Canine Aggression* (Anubis Publishing, 2007), 3–4.

76. Arnold Arluke, Donald Cleary, Gary Patronek, and Janis Bradley, "Defaming Rover: Error-Based Latent Rhetoric in the Medical Literature on Dog Bites," *Journal of Applied Animal Welfare Science* 21:2 (October 2017): 211–23.

77. For example, a 2007 paper by Douglas Dwyer As Van claimed that "pit bull terriers" and German Shepherd Dogs were the most common breeds in their study to "attack" children but they explained that only 1% of their sample reported the presumed breed of the dog, a low percentage to allow generalizations about the other 99%. See Arluke, et.al., 213.

78. Deborah Wells, Deborah Morrison and Peter Hepper, Peter, "The Effect of Priming on Perceptions of Dog Breed Traits," *Anthrozoos* 25:3 (2012): 369.

79. See B. Bushman, "Priming Effects of Media Violence on the Accessibility of Aggressive Constructs in Memory," *Personality and Social Psychology Bulletin* 24 (1998): 537–545 and N. Valentino, V. Hutchings, and I. White, "Cues That Matter: How Political Ads Prime Racial Attitudes During Campaigns," *American Political Science Review* 96 (2002):75–90.

80. Sarah Batt, "Human Attitudes Towards Animals in Relation to Species Similarity to Humans: A Multivariate Approach," *Bioscience Horizons*. 2:2 (June 2009): 184.

81. *Ibid.*, D. Wells, et al. The Wells' study extends earlier work, which revealed that adopters' brief exposure to a video of a misbehaving German Shepherd Dog affected their subsequent perceptions of that dog and other dogs' adoptability. Those who watched a video of the GSD acting aggressively were less likely to report wanting to adopt the breed than those who viewed a video of the breed acting sociable. Video footage offers more dramatic cues and the Wells et al. study wanted to find out if written words and pictures had a similar impact. See John Wright, Alison Smith, Kate Daniel Karen Adkins, "Dog Breed Stereotype and Exposure to Negative Behavior: Effects on Perceptions of Adoptability," *Journal of Applied Animal Welfare Science* 10: 3 (2007): 255–265.

82. Bronwen Dickey, *Pit Bull: The Battle Over an American Icon*, 17.

83. *Ibid.*, 11.

84. David Mikkelson, "Is a 'Do Not Adopt a Pitbull' Ad Airing During the Super Bowl?" (January 20, 2018) https://www.snopes.com/fact-check/pitbull-super-bowl/

85. Bronwen Dickey, 11.

86. Quoted in Bronwen Dickey, *Pit Bull*, 127.

87. Karen London, "Peeved Pups." *Bark* (Fall 2017) https://thebark.com/content/peeved-pups-can-dogs-be-angry..

88. Quoted in Bronwen Dickey, *Pit Bull*, 129.

89. Lindsay Mehrkam and Clive Wynne, "Behavorial Differences Among Breeds of Domestic Dogs (Canis Lupus Familiaris): Current Status of the Science," *Applied Animal Behavior Science* (2014): 14 http://dx.doi.org/10.1016/j.applanim.2014.03.005..

90. Bronwen Dickey, *Pit Bull*, 129.

Chapter Two

1. "Concerning Dogs," *New York Times*, September 27, 1868, 4.

2. James Serpell and Elizabeth Paul, "Pets in the Family: An Evolutionary Perspective," in C. Salmon and T. Shackleford (eds.), *The Oxford Handbook of Evolutionary Family Psychology* (Oxford: Oxford University Press, 2011), 298.

3. Albert Goetze, trans. "The Laws of Eskunna," in James B.Pritchard (ed.),

Ancient Near Eastern Texts Relating to The Old Testament (Princeton, NJ: Princeton University Press, 1955): 161–165. Quoted in John Blaisdell, "A Frightful, But Not Necessarily Fatal, Madness: Rabies in Eighteenth-Century England and English North America." Doctoral dissertation, Iowa State University, http://lib.dr.iastate.edu/rtd/11041 1995. P.10.

4. Gordon Harris, "A Short History of Ipswich Dog Laws," *Historic Ipswich*. The Ipswich Town Historian for the Historical Commission and Department of Recreation and Culture, www.historicipswich.org.

5. *Ibid.*

6. Jessica Wang, "Dogs and the Making of the American State: Voluntary Association, State Power, and the Politics of Animal Control in New York City, 1850–1920," *The Journal of American History* (March 2012): 1001–1002.

7. "Scientific Miscellany," *Virginia Clinical Record*, 2:5 (1872), *Nineteenth Century Collections Online*, http://tinyurl.galegroup.com/tinyurl/8wMsV2.

8. "Hydrophobia," *New York Times*, September 10, 1881, 4.

9. *Ibid.*

10. "A Venomous Beast," *New York Times*, November 17, 1876.

11. *Ibid.*

12. Katherine Grier notes that most people probably did not license their dogs. City police forces were small, and the cost of licenses was high. In many smaller communities, licensing laws only required that dogs be registered, not confined. See *Pets in America*, 215.

13. "A Short Chapter on Dogs," *Baltimore Sun*, May 29, 1840, 2.

14. "The Hydrofobiac Scare," *Hall's Journal of Health*, 33:1 (1886), *Nineteenth Century Collections Online*, http://tinyurl.galegroup.com/tinyurl/8wSsu0.

15. "A Hydrophobia Boom: Hundreds of Mad Dogs Running Wild in West Virginia," *San Francisco Chronicle*, March 7, 1889, 1.

16. "Minor Topics," *New York Times*, July 16, 1868, 4.

17. "The Dogs," *New York Tribune*, April 30, 1845.

18. "Dogs Rampant—To the Rescue," *New York Daily Times*, July 11, 1856, 8. Quoted in Jessica Wang, "Dogs and the Making of the American State."

19. In the early nineteenth century, New York City's mayor ordered that anyone catching an unmuzzled dog would be paid fifty cents. The dogs, who were put down, were typically caught by the city's poor street kids, who saw it as a business opportunity. The policy lead to some public concern over the morals of the young and was changed by 1868, when the mayor lowered the payment and raised the age of eligible catchers to 18. See "Concerning Dogs," *New York Times*, September 27, 1868, 4. New York City's dog ordinances were also seasonal throughout the nineteenth century. It was popularly believed that rabies was most rampant in the summer months despite studies that proved otherwise.

20. "Dog Law," *The Evening Post* (New York, New York), July 1, 1845, 2.

21. "City Dogs," *New York Times*, June 26, 1857, 8.

22. *Ibid.*

23. "Concerning Dogs," *New York Times*, September 27, 1868, 4.

24. Katherine Grier, *Pets in America*, 155–156.

25. *Ibid.*, 12, 74.

26. Quoted in Stanely Coren, *How Dogs Think: What the World Looks Like to Them and Why They Act the Way They Do* (New York: Atria Books, 2005), 218.

27. "How to Train the Dog," *Christian Statesman*, October 3, 1896, 7, *Nineteenth Century Collections Online*, http://tinyurl.galegroup.com/tinyurl/8wTHt2.

28. Jessica Wang, "Dogs and the Making of the American State," 1002.

29. "Incidents Connected with the Great Dog War of 1848," *New York Daily Herald*, July 29, 1848, 1.

30. "Dog Laws," *New York Daily Herald*, August 10, 1848, 1.

31. Jessica Wang, "Dogs and the Making of the American State," 1004.

32. "Bergh and the Dogs," *New York Daily Herald*, June 17, 1874, 9.

33. Jessica Wang, *ibid.*, 1007.

34. "To Catch Dogs Politely: There Are To Be No More Brutal Agents And No Pound," *New York Times*, March 11, 1894, 3.

35. *Ibid.*

36. Katherine Grier, *ibid.*, 217.

37. "Killing Dogs in Philadelphia," *The Daily Republican* (Monongahela, Pennsylvania), July 10, 1882, 2.

38. *Ibid.*

39. Bernard Unti, "The Quality of Mercy: Organized Animal Protection in the United States 1866–1930," Ph.D. Dissertation, American University, 2002, 471.

40. *Ibid.*, 478.

41. Wang, *Ibid.*, 1013.

42. Bob Becker, "Mostly About Dogs," *Chicago Tribune*, August 23, 1936, 79.

43. "Hydrophobia Epidemics and Dog Quarantine," *Honolulu Advertiser*, January 29, 1916, 2.

44. Philip Hadley, "What NOT to Do If You're Bitten By Dog with Rabies Is Explained," *Pittsburgh Press*, May 7, 1944, 14.

45. Harold Price, "Rabies-Hydrophobia-Dog Madness," *The Marion County Standard* (Palmyra, Missouri), January 18, 1939, 3. See also H.C. Kutz, "Diseases of Animals Affecting Man," *Mansfield Advertiser* (Mansfield, Pennsylvania), August 14, 1946, 4.

46. The involvement of animal-welfare groups in the administration of canine control had a noticeable impact on a city's humane treatment of dogs. In a letter to the editor of the *Minneapolis Star*, an independent investigator for the Chicago Anti-Cruelty Society wrote about the difference he/she witnessed between the "horrible treatment" St. Paul's stray dogs received at the hands of "brutal catchers" and the humane approach taken in Minneapolis where The Animal Rescue League had control of dogs' capture. It was, the editorial states, "an unspeakable outrage." See "Cities Cruelty to Dogs," *The Minneapolis Star*, October 31, 1928, 14.

47. Bernard Unti, 493.

48. Clarissa Start, "It's a Tough Job and He Loves It," *St. Louis Post-Dispatch*, April 4, 1948, 3–1.

49. "The Saga of Rin Tin Tin," *Pittsburgh Press*, August 4, 1957, 10.

50. Leonard Barrett, "For Meditation: A Famous Dog," *The Roberts Herald* (Roberts, Illinois), May 27, 1931, 3.

51. *Ibid.*

52. "Dog Park Rankings for the 100 Largest U.S. Cities, 2018," *The Trust for Public Land*, https://cloud-tpl.s3.amazonaws.com/images/landing-pages/ccpf/2018/City%20Park%20Facts_Dog%20Parks%202018.pdf.

53. Patrick Jackson, "Situated Activities in a Dog Park: Identity and Conflict in Human-Animal Space," *Society & Animals* 20 (2012): 258.

54. Lee et al. in Edwin Gomez, Joshua Baur and Ron Malega, "Dog Park Users: An Examination of Perceived Social Capital and Perceived Neighborhood Social Cohesion," *Journal of Urban Affairs* (August 2017): 2.

55. Nancy Deville, "Centennial Dog Park Creates a Popular Place for Pups," *The Tennessean*, April 27, 2007, 11.

56. Quoted in Taryn Graham and Troy Glover, "On the Fence: Dog Parks in the (Un)Leashing of Community and Social Capital," *Leisure Sciences* 36:3 (2014): 218.

57. Frank Robertson, "The Dog Days," *Sonoma West Times & News* (Sebastopol, California), July 8, 2004, D2.

58. Nelson Price, "Pooch Paradise," *The Indianapolis News*, July 21, 1999, D2.

59. Lesley Instone and Kathy Mee, "Companion Acts and Companion Species: Boundary Transgressions and the Place of Dogs in Urban Public Space," in Jacob Bull (ed.), *Animal Movements, Moving Animals: Essays on Direction, Velocity and Agency in Humanimal Encounters* (Uppsala, Sweden: University Printers, 2011): 239–240.

60. Patrick Jackson, "Situated Activities in a Dog Park: Identity and Conflict in Human-Animal Space," *Society & Animals* 20 (2012): 254–272.

61. Nancy Deville, "Centennial Dog Park Creates a Popular Place for Pups," *ibid.*

62. State preemption laws that prevent local governments from adopting breed specific ordinances are on the books in several states but private rental properties and HOAs are not impacted.

63. Deville, *Ibid.*, 29, 31–32.

64. Winifred Ward, "The Horror of 1868 Over the Sins of the Great City," *New York Herald Tribune*, February 9, 1919, 3.

65. "Dog Fighting," *Chicago Tribune*, October 12, 1866, Reprinted from the *New York Herald*, October 9, 1866, 2.

66. Richard Fox, "Dog Fighting," *National Police Gazette*, February 2, 1889, 7.

67. Richard Fox, "Here's a Fighting Dog of Detroit, Michigan, Worth Reading About," *National Police Gazette*, August 19, 1905, 3.

68. *Ibid.*

69. Bronwen Dickey, *Pit Bull*, 68–69.

70. *The Augusta Bugle* (Augusta, Kansas), September 21, 1916, 2.

71. *Ibid.*

72. "The Best Fellow in the World,"

Okolona Messenger (Okolona, Mississippi), December 1, 1909, 2.

73. *Ibid.*

74. "Pet Pit Bulls Will Form New Dog Show Class," *The Evening World*, February 11, 1911, 4.

75. *Ibid.*

76. "Pet Stock Will Form Interesting Exhibit," *Houston Daily Post*, November 7, 1915, 41.

77. "Pit Bull Terrier Show Will Be Held at Houston," *The Galveston Daily News*, March 29, 1925, 13.

78. Bronwen Dickey notes in her history of the pit bull that breed labels were as "loosely applied" in the late 19th and early 20th century as they are now. Dogs that would be considered pit bulls today were variously called bulldogs, pit dogs, pit bulldogs, American bulldogs, Boston bulldogs, Boston bull terriers, American bull terriers, and pit bull terriers, among other names. See *Pit Bull*, 70–71.

79. *Ibid.*, 14.

80. See Joanna Rapf, "Answering a Growl: Roscoe Arbuckle's Talented Canine Co-star, Luke," in Adrienne McLean (ed.), *Cinematic Canines: Dogs and Their Work in the Fiction Film* (New Jersey: Rutgers University Press, 2014), 33–53.

81. "Fatty Arbuckle's Famous Dog 'Luke' is Lost and Found," *Pittsburgh Daily Post*, July 14, 1918, 7. "Fast Movers of the Movies," *Fremont Tribune* (Fremont, Nebraska), July 8, 1915, 5.

82. Arbuckle was charged with manslaughter over the death of Virginia Rappe, a 25-year-old actress who suffered an abdominal attack while attending a party for Arbuckle. She died in hospital days later. An unreliable witness who never testified claimed that Arbuckle had sexually assaulted Rappe, leading to her death. An autopsy disproved this theory and three juries acquitted Arbuckle of the crime but his reputation was ruined and he never appeared on screen again. "Bulldog Mourns for Arbuckle," *Los Angeles Times*, September 14, 1921, 1.

83. Joanna Rapf, "Answering a Growl," 50.

84. Associated Press, "Florida Sheriff Warns Against Pit Bull Fights," *The Times and Democrat* (Orangeburg, South Carolina), August 31, 1971, 3.

85. *Ibid.*

86. Wayne King, "Dog Fighting Hearings Set," *The Lincoln Star* (Lincoln, Nebraska), September 3, 1974, 18. The hearings focused on an anti-dog fighting amendment to the Animal Welfare Act that made transporting dogs across state lines for fighting purposes a federal crime enforceable by the U.S. Department of Agriculture. It was signed into law in 1976.

87. Wayne King, "Sport of Dog Fighting Remains a Grisly Reality," *The Missoulian* (Missoula, Montana), August 31, 1974, A6.

88. Wayne King, "Dog Fighting Thrives in Texas in a Secret, Violent Hinterland," *Arizona Daily Star*, September 17,1974, A7.

89. Mike Kelley, "Dog Fighting in America: Cruel, Brutal—and Illegal," *The Austin American-Statesman*, October 27, 1974, B1.

90. *Ibid.*

91. Associated Press, "Florida Ranks Among Top 5 in Dog Fighting, Paper Says," *Fort Lauderdale News*, September 22, 1974, 4C.

92. Associated Press, "House Unit Sees Gory Movie on Dog Fighting," *Des Moines Register*, October 1, 1974, 8.

93. Bronwen Dickey, *Pit Bull*, 138.

94. Wayne King, *Ibid.*, "Sport of Dog Fighting Remains a Grisly Reality."

95. *Ibid.*

96. Dickey, *Ibid.*, 139.

97. Wes Hills, "Dog Fights Held in Dayton, Suburbs, Local Fighters Say," *Dayton Daily News*, May 25, 1979, 15.

98. *Ibid.*

99. Hills' article did note that there were conflicting accounts about the use of small animals as bait and quoted one owner who said experienced and professional dog fighters did not engage in such gruesome baiting practices. This owner conditioned her dogs with sparring matches against other pit bulls and by "letting them hang by their jaws on a suspended tire." Her dogs, she said, "love fighting." The Humane Society director disputed the idea that pit bulls enjoyed fighting but told the reporter that the dogs "instinctively want to fight other animals."

100. Dickey also notes that, "Nowhere in the underground fighting literature, in which training regimens are painstakingly detailed, are these practices ever mentioned." *Pit Bull*, 139.

101. Jack Roberts, "Humane Society Goes to War on Pit Bull Dog Fights," *The Miami News*, March 5, 1980, 5A.

102. Quoted in E.M. Swift, "The Pit Bull Friend and Killer," *Sports Illustrated*, July 27, 1987, https://www.si.com/vault/1987/07/27/115813/the-pit-bull-friend-and-killer-is-the-pit-bull-a-fine-animal-as-its-admirers-claim-or-is-it-a-vicious-dog-unfit-for-society.

103. Jack Roberts, "Pit Bulldogs: Are They Good Pets or a Bodily Menace?" *The Miami News*, January 30, 1979, 5A.

104. Ron Avery, "Pit Bull Terriers Under Fire For Recent Violent Incidents," *Philadelphia Daily News*, June 25, 1987, 6.

105. Quoted in Michael Ruane, "Pit Bull Dogs: On City Streets, A Fad Becomes a Menace," *Philadelphia Inquirer*, August 26, 1985, 1.

106. "Muzzling the Pit Bull," *Los Angeles Times*, July 1, 1987, Part II, 4.

107. Paul Kaplan, Paul, "Shepherds More Aggressive, Vet Says," *The Miami News*, January 16, 1980, 4A.

108. Ana Veciana, "Pet Shop Owners Getting Request for 'Dog That Bit the Old Lady,'" *The Miami News*, January 16, 1980, 4A.

109. A misdemeanor, the fines were typically small.

110. Bronwen Dickey, *ibid.*, 146.

111. Neil Peirce, "How to Deal with Pit Bull Menace," *The Tampa Tribune*, July 29, 1987, 7A.

112. Marilee Loboda Braue, "Pit Bull Attacks on People Spurs Concern," *Asbury Park Press* (Asbury Park, New Jersey), August 17, 1986, A2.

113. Hector Santos, "Letters," *Los Angeles Times*, July 11, 1987, Part II, 2.

114. J. Cohen and J. Richardson, "Pit Bull Panic," *Journal of Popular Culture* 36:2 (2002): 285–317.

115. Ron Avery, "Pit Bull Terriers Under Fire For Recent Violent Incidents," *Philadelphia Daily News*, June 25, 1987, 6.

116. E.M. Swift, *Ibid.*, "The Pit Bull Friend and Killer."

117. David Brand, "Behavior: Time Bombs on Legs," *Time*, July 27, 1987, http://content.time.com/time/magazine/article/0,9171,965065,00.html

118. *Ibid.*

119. More specifically, the stage was reset. America has historically used the treatment of animals in the context of race. Laws prohibiting cruelty to animals often used ideas about the white man's obligation to educate people of color with a "gospel of kindness." See Janet Davis, "Cockfight Nationalism: Blood Sport and the Moral Politics of American Empire and Nation Building," *American Quarterly* 65:3 (2013), 555.

120. Bronwen Dickey, *Pit Bull*, 221.

121. Arnold Arluke, "Our Animals, Ourselves," *Contexts*, 9:3 (2010):39.

122. *Ibid.*

123. *Ibid.*, 38.

124. Gloria Campisi, "Cities Wage War Against Pit Bulls," *Philadelphia Daily News*, April 19, 2000, 7.

125. Leon Taylor and Gloria Campisi, "Despite Popularity Among City Kids, Some Say It's Time to Ban Dogs of War," *Philadelphia Daily News*, August 8, 1997, 33.

126. Quoted in Bronwen Dickey, *Pit Bull*, 226–227.

127. Deborah Lawson, "Bull Terrier Owners Fight Ordinances," *The Atlanta Constitution*, February 5, 1984, F1.

128. Ron Avery, "Pit Bull Terriers Under Fire For Recent Violent Incidents," *Philadelphia Daily News*, June 25, 1987, 6.

129. Michael Vick, Indictment, 17. https://www.animallaw.info/sites/default/files/vick_indictment.pdf. See also Megan Glick, "Animal Instincts: Race, Criminality and the Reversal of the "Human," *American Quarterly* 65: 3 (September 2013): 639–659. As Glick notes, Vick admitted to killing only two dogs.

130. Megan Glick, *ibid.*, 648.

131. *Ibid.*

132. *Ibid.*, 640.

133. *Ibid.*, 656, 649.

134. Associated Press, "Vick Case Illustrates Pit Bull's Changing Status," *NBCnews.com* http://www.nbcnews.com/id/19937995/ns/us_news/t/vick-case-illustrates-pit-bulls-changing-status/#.XKfShC_MxBw.

135. *Ibid.*

136. Steve Visser, "The Michael Vick Case: Disagreement Over Whether to Condemn Dogs," *The Atlanta Constitution*, August 25, 2007, A10.

137. *Ibid.*

138. Harlan Weaver, "Becoming in Kind": Race, Class, Gender, and Nation

in Cultures of Dog Rescue and Dogfighting," *American Quarterly* 65: 3 (September 2013): 696–698.

139. Rebecca Pickens, "Michael Vick's Pit Bulls & Dogfighting: Ramifications of Media Coverage," *Journal of Student Research* 2:1 (2013):33.

140. *Ibid.*

141. Bronwen Dickey, *Pit Bull*, 289.

142. Rebecca Wisch, "Overview of States the Prohibit Breed-Specific Legislations by State Law," *Animal Legal & Historical Center*, Michigan State University College of Law, 2018, https://www.animallaw.info/article/overview-states-prohibit-bsl.

143. Consider these from February 2019: Associated Press, "Suit: Emotional Support Dog Mauls Girl at Portland Airport," *Statesman Journal* (Salem, Oregon), February 28, 2019, 3A. Jenna Lawson, "Dog to be Put Down After Attacking Two People," *Dayton Daily News*, February 5, 2019, B8.

144. Tom Junod, "The State of the American Dog," *Esquire*, July 14, 2014, https://www.esquire.com/news-politics/a23731/american-dog-0814/.

145. Associated Press, "Jailed Dog Owner Blames Boy's Parents in Fatal Attack by Pit Bull," *The Journal News* (White Plains, New York) June 16, 1987, A12. Associated Press, "Dog Officer Mauled By Bull Terrier," *The Boston Globe*, June 24, 1987, 3.

146. Peter Larson, "Contention," *The Orlando Sentinel*, May 16, 1982, 18.

147. *Ibid.*

148. *Ibid.*, 17.

Chapter Three

1. Stubby's story is recounted in several children's books and one for adults. See: Ann Bausum, *Sergeant Stubby: How a Stray Dog and His Best Friend Helped Win World War I and Stole the Heart of a Nation* (New York: Penguin Random House, 2014). For Pancho the police dog, see: Raisa Bruner, "Enthusiastic Hero Dog Has Been Trained to Perform CPR on a Police Officer," *Time.com* (June 27, 2018). For Max the bomb-sniffing dog, see: Ana Calderone, et al., "Hero Dogs" *People* 84:16 (October 19, 2015). Unemployed family pets also make the pages of magazines for their brave behaviors. Hank alerted his owner to a burning shed in the backyard, which allowed the family time to get to safety and call emergency services. He was credited with "putting the rescue into motion." See: Rais Bruner, "This Midnight Hero Dog That Saved His Family from a Fire Is Getting the Recognition He Deserves," *Time.com* (March 25, 2019).

2. Chis Pearson, "Dogs, History, and Agency," *History and Theory* 52:4 (December 2013):143.

3. *Ibid.*, 142.

4. Quoted in Oscar Sherwin, "Stop the Runaway!" *Negro History Bulletin* 8:6 (March 1945): 129.

5. John Campbell, "The Seminoles, the 'Bloodhound War,' and Abolitionism, 1796–1865," *The Journal of Southern History* LXXII: 2 (May 2006): 301. The term "bloodhound" often referred to a type of dog valued for its scent tracking abilities rather than a physically identifiable breed.

6. Frederick Law Olmsted, *A Journey in the Seaboard Slave States: With Remarks on Their Economy* (New York: Dix & Edwards, 1856), 160–161. https://archive.org/details/journeyinseaboarolms/page/160. Olmsted's description of training methods was similar to one recalled by an earlier slave narrative. In it, James Williams said that when the hounds were young, they were "taught to run after the negro boys and being always kept confined except when let out in pursuit of runaways, they seldom fail of overtaking the fugitive." See: *Narrative of James Williams, An American Slave, Who Was for Several Years a Driver on a Cotton Plantation in Alabama.* (New York: The American Anti-Slavery Society, 1838). Available at: Docsouth.unc.edu.

7. Charles Stearn, "Facts in the Life of Gen. Taylor; the Cuba Blood-Hound Importer, the Extensive Slave-Holder, and the Hero of the Mexican War," 1848. Quoted in John Franklin and Loren Schweninger, *Runaway Slaves: Rebels on the Plantation* (New York: Oxford University Press, 1999): 161.

8. David Turner, *West Tennessee Democrat*, March 2, 1853. In Oscar Sherwin, "Stop the Runaway!" 130.

9. J.C. Hardy, Advertisement in *The Daily Clarion* (Meridian, Mississippi) reprinted in *The Times-Democrat* (New Orleans, Louisiana), November 5, 1863, 1.

10. *Sumter County Whig* (Livingston, Alabama), June 11, 1844.

11. Quoted in Larry Spruill, "Slave Patrols, "Packs of Negro Dogs" and Policing Black Communities," Phylon 53:1 (Summer 2016): 53.

12. Quoted in Franklin and Schweninger, *Runaway Slaves*, 161.

13. James Mellon (ed.), *Bullwhip Days, The Slaves Remember, an Oral History* (New York: Avon Books, 1990). Quoted in Spruill, 53.

14. Harriet Jacobs, *Incidents in the Life of a Slave Girl. Written by Herself. Boston 1861.* https://docsouth.unc.edu/fpn/jacobs/jacobs.html#jac145 , 186–187.

15. *Ibid.*, 36.

16. David Wilson (ed.), *Twelve Years a Slave: Narrative of Solomon Northup* (Auburn: Derby and Miller, 1853). https://docsouth.unc.edu/fpn/northup/northup.html. 136–137.

17. *Ibid.*, 137–138.

18. Bloodhound "experts" would often dispute stories about the cruelty of Bloodhounds in editorials defending the dogs' noble and gentle characteristics.

19. Quoted in Franklin and Schweninger, *Runaway Slaves*, 164.

20. *Narrative of James Williams, An American Slave, Who Was for Several Years a Driver on a Cotton Plantation in Alabama* (New York: The American Anti-Slavery Society, 1838), 50–51. Docsouth.unc.edu.

21. *Ibid.*, 85–87.

22. *Ibid.*, xviii–xix.

23. *Ibid.*, xv.

24. *Narrative of the Life of J.D. Green, a Runaway Slave, from Kentucky, Containing an Account of His Three Escapes, in 1839, 1846, and 1848* (Huddersfield: Henry Fielding, Pack Horse Yard, 1864), 25. https://docsouth.unc.edu/neh/greenjd/greenjd.html.

25. John Campbell, "The Seminoles," 260.

26. George W. Carleton, *The Suppressed Book About Slavery! Prepared for Publication in 1857. Never Published Until the Present Time* (New York: Carleton, 1864), 338. https://archive.org/details/suppressedbookab1864carl/page/n10/mode/2up.

27. Quoted in Campbell, 298.

28. Frederick Douglass, "Resistance to Blood-Houndism: Addresses Delivered in Syracuse, New York, On 7–8 January 1851," *Frederick Douglass Papers. Series One: Speeches, Debates, and Interviews*

Volume 2: 1847–1854. Digital Edition. https://frederickdouglass.infoset.io/islandora/object/islandora%3A1153?solr_nav%5Bid%5D=ecf2ad4bc979977f4ba4&solr_nav%5Bpage%5D=0&solr_nav%5Boffset%5D=19#page/1/mode/1up/search/bloodhound.

29. Campbell, 259.

30. "From Washington; Charles Sumner on the Barbarism of Slavery. The Social Tendencies of the Institution Argued. Bitter Reply of a South Carolina Senator. The House on Post-office Business and Public Printing," *New York Times*, June 5, 1860. https://www.nytimes.com/1860/06/05/archives/from-washington-charles-sumner-on-the-barbarism-of-slavery-the.html.

31. Charles Sumner, *Charles Sumner: His Complete Works*. Statesman Edition. Vol. IV. (Boston: Lee and Shepherd, 1900), 178. https://archive.org/details/completeworks04sumnuoft/page/178?q=%22kennel+of+Carolina+bloodhounds%22.

32. "Col. Butler's "Hounds,'" *New York World*, October 19, 1879. Reprinted in *The Livingston Journal* (Livingston, Alabama), November 7, 1879, 15:45, 1.

33. "Southern Bloodhounds," *Chicago Tribune*, October 8, 1879, 7. Originally from *New York Herald*, October 5, 1879.

34. "Col. Butler's "Hounds." Witnessing the 'Hunting of the Negro,'" *New York World*. Reprinted in *The Raleigh News* (Raleigh, North Carolina), October 23, 1879, 1.

35. The "Tom Shows," as they were known, would be performed by more than 400 separate travelling theater companies. See Jane Ford, "The Story of 'Uncle Tom's Cabin' Spread from Novel to Theater and Screen," *UVA Today*, November 12, 2012.

36. Damon Runyon, "My Old Home Town," *The Buffalo Times*, January 27, 1924, 13.

37. In Stowe's novel, the slave merchant mentions the possibility of using dogs to chase Eliza but decides against it because "dogs might damage the gal."

38. Quoted in Delise, *Pitbull Placebo*, 30.

39. Campbell, "The Seminoles," 261.

40. Taylor's letter was dated July 28th, 1839. "Those Blood Hounds Again," *Wayne County Herald* (Honesdale, Pennsylvania), June 21, 1848, 2.

41. Quoted in Campbell, 281.

42. "Pursued by Bloodhounds," *The Daily Republic* (Monongahela, Pennsylvania), May 21, 1895, 3.

43. Henry C. Wright, "Is This Infidelity and Atheism? Then Am I an Infidel and an Atheist," Painesville, Ohio, June 29, 1848. Letter to James Haughton, Dublin Ireland. Reprinted in *The Liberator* (Boston, Massachusetts), August 11, 1848, 127.

44. Campbell, 282.

45. *Ibid.*

46. See *The Vermont Patriot and State Gazette*, June 22, 1848, 2. https://www.newspapers.com/image/488948954/?terms=%22zachary%2Btaylor%22%2B%22bloodhounds%22.

47. Campbell, 287.

48. Samuel Ringgold Ward, *Autobiography of a Fugitive Negro* (London: John Snow, 1855), 21. https://docsouth.unc.edu/neh/wards/ward.html.

49. Campbell, 262.

50. *Ibid.*

51. *Ibid.*

52. Spruill, 56.

53. Thomas Wentworth Higgins, *Army Life in a Black Regiment* (Boston: Fields, Osgood, & Co., 1870), 71.

54. *Ibid.*, 230.

55. Charles Fowler, *Historical Romance of the American Negro* (Baltimore: Press of Thomas & Evans, 1902), 84–85. http://www.gutenberg.org/files/35189/35189-h/35189-h.html.

56. *Trial of Henry Wirz: Letter from the Secretary of War Ad Interim, in Answer to a Resolution of the House of April 16, 1866, Transmitting a Summary of the Trial of Henry Wirz* (Washington, D.C.: United States Congress, 40th, 2nd session: 1867–1868), 5. https://archive.org/details/trialofhenrywirz00unit/page/4.

57. *Ibid.*, 196.

58. *Ibid.*, 809.

59. *Ibid.*, 811.

60. Robert Gersbach and Theo Jager, *The Police Dog in Word and Picture: The Trainer's Hand-Book, the Breeder's Guide, The Officer's Vade Mecum* (New York: The Deming Press, 1910), 73.

61. *Ibid.*, preface.

62. *Ibid.*, 70.

63. *Ibid.*

64. *Ibid.*

65. *Ibid.*

66. *Ibid.*, 11.

67. Samuel Chapman, *Police Dogs in North America* (Springfield, IL: Charles C. Thomas, 1990), 15.

68. Quoted in Chapman, 16.

69. "Nothing Like a Canine Sherlock Holmes: In Flatbush at Any Rate Burglars Have Learned to Beware the Barking Squad," *New York Times*, September 6, 1908, 46.

70. "Police Dogs of New York City," *The Tennessean*, October 10, 1908, 3.

71. *Ibid.*, 35.

72. Kellogg Durland, *Boston Evening Transcript*, 1911, Quoted in Chapman, 17.

73. "Fine Scouts They Say, These Police Dogs: Baltimore Will Test Them in Lonely Suburbs, Tales of Criminals They Have Caught in New York," *The Baltimore Sun*, November 1, 194, 15.

74. Bob Becker, "Mostly About Dogs: The Bloodhound Is a Gentle Dog But It 'Gets Its Man,'" *Chicago Tribune*, May 3, 1936, 10.

75. "The Bloodhound in Criminal Cases," *The Press and Sun Bulletin* (Binghamton, New York), March 12, 1932, 6.

76. Anthony Burnell, "On the Trail with Bloodhounds," *Cincinnati Enquirer*, April 16, 1933, 2.

77. "The Police Dog—Pal or Peril?" *The Indianapolis Star*, February 8, 1925, 86.

78. J. P. L., "Strongheart Police Dog Farm," *Rutland Daily Herald*, June 4, 1926, 9.

79. Charles Sloane, "Police Science: Dogs in War, Police Work and on Patrol," *Journal of Criminal Law and Criminology.* 46:3 (1955): 395.

80. *Ibid.*

81. J.C. Furnas, "Four-Footed Cops," *Saturday Evening Post*, September 22, 1956, 80.

82. *Ibid.*, 38.

83. "Police Dogs Show Mettle: Nab Hundreds of Criminals," *The Evening Sun* (Baltimore Maryland) December 11, 1956, 25.

84. *Ibid.*, 4.

85. "2 Dogs Will Go on Patrol in Test of Aid to Police," *The Evening Sun*, December 19, 1956, 83.

86. Tyler Wall, 864.

87. Helen Shaffer, "Control of City Crime," *CQ Researcher: In-Depth Reports on Today's Issues* (October 18, 1961): 3. http://library.cqpress.com/cqresearcher/cqresrre1961101800.

88. *Ibid.*

89. *Ibid.*, 7.

90. Robert Gannon, "Canine Cops: Can They Put Teeth in the Law?," *Popular Science* (January, 1963): 186.

91. *Ibid.*, 101.

92. Wall, 867.

93. *Ibid.*

94. Paul Moore, "Police Dogs Trained to Leap on Criminals," *The Evening Sun* (Baltimore Maryland) February 27, 1957, 37.

95. James Parks, "More Cities Enlist Dogs to Help Police Nip Crime Rate Rise," *Wall Street Journal*, January 28, 1960. Archived in Eugene Connor Papers Collection, Police Department K-9 Corps, Birmingham Public Library Digital Collections, http://bplonline.cdmhost.com/digital/collection/p16044coll1/id/12746/rec/2.

96. Don Bedwell, "Police Report Canine Aides Are Proving Their Worth," *The Springfield News-Leader* (Springfield, Missouri), January 11, 1960, 11.

97. "Thefts Halted in Areas Worked by Police Dogs," *St. Louis Post-Dispatch*, October 26, 1958, 1.

98. *Ibid.*, 3.

99. Wall, 870.

100. *Ibid.*

101. Charles Holcomb, "The K-9 Corps—A Crime Deterrant," *The Evening Sun* (Baltimore, Maryland) March 13, 1958, 37.

102. Chuck Edwards, "Dog Helps Marshal Protect Lexington," *News-Journal* (Mansfield, Ohio) March 5, 1958, 3.

103. Martin Luther King Jr., *Why We Can't Wait* (New York: Signet Books/New American Library, 1964): 43.

104. See Davi Johnson, "Martin Luther King Jr.'s 1963 Birmingham Campaign as Image Event," *Rhetoric and Public Affairs* 10:1 (Spring 2007): 22.

105. *Ibid.*

106. Quoted in Meg Spratt, "When Police Dogs Attacked: Iconic New Photographs and Construction of History, Mythology, and Political Discourse," *American Journalism* 25:2 (Spring 2008): 93.

107. "Birmingham Negroes Sound New Rallying Cry," *The Miami News*, April 8, 1963, 4.

108. *Ibid.*

109. Gadsden, who was fifteen at the time and watching his classmates protest, was crossing the street when Leo, the police dog of Officer R. E. Middleton, lunged at him. Gadsden later said he was not afraid of large dogs because he had one at home and he knew to reflexively raise his knee into the dog's chest. In the photo, however, it looks like Gadsden's body is bent into a nonviolent posture. See Diane McWhorter, "The Moment That Made a Movement," *Washington Post*, May 2, 1993. https://www.washingtonpost.com/archive/opinions/1993/05/02/the-moment-that-made-a-movement/20eef454-daa6-45f3-a29a-4b03b9d16097/?utm_term=.7db9349c0f7b.

110. "Violence Explodes at Racial Protests in Alabama," *New York Times*, May 4, 1963, 1.

111. *Ibid.*

112. Quoted in Davi Johnson, 18.

113. Quoted in Steven Kasher, *The Civil Rights Movement, A Photographic History, 1954–68* (New York: Abbeville Press, 1996), 90.

114. Johnson, 19.

115. Taylor Branch, *Parting the Waters: America in the King Years 1954–1963* (New York: Simon and Schuster, 1988), 761.

116. Wolf Levitan, "Letter," *The Detroit Tribune*, May 11, 1963, 4.

117. Quoted in Spruill, 61.

118. Johnson, 5.

119. Quoted in Johnson, 14.

120. "The Dogs' Attack Is Negroes' Reward," *Life*, May 17, 1963, 30.

121. "Freedom—Now," *Time*, May 17, 1963, 26.

122. Martha Cole, "Use of Police Dogs Stire [*sic*] Controversy," *Del Rio New Herald* (Del Rio, Texas), May 14, 1963, 3.

123. "Birmingham, U.S.A.: 'Look at Them Run,'" *Newsweek*, May 13, 1963, 27–29.

124. Glenn Eskew, *But for Brimingham: The Local and National Movements in the Civil Rights Struggle* (Chapel Hill: University of North Carolina Press, 1997), 6.

125. "Race Riot Reflections," *The Oneonta Star* (Oneonta, New York) May 13, 1963, 1.

126. "Food for Thought," *The York Daily Record* (York, Pennsylvania) June 5, 1963, 18.

127. This is especially evident in the current artistic representations of the dog

photos, which include a sculpture instal-
lation in Birmingham's Kelly Ingram Park.
The "Foot Soldier" monument recreates the
Gadsden photo with an interpretation that
has Gadsden leaning back and the police
officer who holds his shirt standing with
commanding authority. Another piece, by
James Drake, dramatically depicts three
metal dogs lunging from two metal walls.
They are leashed, which invokes the police
officers, but the figures of the police are
absent. A path between the walls allows the
visitor to walk between the dogs, recreat-
ing the experience of being attacked from
all sides.

128. Quoted in Wall, 877.

129. In some southern media outlets,
this interpretation was reversed and the
authorities and the dogs were heroes fighting the disruptors of social order. The photographs were rarely published with the
written accounts of events. See Johnson, 17.

130. "Nazi Tactics in the 'Free State,'"
Saturday Evening Post, March 28, 1964.

131. "Crowds Battle Police In Chicago
and Florida," *The Boston Globe*, June 13,
1966, 19.

132. Wall, 873.

133. Martha Cole, "Use of Police Dogs
Widespread," *Birmingham News*, May 14,
1963. Archived in Eugene Connor Papers
Collection, Police Department K-9 Corps,
Birmingham Public Library. Digital Collections, http://bplonline.cdmhost.com/
digital/collection/p16044coll11/id/12746/
rec/2.

134. George Newman, "Police Dogs
Vs. Mobs: Is It Morally Right?" *The Miami
News*, May 26, 1963, 1.

135. Dickey, *Pit Bull*, 130–131.

136. Toni Splichal, "Guard Dogs:
Trained or Abused?" *Fort Lauderdale News*,
September 15, 1974, 1C.

137. *Ibid.*

138. David Correia and Tyler Wall,
Police: A Field Guide (London, New York:
Verso, 2018). https://www.amazon.com/-
Police-Field-Guide-David-Correia/dp/
1786630141.

139. David Beers, "Police Dogs Bite
Hundreds of People Every Year, Many of
Them Never Charged with a Crime. Officials Say the Dogs Are Just Doing Their
Job. The Victims Say They Are Instruments of Terror," *Los Angeles Times*, February 9, 1992, https://www.latimes.com/

archives/la-xpm-1992-02-09-tm-3238-
story.html.

140. *Ibid.*

141. *Ibid.*

142. Andrea Ford, "Video of Police Dog
Attack on Unarmed Theft Suspect Prompts
Panel Inquiry," *Los Angeles Times*, December 12, 1991, https://www.latimes.com/
archives/la-xpm-1991-12-12-me-343-story.
html.

143. "LAPD, Dogs and Video Tape:
Police Commission Must Fully Examine
Allegations About Police Dog Attacks," *Los
Angeles Times*, December 27, 1991, B10.

144. David Beers, *ibid.*

145. Tyler Wall, "Legal Terror and the
Police Dog," *Radical Philosophy* 188 (Nov/
Dec 2014): 3.

146. Beers, 24.

147. *Ibid.*

148. *Ibid.*

149. *Ibid.*, 25.

150. Victor Merina, "Police K-9 Unit in
Dog Fight with Critics," *Los Angeles Times*,
July 8, 1991, B1.

151. *Ibid.*

152. David Savage, "Necessary Weapons, or Excessive Force?" *Los Angeles Times*,
February 29, 1996, https://www.latimes.
com/archives/la-xpm-1996-02-29-mn-
41386-story.html.

153. Jason Henry, "Bark vs. Bite: Los
Angeles Police, Sheriff's Department Dif-
fer When It Comes to K-9 Strategies,"
Pasadena Star News, November 26, 2013,
https://www.sgvtribune.com/2013/11/26/-
bark-vs-bite-los-angeles-police-sheriffs-
department-differ-when-it-comes-to-k-9-
strategies/.

154. Colleen Heild, "APD Dog Bites
Cost City Over $940,000," *Albuquerque
Journal*, May 26, 2002, 1.

155. Joanne Cavanaugh and Dana
Banker, "K-9s Used Recklessly, Reports
Say," *South Florida Sun Sentinel*, May 12,
1991, 1.

156. *Ibid.*

157. Quoted in Dickey, 310. The report
also noted that "in every canine bite incident for which racial information is available, the subject was African American."

158. Joel Grover and Matthew Glasser,
"Cops Allow Police Dog to Bite Naked,
Unarmed Man," *NBC Los Angeles*,
December 12, 2016, https://www.nbc
losangeles.com/news/local/Cops-Allow-

Police-Dog-Bite-Naked-Unarmed-Man-406122445.html.

159. Brooks Barnes, "The True Story of Sergeant Goosby and His 19 Dogs," *New York Times*, November 21, 2015, https://www.nytimes.com/2015/11/22/fashion/-michael-goosby-lapd-dogs.html.

160. *Ibid.*

161. Aaron Skabelund, "Breeding Racism: The Imperial Battlefields of the "German" Shepherd Dog," *Society and Animals* 16 (2008): 357.

162. Quoted in William Putney, *Always Faithful: A Memoir of the Marine Dogs of WWII* (New York: Free Press, 2002), 165. See Fiona Allon and Lindsay Barrett, "That Dog Was a Marine! Human-Dog Assemblages in the Pacific War," *Animal Studies Journal* 4:1 (2015), 126–147.

163. Allon and Barrett, 136.

164. See Robert Lilly and Michael Puckett, "Social Control and Dogs: A Sociohistorical Analysis," *Crime & Delinquency* 43: 2 (April 1997): 129.

165. Mark Derr, *A Dog's History of America* (New York: North Point Press, 2004), 257–258.

166. Michael Lemish, *War Dogs: A History of Loyalty and Heroism* (Washington, D.C.: Brassey's, 1996), 6.

167. *Ibid.*, 13. Trainers would later change the method the dogs used to alert so that they would lie down if no one was found or urge their handlers to return to the site, if there were wounded.

168. Lemish, 20.

169. When the United States entered WWI in 1917, it did so without war dogs in the military. The exception was sled dogs that were kept in Alaska. Four hundred were delivered to the French army to help haul ammunitions and supplies in areas that snowed. See Lemish, 21.

170. This number also included police dogs. See Lilly and Puckett, 129.

171. Quoted Skabelund, 359.

172. *Ibid.*, 361.

173. *Ibid.*, 360.

174. *Ibid.*

175. Abba Solomon Eban, *Heritage: Civilization and the Jews* (New York: Summit Books, 1984): 305.

176. Skabelund, 364. This statistic does not include dogs in the navy, constabulary, colonial police forces or other organizations.

177. Quoted in Rebecca Frankel, *War Dogs: Tales of Canine Heroism, History and Love* (New York: St. Martin's Griffin, 2015): 108.

178. "Dogs to Have Place in Nation's Service," *The Cincinnati Enquirer*, April 12, 1942, 6.

179. "War Dogs," *The Clearing House*, 16:7 (March 1942): 446.

180. Advertisement for Sparton Precision Electrical Manufacturers from the National Museum of American History's Division of Armed Forces History. Italics in the original. https://americanhistory.si.edu/blog/dogs-defense.

181. Purina Dogs for Defense advertisement. https://americanhistory.si.edu/blog/dogs-defense.

182. Quoted in Aaron Skabelund, "Dogs at War: Military Dogs in Film," in Adrienne McLean (ed.), *Cinematic Canines: Dogs and Their Work in the Fiction Film* (New Brunswick, NJ: Rutgers University Press, 2014), 127.

183. "Pets Assist Dogs for Defense," *The Journal Herald* (Dayton, Ohio) May 30, 1943, 19.

184. "Dogs For Defense," *Beatrice Daily Sun* (Beatrice, Nebraska) June 4, 1943, 1.

185. Fairfax Downey, "War Dogs," *The Birmingham News*, June 7, 1942, 12.

186. Bob Becker, "Mostly About Dogs," *Chicago Tribune*, October 17, 1943, 8.

187. Ben Markland, "Chicago Area's Dogs of War Go Off to Battle," *Chicago Tribune*, November 8, 1942, Part 3, 5.

188. Potts Boswell, "Dogs For Defense, Inc., Takes Sissified Pooches, Turns Out Fighting Beasts," *The Tampa Tribune*, August 30, 1942, Part 2, 8.

189. "War Dogs Taught to Honor Uniform," *Tucson Daily Citizen*, June 14, 1943, 4.

190. Robert Ruark, "Have the War Dogs Been Good Soldiers?" *Saturday Evening Post* 217:22 (November 25, 1944): 18.

191. *Ibid.*

192. Ward Walker, "Four Footed Fighters!" *Chicago Tribune*, May 20, 1945, 9.

193. Bonnie Wiley, Bonnie, "Returned GI's High In Praise of Dog's Work in Jungle War," *The Birmingham News*, May 7, 1944, 3D.

194. *Ibid.*

195. Jack Cuddy, "Marines Pay in Cigarettes Just to Be Near War Dogs," *The Boston Daily Globe*, April 6, 1944, 17.

196. Eileen Callahan, "Nippees Treasure Teeth-Marks from Thrice-Cited Chips," *Daily News* (New York) January 23, 1944, 50.

197. Bonnie Wiley, "U.S. War Dogs Prove Their Worth in Combat in Jungles of New Britain and New Guinea," *The Courier-Journal* (Louisville, Kentucky) May 7, 1944, 11.

198. Allon and Barrett, "That Dog was Marine!" 142.

199. Quoted in Lemish, *War Dogs*, 142.

200. *Ibid.*, 143.

201. *Ibid.*, 145.

202. John Casserly, "War Dogs Pay High Price in Korea, Too," *The Times* (Shreveport, Louisiana) January 19, 1953, 16.

203. "Air Force Sentry Dogs in Vietnam Prove Courageous," *Valley News* (Van Nuys, California) June 10, 1966, 25.

204. Lemish, 181.

205. "Sunday: Beware of the Dogs," *Star Tribune*, October 3, 1969, 22.

206. Richard Saltus, "Gung-Ho Dog Makes Mark in Vietnam," *Arizona Daily Star*, September 17, 1970, B1.

207. "GI Praises Scout Dog For Foiling VC Sniper," *The Springfield News-Leader* (Springfield, Missouri) April 4, 1970, 7.

208. See Michael Delli Carpini (1990). "Vietnam and the Press," in D. M. Shafer (ed.), *Legacy: The Vietnam War in the American Imagination* (Boston, MA: Beacon Press, 1990), 132–133.

209. *Ibid.*, 136.

210. *Ibid.*, 137.

211. *Ibid.*, 139.

212. *Ibid.*, 144.

213. George McArthur, "Strange Diseases Are Added Hazards for Viet War Dogs," *Los Angeles Times*, December 1, 1970, 14.

214. *Ibid.*

215. The main concern was a deadly disease called Tropical Canine Pancytopenia or TCP, which originated from ticks on tracker dogs obtained from the British in Malaysia. It was later found to have existed in the United States for years. See Lemish, 227, 236.

216. Lemish, 233.

217. *Ibid.*, 236.

218. De. M. Miller, "Cruel Reward for Faithful War Dogs," *The Kansas City Times*, September 21, 1970, 30.

219. "Military Dogs Get 1-Way Ticket to Vietnam," *Orlando Evening Star*, April 3, 1970, 4.

220. Curt Matthews, "GI Losing Plea for War Dog," *St. Louis Post-Dispatch*, December 11, 1970, 1.

221. Sterling Colthurst, "To Save Army Dogs," *Los Angeles Times*, November 15, 1970, 90.

222. The military's reasoning for not allowing the dogs to be adopted was based on liability. The dogs were trained to attack, making the federal government potentially responsible.

223. "U.S. Sentry Dogs Leaving Vietnam," *The Dispatch* (Moline, Illinois) September 11, 1971, 17.

224. "Dogs Save Lives in Viet Fighting," *Austin American-Statesman*, December 6, 1970, G-7.

225. Guy Wright, "The Dogs of War," November 22, 1970, B3.

226. Lemish, 243.

227. James Vaznis, "Fido, You're in the Army Now," *The Boston Globe*, September 12, 2004, 3.

228. Penny Owen, "Former Airman Fights to Adopt Military Dog," *The Daily Oklahoman*, May 7, 2000, 1.

229. *Ibid.*, 10A.

230. Laurie Denger, "Retirement From Marines Means Model Canine Must Be Destroyed," *Dayton Daily News* July 16, 2000, 4E.

231. Seymour Hersh, "Torture at Abu Ghraib," *The New Yorker*, May 10, 2004 https://www.newyorker.com/magazine/2004/05/10/torture-at-abu-ghraib.

232. *Ibid.*

233. *Ibid.*, 87.

234. Josh White, "Abu Ghraib Dog Tactics Came From Guantanamo," *Washington Post*, July 27, 2005 http://www.washingtonpost.com/wp-dyn/content/article/2005/07/26/AR2005072601792.html.

235. Cardona was convicted of dereliction of duty and aggravated assault while Smith was found guilty of six counts including maltreatment of prisoners and dereliction of duty.

236. "Army Dog Handler at Abu Ghraib Convicted," *Los Angeles Times*, June 2, 2006, A18.

237. "Dog Handler at Abu Ghraib Convicted," *Sioux City Journal* (Sioux City, Iowa) March 22, 2006, A9.

238. See Sara Johnson, "'You Should Give Them Blacks to Eat' Waging Inter-

American Wars of Torture and Terror," *American Quarterly* 61:1 (March 2009).

239. Gardiner Harris, "A Bin Laden Hunter on Four Legs," *New York Times*, May 4, 2011 https://www.nytimes.com/2011/05/05/science/05dog.html.

240. Ben Forer, "Osama Bin Laden Raid: Navy SEALS Brought Highly Trained Dog with Them into Compound," *ABC News*, May 5, 2011 https://abcnews.go.com/U.S./osama-bin-laden-raid-navy-seals-military-dog/story?id=13535070.

241. Rebecca Frankel, *War Dogs: Tales of Canine Heroism, History and Love* (New York: St. Martin's Griffin, 2015), 151.

242. Alex Danchev, "'Like a Dog!': Humiliation and Shame in the War on Terror," *Alternatives: Global, Local, Political* 31:3 (July-September 2006): 273.

243. Quoted in Frankel, 228.

244. *Ibid.*, 229.

245. *Ibid.*

246. While dogs behave badly in live action narrative films and animated cinema, their actions are typically depicted as mischievous rather than dangerous. I have narrowed the discussion to animal horror films where a dog is the central character because these films tell a story of how a dog commits a transgression against humanity and must be punished.

Chapter Four

1. Adrienne McLean (ed.), *Cinematic Canines: Dogs and Their Work in the Fiction Film* (New Brunswick, NJ: Rutgers University Press, 2014): 13.

2. Jim Doherty, "Tigers at the Gate," *Smithsonian Magazine*, January 2002, https://www.smithsonianmag.com/science-nature/tigers-at-the-gate-57966637/.

3. See Ashely May, "Toddler Killed By Alligator Near Disney Resort Honored with Statue," *USA Today*, August 9, 2017 https://www.usatoday.com/story/news/nation-now/2017/08/09/toddler-killed-alligator-near-disney-resort-honored-statue/553497001/. David Harris, "Parents of Boy Who Died in Alligator Attack at Disney Have Another Son," *Orlando Sentinel*, September 12, 2018 https://www.orlandosentinel.com/news/-breaking-news/os-lane-graves-brother-born-20180912-story.html.

4. Dominic Lennard, *Brute Force:*

Animal Horror Movies (New York: SUNY Press, 2019), 5.

5. *Ibid.*, 26.

6. *Ibid.*, 21.

7. *Ibid.*, 12.

8. *Ibid.*

9. Laurent Bouzereau, Director, *Dog Days: The Making of Cujo*, 42nd Street Films, 2007.

10. *Ibid.*

11. Mark Browning, *Stephen King on the Big Screen* (Wilmington, NC: Intellect Books, 2009), 188.

12. Tony DeSena, "Cujo Should Have Met a Quick Death," *Daily Record* (Morristown, New Jersey) August 18, 1983, 35.

13. Jack Garner, "Horror-Movie Lovers Can Really Sink Their Teeth Into Cujo," *Courier-Post* (Camden, New Jersey) August 19, 1983, 4C.

14. Linda Gross, "Rabid Dog on the Rampage in Cujo," *Los Angeles Times*, August 15, 1983, Part VI, 4.

15. Laurent Bouzereau, *Dog Days.*

16. Lennard, *Brute Force*, 172.

17. Browning, *Stephen King*, 191.

18. *Ibid.*

19. Lou Cedrone, "Stars of 'The Pack' Come Here to Bark About Their New Film," *The Evening Sun* (Baltimore, Maryland) September 1, 1977, 12. Miller also anthropomorphized the lead dog in the press. Discussing "Josh's" acting motivation, he told a reporter, "Discipline, yes. But love. Do you think Josh does this just to get a piece of meat?" See: Henry Mitchell, "Josh Vicious? He's a Pussycat," *Washington Post* reprinted in *The Courier-Journal* (Louisville, Kentucky) August 30, 1977, C1.

20. Associated Press, "Pack of Wild Dogs Stars in Thriller," *The Boston Globe*, January 14, 1977, 19.

21. Judy Stone, "Hope's Delighted to be Frightened by a Pack of Dogs," *San Francisco Examiner*, April 10, 1977, 17.

22. Betsy Light, "Whimper Replaces Snarl in 'The Pack'" *Journal and Courier* (Lafayette, Indiana), September 4, 1977, 4.

23. *Ibid.*

24. Lou Cedrone, "'Pack' Goes to the Dogs," *The Evening Sun* (Baltimore, Maryland), August 30, 1977, B5.

25. Scott Hammen, "'The Pack' Falls Into the Category of Beastly Stories–They're All Alike," *The Courier-Journal* (Louisville, Kentucky), August 26, 1977, C7.

26. Elizabeth Duff, "The Wild Dogs: They're Appearing More and More in the Phila. Area," *Philadelphia Inquirer*, May 14, 1977, 3.

27. *Ibid.*

28. Keith Takahashi, "Animal Control Agency Wages War on Southeast Dog Packs," *Los Angeles Times*, May 19, 1977, 2.

29. Wally Dillon, "Sheriff Hunts for Wild Dogs," *The Tampa Tribune*, September 16, 1977, 1.

30. *Ibid.*, 3.

31. James McTague, "Dog Hunter Has Trophies—And Scars," *Asbury Park Press* (Asbury Park, New Jersey), June 1, 1977, 1.

32. *Ibid.*

33. Lisa Dombrowski, "Every Dog Has Its Day: The Muzzling of Samuel Fuller's White Dog," *Film Comment* (November-December, 2008): 48.

34. Robert Price, "Black Writers," Letter to the Editor, *Los Angeles Times*, January 24, 1982, 91.

35. Same Fuller, Response to "Black Writers," Letter to the Editor. *Los Angeles Times*, February 21, 1982, 103.

36. Dombrowski, 48.

37. Eric Kasum, "White Dog—No Lassie Movie This," *Los Angeles Times*, April 11, 1982, 18.

38. *Ibid.*, 19.

39. Associated Press, "NBC Drops Plan to Show Film White Dog," *New York Times*, January 20, 1984, 23C.

40. Dombrowski, 47.

41. Don Ranvaud, "An Interview with Sam Fuller," *Framework: The Journal of Cinema and Media*. 19 (1982): 26.

42. Quoted in J. Hoberman, "Sam Fuller, Unmuzzled," Essay in Criterion Collection DVD Booklet, 2008, 6.

43. Samuel Fuller, "The White Dog Talks—To Sam Fuller," *Framework: The Journal of Cinema and Media*, 19 (1982): 25.

44. Hoberman, 8.

45. Brett Mills, *Animals on Television*, 154.

46. *Ibid.*, 152.

47. *Ibid.*

48. Kim Hoh Wong, "It Changed My Life: Cesar Millan Back to Being Top Dog After Very Low Point," *The Straits Times*, July 2, 2017, https://www.straitstimes.com/singapore/it-changed-my-life-cesar-millan-back-to-being-top-dog-after-very-low-point.

49. Bettijane Levine, "Redeeming Rover," *September 25, 2002, Los Angeles Times*, E3.

50. Nina Metz, "Dog Whisperer Cesar Millan on Why Americans Have So Many Problems with Their Dogs," *Chicago Tribune*, February 16, 2017 https://www.chicagotribune.com/entertainment/tv/ct-cesar-millan-tv-chicago-0217-2017 0216-column.html.

51. Mark Derr, "Pack of Lies," *New York Times*, August 31, 2006. https://www.nytimes.com/2006/08/31/opinion/31derr.html.

52. Andra Park, "Owner in Cesar 91 Animal Cruelty Case Defends Millan: His Help is 'The Best Thing That Ever Happened' to Us," *People*, March 12, 2016 https://people.com/crime/cesar-millan-animal-cruelty-case-owner-defends-dog-whisperer/.

53. *Ibid.*

54. Mills, 168.

55. Millan's superior expertise is apparently so accepted that even dog trainers will call him admitting failure in dealing with a client's dog, as happened in an episode of *Cesar 911* titled "Who's the Boss."

56. Cesar Millan (Host), February 3, 2012, "Hounded by Fear," *Dog Whisperer*.

57. Mills, 171.

58. See Mills, 168.

59. Cesar Millan (Host), May 1, 2015, "Not So Gentle Giant," *Cesar 911*.

60. As of this writing, *Dog: Impossible* has not been renewed for a second season. The show was the subject of a petition on change.org, which urged signers to send a message to Nat Geo Wild to stop the series because it "showed outdated and fear based techniques but never fully resolved any behavioral issues with the dogs." It has received over 17,000 signatures. See: https://www.change.org/p/nat-geo-wild-stop-dog-impossible-on-nat-geo-wild

61. Pre-meeting footage shows similar misbehavior.

62. Matt Beisner (Host), September 8, 2019 "Don't Fear the Collar," *Dog: Impossible*.

63. Beisner, September 2, 2019, "The Tormentor," *Dog: Impossible*.

64. Beisner, September 22, 2019, "Brink of Disaster," *Dog: Impossible*.

65. "Don't Fear the Collar."

66. "Brink of Disaster."

67. "The Tormentor."
68. "Brink of Disaster."
69. "Don't Fear the Collar."
70. "The Tormentor."
71. Beisner, October 6, 2019, "Breaking Fear," *Dog: Impossible.*
72. "Brink of Disaster."
73. "Breaking Fear."
74. *Ibid.*
75. *Ibid.*
76. "Brink of Disaster."
77. "The Tormentor."
78. *Ibid.*
79. Tia Torres (Host), November 6, 2010, "A Battle of Wills," *Pit Bulls & Parolees.*
80. Sue Manning, "Champion of Underdogs Rescues Pit Bulls, Parolees," *Rocky Mount Telegram* (Rocky Mount, North Carolina), August 19, 2009, 4B.
81. Villalobos Rescue Center Website. FAQ. https://www.vrcpitbull.com/about/faq/.
82. Manning, *ibid.*
83. Torres, January 18, 2020, "Saved from the Fight," *Pit Bulls & Parolees.*
84. Torres, November 6, 2010, "A Battle of Wills."
85. Villalobos Rescue Center Website, Adoption Process, "Pit Bull Facts" https://www.vrcpitbull.com/pit-bull-facts/.
86. Torres, "A Battle of Wills."
87. Jennifer Gee, "Judge Rules 4 Pitbulls Vicious," *Gold Country Media*, November 5, 2009 https://goldcountrymedia.com/news/21805/judge-rules-4-pitbulls-vicious/.
88. Gee, "APD Investigating Pitbull Attack in Downtown," *Gold Country Media*, September 18, 2009 https://goldcountrymedia.com/news/5282/apd-investigating-pitbull-attack-in-downtown/.
89. Gee, "Hearing Reveals Details of Pitbull Seizure," *Gold Country Media*, September 23, 2009 https://goldcountrymedia.com/news/3089/hearing-reveals-details-of-pitbull-seizure/.
90. *Ibid.*
91. Gee, "Owner Says Dogs Are 'Very Kind,'" *Gold Country Media*, September 24, 2009 https://goldcountrymedia.com/news/1082/owner-says-dogs-are-very-kind/
92. Gee, "Hearing Reveals"
93. The main reporter for the series is Jenifer Gee. *The Auburn Journal* is owned by Gold Mountain Media.

94. Barbara Lacy, "Protect Citizens from Violent Pitbulls," *Gold Country Media*, September 28, 2009 https://goldcountrymedia.com/news/134260/-protect-citizens-from-violent-pitbulls/
95. Marilyn Carter, "How Many Pets Are Permitted?" *Gold Country Media*, September 28, 2009 https://goldcountrymedia.com/news/134267/how-many-pets-are-permitted/
96. Ron Paitich, "Give 4 Dogs No Second Chance," *Gold Country Media*, September 29, 2009 https://goldcountrymedia.com/news/133780/give-4-dogs-no-second-chance/.
97. Dan Lucas, "Euthanize the Attack Pitbull," *Gold Country Media*, November 3, 2009 https://goldcountrymedia.com/news/21679/euthanize-the-attack-pitbull/.
98. Tony Hazarian, "Love Your Dog But Not at the Expense of Fellow Humans," *Gold Country Media*, September 30, 2009 https://goldcountrymedia.com/news/128798/love-your-dog-but-not-at-expense-of-fellow-humans/.
99. Matt Green and Frank Ford, "Pitbulls Spark Controversy," *Gold Country Media*, December 17, 2009 https://goldcountrymedia.com/news/23746/pitbulls-spark-controversy/.
100. Misty Green, "Have We Forgotten About Education?" *Gold Country Media*, December 11, 2009 https://goldcountrymedia.com/news/23500/have-we-forgotten-about-education/.
101. "Our View: City Should Look at Vicious Dog Policies After Attack," *Gold Country Media*, October 9, 2009 https://goldcountrymedia.com/news/20578/our-view-city-should-look-at-vicious-dog-policies-after-attack/.
102. Jenifer Gee, "Councilman Proposes Pitbull Ordinance," *Gold Country Media*, October 23, 2009 https://goldcountrymedia.com/news/21228/-councilman-proposes-pitbull-ordinance/.
103. "Our View: City Should Look at Vicious Dog Policies After Attack." *Gold Country Media.* Coverston's lawyer Dean Starks told the paper that the anti-aggression shots were on the advice of Coverston's veterinarian but a representative of the clinic where he or she works, declined to comment. See Gee, "Court Hearing Coming Up in Pitbull Attack," October 12, 2009. https://

goldcountrymedia.com/news/20613/court-hearing-coming-up-in-pitbull-attack/.

104. Gee, "Pitbull Hearing Debates 'Vicious' Label for Dogs," *Gold Country Media*, October 16, 2009 https://gold countrymedia.com/news/20869/pitbull-hearing-debates-vicious-label-for-dogs/.

105. Gee, "Judge Rules One Pitbull Can Live," *Gold Country Media*, January 29, 2010 https://goldcountrymedia.com/news/25493/pitbull-to-go-to-tv-stars-rescue-center/.

106. *Ibid.*

107. Gee, "Pitbull Trial Reveals Alleged $10,000 Bribe," Gold Country Media, January 30, 2010 https://goldcountrymedia.com/news/25472/pitbull-trial-reveals-alleged-10000-bribe/.

108. Gee, "Pitbull to Go to TV Star's Rescue Center," *Gold Country Media*, January 31, 2010 https://goldcountrymedia.com/news/25493/pitbull-to-go-to-tv-stars-rescue-center/.

109. Bridget Jones, "Pitbull Regulations Nixed," *Gold Country Media*, June 14, 2010 https://goldcountrymedia.com/news/30954/pitbull-regulations-nixed/

110. Gee, "Pitbull Trial Reveals Alleged $10,000 Bribe."

111. Clariss Smith, "Lock Up Those Pit Bulls, Or the Owner," *Gold Country Media*, October 8, 2009 https://goldcountrymedia.com/news/20454/lock-up-those-pit-bulls-or-the-owner/.

112. Grace Blackburn, "Dog Owners at Fault, Not Pedestrians," *Gold Country Media*, September 21, 2009 https://goldcountrymedia.com/news/5044/dog-owners-at-fault-not-pedestrians/.

113. Daniel Chauvin, "Common Sense Sadly Missing," *Gold Country Media*, September 30, 2009 https://goldcountrymedia.com/news/130968/common-sense-sadly-missing/.

114. Gee, "TV Star Says 'Vicious' Pitbull is a 'Gentleman'" *Gold Country Media*, March 5, 2010 https://goldcountrymedia.com/news/26945/tv-star-says-vicious-pitbull-is-a-gentleman/.

Endings

1. Jon Katz, *The New Work of Dogs: Tending to Life, Love and Family* (New York: Random House, 2004), xxi.

2. James Serpell, *The Domestic Dog: Its Evolution, Behavior and Interactions with People* (Cambridge: Cambridge University Press, 2017): 311.

3. *Ibid.*

4. Nicholas Schmidle, "Getting Bin Laden," *The New Yorker*, August 1, 2011 https://www.newyorker.com/magazine/2011/08/08/getting-bin-laden.

5. Katie Rogers, Katie, "Trump Says 'Beautiful' and 'Talented' Dog Injured in al-Baghdadi Raid," *New York Times*, October 27, 2019 https://www.nytimes.com/2019/10/27/us/politics/trump-dog-al-baghdadi-raid.html?search ResultPosition=3.

6. Katie Rogers, "Trump Shares Photo of 'Wonderful' Dog in ISIS Raid, but Not a Name," *New York Times*, October 28, 2019 https://www.nytimes.com/2019/10/28/us/politics/trump-baghdadi-dog-conan.html?searchResultPosition=1.

7. Niraj Chokshi and Karen Zraick, "Trump Tweets Fake Photo of Hero Dog Getting a Medal," *New York Times*, October 30, 2019 https://www.nytimes.com/2019/10/30/us/politics/trump-dog.html?searchResultPosition=5.

8. Eileen Sullivan, "Trump Praises Military Dog Conan Amid Fight with Navy," *New York Times*, November 11, 2019 https://www.nytimes.com/2019/11/25/us/politics/trump-dog-conan.html?searchResultPosition=2.

9. *Ibid.*

10. Katie Rogers, "Trump Says."

11. Rogers, "Trump Shares Photo."

12. Keith Olbermann, "WTF? Why is Trump Such a Weirdo About Dogs?" *The Closer with Keith Olbermann*, https://www.youtube.com/watch?v=M8xKAY LXbYA&list=PL0hKMB1-xkc_5ES_PEDgr 8VjMpQ5haPD6&index=29&t=0s.

13. Edward Hoyt, "To Die Like a Dog: President Trump Needs a Canine Correction," November 2019, *The Bark.com*, https://thebark.com/content/die-dog.

14. At least one research study found this to be true. Academics investigated how prominent dog stories were relative to other news stories and concluded that events featuring dogs printed in the *New York Times* were more likely to be reported by other newspapers than non-dog events. See Matthew Atkinson, Maria Deam and Joseph Uscinski, "What's a Dog Story Worth?" *PS:*

Political Science and Politics 47:4 (October 2014): 821.

15. Yi-Fu Tuan, *Dominance and Affection: The Making of Pets* (New Haven: Yale University Press, 1984), 88.

16. It should be noted that this number, as part of the total of 1.5 million dogs and cats euthanized, has declined annually from approximately 2.6 million in 2011.

17. See: https://www.aspca.org/-animal-homelessness/shelter-intake-and-surrender/pet-statistics.

18. Karla Armbruster, "Good Dog": The Stories We Tell About Our Canine Companions and What They Mean for Humans and Other Animals," *PLL* (2002): 354.

19. Bradford Betz, "Denver to End 30-Year Pit Bull Ban, Require License for Owners," *Foxnews.com*, February 11, 2020 https://www.foxnews.com/us/denver-end-pit-bull-ban-require-license.

20. Kate Ryan, "Pit Bull Ban Stands in Prince George's Co.," *WTOP.com*, October 22, 2019 https://wtop.com/prince-georges-county/2019/10/pit-bull-ban-stands-in-prince-georges-county/.

21. Rachel Chason, "About 400 Pit Bulls Euthanized Last Year in Prince George's, Officials Say," *Washington Post*, October 7, 2019 https://www.washingtonpost.com/local/md-politics/about-400-pit-bulls-euthanized-last-year-in-prince-georges-officials-say/2019/10/07/7f95c83a-e90e-11e9-9306-47cb0324fd44_story.html.

22. Jennier Earl, "Meet The First Official "Pit Bull" Police Dog in the State of New York," CBSnews.com, November 15, 2016 https://www.cbsnews.com/news/meet-the-first-official-pit-bull-police-dog-in-the-state-of-new-york/.

23. See Helen Steward, "Animal Agency," *Inquiry* 52:3 (2009): 226. Tim Ingold, "The Animal in the Study of Humanity," in *What is Animal?* Tim Ingold (ed.) (London: Unwin Hyman, 1988), 95.

Bibliography

Allon, Fiona and Lindsay Barrett. "That Dog Was Marine! Human-Dog Assemblages in the Pacific War." *Animal Studies Journal* 4: 1 (2015): 126–147.

Amiot, Catherine, Brock Bastian and Pim Martens. "People and Companion Animals: It Takes Two to Tango." *BioScience* 66: 7 (July 2016): 552–560.

Arluke, Arnold, Donald Cleary, Gary Patronek and Janis Bradley. "Defaming Rover: Error-Based Latent Rhetoric in the Medical Literature on Dog Bites." *Journal of Applied Animal Welfare Science* 21: 3 (2018): 211–223.

Armbruster, Karla. "Good Dog": The Stories We Tell About Our Canine Companions and What They Mean for Humans and Other Animals." *Papers on Language and Literature* 38: 4 (2002): 351–376.

Atkinson, Matthew, Maria Deam and Joseph Uscinski. "What's a Dog Story Worth?" *PS* (October 2014): 1–5.

Bao, Katherine and George Schreer. "Pets and Happiness: Examining the Association Between Pet Ownership and Wellbeing." *Anthrozoos* 29: 2 (2016): 283–296.

Batt, Sarah. "Human Attitudes Towards Animals in Relation to Species Similarity to Humans: A Multivariate Approach." *Bioscience Horizons* 2: 2 (June 2009): 180-190.

Beatson, Ruth and Michael Halloran. "Humans Rule! The Effects of Creatureliness Reminders, Mortality Salience and Self-Esteem on Attitudes Towards Animals." *British Journal of Social Psychology* 46 (2007): 619–632.

Boisseron, Benedicte. "Afro-Dog." *Transition* 118 (2015): 15–31.

Bradley, Janis. *Dogs Bite: But Balloons and Slippers Are More Dangerous.* Berkeley: James & Kenneth Publishers, 2005.

Brown, Royal. "Reviewed Works: *White Dog* by Sam Fuller, Jon Davison and Curtis Hanson." *Cineaste* 34: 3 (Summer 2009): 54–55.

Brown, Simon. *Screening Stephen King: Adaptation and the Horror Genre in Film and Television.* Austin: University of Texas Press, 2018.

Browning, Mark. *Stephen King on the Big Screen.* Bristol, UK: Intellect Books, 2009.

Campbell, John. "The Seminoles, the "Bloodhound War," and Abolitionism, 1796-1865." *The Journal of Southern History* LXXII: 2 (May 2006): 259–302.

Cohen, Judy and John Richardson. "Pit Bull Panic." *Journal of Popular Culture* 36: 2 (November 2002): 285–317.

Coren, Stanley. *The Pawprints of History: Dogs and the Course of Human Events.* New York: Free Press, 2002.

Cudworth, Erika and Tracey Jensen. "Puppy Love? Animal Companions in the Media." In *Critical Animal and Media Studies: Communication for Nonhuman Animal Advocacy*, ed. Nuria Almiron, Matthew Cole and Carrie Freeman. New York: Routledge, 2016.

Danchev, Alex. "Like A Dog!": Humiliation and Shame in the War on Terror." *Alternatives: Global, Local, Political* 31: 3 (July-September 2006): 259–283.

Deane, Samantha and Amy Shuffleton. "Plate and the Police: Dogs, Guardians, and Why Accountability Is the Wrong Answer." *Educational Studies* (2016): 491–505.

Dickey, Bronwen. *Pit Bull: The Battle Over an American Icon.* New York: Vintage Books, 2017.

Dombrowski, Lisa. "Every Dog Has Its Day." *Film Comment* 44: 6 (November/ December 2008): 46–49.

Evans, Rhonda an Craig Forsyth. "Entertainment to Outrage: A Social Historical View of Dogfighting." *International Review of Modern Sociology* 27: 2 (Autumn 1997): 59–71.

Fox, Richard. "Dog Eat Dog." *National Police Gazette* (October 8, 1881): 11.

_____. "Dog Fighting." *National Police Gazette* (February 2, 1889): 7.

_____. "Here's a Fighting Dog of Detroit, Michigan, Worth Reading About." *National Police Gazette* (August 19, 1905): 3.

Frankle, Rebecca. *War Dogs: Tales of Canine Heroism, History and Love.* New York: St. Martin's Griffin, 2015.

Franklin, John, and Loren Schweninger. *Runaway Slaves: Rebels on the Plantation.* New York: Oxford University Press, 1999.

Freeman, Carrie, Marc Bekoff and Sarah Bexell. "Giving Voice to the 'Voiceless': Incorporating Nonhuman Animal Perspectives as Journalistic Sources." *Journalism Studies* 12: 5 (2011): 590–607.

Fuchs, Michael and Stefan Brandt. "Animals on American Television: Introduction to the Special Issue." *European Journal of American Studies* 13–1 (2018): 1–7.

Fuller, Sam. "The White Dog Talks—To Sam Fuller." *Framework: The Journal of Cinema and Media* 19 (1982): 21–25.

Gersbach, Robert, and Theo Jager. *The Police Dog in Word and Picture.* New York: The Deming Press, 1910.

Glick, Megan. "Animal Instincts: Race, Criminality, and the Reversal of the "Human."" *American Quarterly* 65: 3 (September 2013): 637–659.

Gomez, Edwin, Ron Malega, and Joshua Baur. "Dog Park Users: An Examination of Perceived Social Capital and Perceived Neighborhood Social Cohesion." *Journal of Urban Affairs* (August 2017): 1–21.

Graham, Taryn and Troy Glover. "On the Fence: Dog Parks in the (Un)Leashing of Community and Social Capital." *Leisure Sciences* 36 (2014): 217–234.

Gregersdotter, Katarina, Johan Hoglund and Nicklas Hallen, eds. *Animal Horror Cinema: Genre, History and Criticism.* New York: Palgrave Macmillan, 2016.

Grier, Katherine. *Pets in America: A History.*

Chapel Hill: University of North Carolina Press, 2006.

Grimm, David. *Citizen Canine: Our Evolving Relationship with Cats and Dogs.* New York: Public Affairs, 2014.

Gunter, Lisa, Rebecca Barber, and Clive Wynne. "What's in a Name? Effect of Breed Perceptions & Labeling on Attractiveness, Adoptions & Length of Stay for Pit-Bull-Type Dogs." *PloS ONE* 11: 3 (March 23, 2016).

Haraway, Donna. *The Companion Species Manifesto: Dogs, People, and Significant Otherness.* Chicago: Prickly Paradigm Press, 2003.

Hearn, Vicki. *Bandit: Dossier of a Dangerous Dog.* New York: The Akadine Press, 2002.

Herzog, Hal. *Some We Love, Some We Hate, Some We Eat: Why It's So Hard to Think Straight About Animals.* New York: Harper Perennial, 2010.

Hesford, Wendy. "Staging Terror." *TDR (1988–)* 50: 3 (Autumn 2006): 29–41.

Hobgood-Oster, Laura. *A Dog's History of the World: Canines and the Domestication of Humans.* Waco, TX: Baylor University Press, 2014.

Holmberg, Tora, ed. *Investigating Human/ Animal Relations in Science, Culture and Work.* Uppsala: Uppsala University, 2009.

Hussain, Safia. "Attacking the Dog-Bite Epidemic: Why Breed Specific Legislation Won't Solve the Dangerous-Dog Dilemma." *Fordham Law Review* 74: 5 (2006): 2847–2887.

"The Hydrofobiac Scare." *Hall's Journal of Health* 33:1 (1886).

Instone, Lesley, and Jill Sweeney. "Dog Waste, Wasted Dogs: The Contribution of Human-Dog Relations to the Political Ecology of Australian Urban Space." *Geographical Research* 52: 4 (November 2014): 355–364.

Instone, Lesley, and Kathy Mee. "Companion Acts and Companion Species: Boundary Transgressions and the Place of Dogs in Urban Space." In *Animal Movements Moving Animals: Essays on Direction, Velocity and Agency in Humanimal Encounters,* ed. Jacob Bull, 229–250. Uppsala, Sweden: University Printers, 2011.

Jackson, Patrick. "Situated Activities in a Dog Park: Identity and Conflict in

Human-Animal Space." *Society & Animals* (2012): 254–272.

Johnson, Davi. "Martin Luther King, Jr.'s 1963 Birmingham Campaign as Image Event." *Rhetoric and Public Affairs* 10: 1 (Spring 2007): 1–25.

Johnson, Sara. "'You Should Give Them Blacks to Eat': Waging Inter-American Wars Of Torture and Terror." *American Quarterly* 61: 1 (March 2009): 65–92.

Kalof, Linda, and Carl Taylor. "The Discourse of Dog Fighting." *Humanity & Society* 31 (November 2007): 319–333.

Katz, Jon. *The New Work of Dogs: Tending to Life, Love, and Family.* New York: Random House, 2004.

Lemish, Michael. *War Dogs: A History of Loyalty and Heroism.* Lincoln, NE: Potomac Books, 2008.

Lennard, Dominic. *Brute Force: Animal Horror Movies.* New York: SUNY Press, 2019.

Levine, Rachel, and Justyna Poray-Wybranowska. "American Bully: Fear, Paradox, and and the New Family Dog." *Otherness: Essays and Studies* 5: 2 (September 2016): 151–200.

Lilly, Robert, and Michael Puckett. "Social Control and Dogs: A Sociohistorical Analysis." *Crime & Delinquency* 43: 2 (April 1997): 123–147.

Lockwood, Randall, and Kate Rindy. "Are 'Pit Bulls' Different? An Analysis of the Pit Bull Terrier Controversy." *Anthrozoos* 1:1 (March 1987): 2–8.

Malamud, Randy. *An Introduction to Animals and Visual Culture.* New York: Palgrave Macmillan, 2012.

McKenna, Erin. *Pets, People and Pragmatism.* New York: Fordham University Press, 2013.

McLean, Adrienne, ed. *Cinematic Canines: Dogs and Their Work in the Fiction Film.* New Brunswick, New Jersey: Rutgers University Press, 2014.

Meacham, Sarah. "Pets, Status, and Slavery in the Late-Eighteenth-Century Chesapeake." *The Journal of Southern History* LXXVII:3 (August 2011): 521–545.

Meade, Peter. "Police and Domestic Dog Bite Injuries: What Are the Differences? What Are the Implications About Police Dog Use?" *Injury Extra* 37 (2006): 395–401.

Medlin, Jamey. "Pit Bulls and the Human Factors Affecting Canine Behavior."

DePaul Law Review 56:4 (Summer 2007): 1285–1319.

Mehrkam, Lindsay and Clive Wynne. "Behavioral Differences Among Breeds of Domestic Dogs (*Canis Lupus Familiaris*): Current Status of the Science." *Applied Animal Behaviour Science* (2014): 10–14.

Merskin, Debra. "Media Theories and the Crossroads of Critical Animal and Media Studies." *Critical Animals and Media Studies: Communication for Nonhuman Animal Advocacy* (January 1, 2016).

Mills, Brett. *Animals on Television: The Cultural Making of the Non-Human.* New York: Palgrave Macmillan, 2017.

Molloy, Claire. *Popular Media and Animals.* New York: Palgrave Macmillan, 2011.

Morell, Virginia. "Going to the Dogs." *Science* 325:5944 (August 28, 2009): 1062–1065.

Pearson, Chris. "Dogs, History and Agency." *History and Theory* 52:4 (December 2013): 128–145.

Pickens, Rebecca Crinean. "Michael Vick's Pit Bulls & Dogfighting: Ramifications of Media Coverage." *Journal of Student Research* 2: 1 (2013): 29–35.

Ranvaud, Don and Samuel Fuller. "An Interview with Sam Fuller." *Framework: The Journal Of Cinema and Media* 19 (1982): 26–28.

St. Michel, Carrie. "Bred for Trouble." *Good Housekeeping* 235:4 (October 2002).

Sanders, Clinton. "'The Dog You Deserve': Ambivalence in the K-9 Officer/Patrol Dog Relationship." *Journal of Contemporary Ethnography* 35 (2006): 148–172.

Schwartz, Marion. *A History of Dogs in the Early Americas.* New Haven: Yale University Press, 1997.

"Scientific Miscellany." *Virginia Clinical Record* 2: 5 (1872).

Serpell, James. "Anthropomorphism and Anthropomorphic Selection—Beyond the "Cute Response." *Society & Animals* 10: 4 (2002): 437–454.

Shaffer, Helen. "Control of City Crime." *CQ Researcher* (October 18, 1961):1–8.

Skabelund, Aaron. "Breeding Racism: The Imperial Battlefields of the 'German' Shepherd Dog." *Society and Animals* 16 (2008): 354–371.

Spratt, Meg. "When Police Dogs Attacked: Iconic News Photographs and Construction of History, Mythology and Political

Discourse." *American Journalism* 25: 2 (Spring 2008): 85–105.

Spruill, Larry. "Packs of Negro Dogs" and "Policing Black Communities." *Phylon* 53: 1 (Summer 2016): 42–66.

Tarver, Erin. "The Dangerous Individual('s) Dog: Race, Criminality and the 'Pit Bull.'" *Culture, Theory & Critique* 55: 3 (November 2014): 273–285.

Tullis, Paul. "The Softer Side of Pit Bulls: A Reviled Breed Gets a Makeover." *Time* 182: 4 (July 22, 2013).

Unti, Bernard. "The Quality of Mercy: Organized Animal Protection in the United States 1866–1930." Ph.D. Dissertation, American University (2002).

Wall, Tyler. "For the Very Existence of Civilization": The Police Dog and Racial Terror." *American Quarterly* 68: 4 (December 2016): 861–882.

_____. "Legal Terror and The Police Dog."

Radical Philosophy 188 (November/December 2014): 2–7.

Wang, Jessica. "Dogs and the Making of the American State: Voluntary Association, State Power, and the Politics of Animal Control in New York City, 1850–1920." *The Journal of American History* (March 2012): 998–1024.

Weaver, Harlan. "'Becoming in Kind': Race, Class, Gender and Nation in Cultures of Dog Rescue and Dogfighting." *American Quarterly* 65: 3 (September 2013): 689–709.

Weil, Harry. "Review: The Aesthetics of Abu Ghraib." *Art Journal* 71: 2 (Summer 2012): 123–126.

Wells, Deborah, Deborah Morrison and Peter Hepper. "The Effect of Priming on Perceptions of Dog Breed Traits." *Anthrozoos* 25: 3 (July 5, 2012): 369–377.

Index

abolitionists 61–63, 67, 70, 171
Abu Ghraib 111–113, 171, 181
aggression 7, 20, 26–28, 42, 57, 70, 77, 79, 92, 96, 114, 130, 159
American Kennel Club 3–4, 46, 97
American Society for the Prevention of Cruelty to Animals 36–38, 52, 56, 169–170
animal horror cinema 10, 115, 117, 131, 164, 189
animal shelter 22, 37–38, 40, 50, 53, 56, 155, 159, 162
animal welfare 35–38, 40–41, 47, 50, 52–55, 172
anthropomorphism 9–12, 14, 17
Arbuckle, Roscoe "Fatty" 46

Beisner, Matt 148–151, 153
Bergh, Henry 36, 44
biophilia 13
Birmingham 79–85, 100, 103, 112–113
bites 20–24, 27–29, 33, 86–89, 92, 118, 121, 127, 139, 152, 157–158
Bloodhound 59–72, 74, 94
The Bloodhound War 66–67
Breed Specific Legislation 22
Burns, Kit 44–45, 48, 57

Connor, Eugene "Bull" 79–80, 82–83
creatureliness 9, 18
criminality 10, 53–54, 57, 154
Cujo 115, 118–123
cute response 13
cynophobia 7

dog catchers 35–38, 41, 59–60, 114, 170
Dog: Impossible 148–153, 163, 172
dog parks 40–43
Dog Whisperer 133–148, 163
dogfighting 26, 44–45, 47, 50, 54–55, 57
Dogs for Defense 97–100, 102, 104–105

ethic of kindness 9, 14, 34, 36

Fuller, Sam Fuller 128–131

Gadsden, Walter Gadsden 80
German Shepherd Dog 1–4, 21–22, 25, 51, 55, 72, 74–81, 83, 85, 92–93, 95–96, 99, 103, 106–107, 123, 127, 130, 144–145, 147, 168, 171

Haraway, Donna 8
hydrophobia 30–32, 39

K-9 76–79, 84–89, 91, 105–106, 111, 113, 167
King, Martin Luther, Jr. 79
Korean War 105–106

Los Angeles Police Department 86–89, 91–92

Marines 93–94, 99, 104–105, 107, 110
McGruff the Crime Dog 85
Millan, Cesar 4, 133–148, 172

National Canine Research Council 23, 27
negro dogs 59–61, 64, 68, 80–83, 114, 171

Olmsted, Frederick Law 59

The Pack 123–127
Pal the Wonder Dog 46
pet keeping 11–13, 29, 34, 40–41, 50, 100, 123, 134, 170
pit bulls 4, 10, 22, 24, 26–27, 43–57, 145, 147, 153–164, 170
Pit Bulls & Paroleees 56, 153–155, 160, 163–164, 170
police 71–93
positive health outcomes 15
priming effect 25–26

rabies 30–34, 38–39, 41, 57, 85, 107, 122, 127, 169–170
race 54–55, 57
reflexive consciousness 11
Rin Tin Tin 40

Second Seminole War 66–67
slave narrative 60–62
social support 15–17, 167
Strongheart 75

Index

ɔr, Zachary 66
ɹrres, Tia 153–154, 159–164

Uncle Tom's Cabin 65

Vick, Michael 54
Vietnam War 106–110, 113

War Dog Fund 99–100
White Dog 127–133
Wirz, Henry 68
World War II 97–106